China's Virtual Monopoly of Rare Earth Elements

Rare Earth Elements are a group of 17 metals which have a central role in modern industry, increasingly used in the fields of green technologies, high technological consumer goods, industrial and medical appliances and modern weapons systems. Although deposits of Rare Earths are globally dispersed, over 90% of global demand has been provided by Chinese mines since the late 1990s, leading to a situation where China has a virtual monopoly. This book surveys the Rare Earths mining industry, discusses the extent to which Rare Earths really are scarce elsewhere in the world and assesses the economics of production, considering arguments for the rationing of supply, for higher pricing and for a total export embargo. This actually occurred in 2010, demonstrating the vulnerability of the rest of the world to China's control of these increasingly vital resources.

Roland Howanietz is a Research Associate and Lecturer in East Asian Economics at the Ruhr University Bochum, Germany.

Routledge Contemporary China Series

China Reclaims World Power Status
Putting an end to the world America made
Paolo Urio

The Economic Roots of the Umbrella Movement in Hong Kong
Globalization and the Rise of China
Louis Augustin-Jean and Anthea H.Y. Cheung

China's Hydro-politics in the Mekong
Conflict and Cooperation in Light of Securitization Theory
Sebastian Biba

Economic Policy Making in China (1949–2016)
The Role of Economists
Pieter Bottelier

The Power of Relationalism in China
Leah Zhu

China's Financial Opening
Coalition Politics and Policy Changes
Yu-Wai Vic Li

Urbanization, Regional Development and Governance in China
Jianfa Shen

Midwifery in China
Ngai Fen Cheung and Rosemary Mander

China's Virtual Monopoly of Rare Earth Elements
Economic, Technological and Strategic Implications
Roland Howanietz

For more information about this series, please visit: www.routledge.com/Routledge-Contemporary-China-Series/book-series/SE0768

China's Virtual Monopoly of Rare Earth Elements

Economic, Technological and Strategic Implications

Roland Howanietz

Routledge
Taylor & Francis Group
LONDON AND NEW YORK

First published 2018 by Routledge

2 Park Square, Milton Park, Abingdon, Oxfordshire OX14 4RN
52 Vanderbilt Avenue, New York, NY 10017

Routledge is an imprint of the Taylor & Francis Group, an informa business

First issued in paperback 2020

British Library Cataloguing-in-Publication Data
A catalogue record for this book is available from the British Library

Library of Congress Cataloging-in-Publication Data
Names: Howanietz, Roland.
Title: China's virtual monopoly of rare earth elements : economic, technological and strategic implications / Roland Howanietz.
Description: 1 Edition. | New York : Routledge, 2018. | Series: Routledge contemporary China ; 192
Identifiers: LCCN 2018005140 | ISBN 9780815363309 (hardback) | ISBN 9781351109918 (ebook) | ISBN 9781351109901 (web pdf) | ISBN 9781351109888 (mobipocket) | ISBN 9781351109895 (epub)
Subjects: LCSH: Mines and mineral resources. | Mines and mineral resources—China. | Rare earth metals—China. | Nonferrous metals—China.
Classification: LCC HD9506.A2 H69 2018 | DDC 333.8/54940951—dc23
LC record available at https://lccn.loc.gov/2018005140

ISBN: 978-0-8153-6330-9 (hbk)
ISBN: 978-0-367-59013-0 (pbk)

Typeset in Times New Roman
by Apex CoVantage, LLC

Contents

Figures and map

Figures

Map

Tables

Abbreviations

AMD	Acid mine drainage
BGS	British Geological Survey
CCP	Chinese Communist Party
CRIRSCO	Committee for Mineral Reserves International Reporting Standards
DoE	Department of Energy
EC	European Commission
EPA	Environmental Protection Agency
EPB	Environmental protection bureaus
FDI	Foreign direct investment
GDP	Gross domestic product
GFC	Global Financial Crisis
GNI	Gross national income
HHI	Herfindahl-Hirschman-Index
IT	Information technology
JOGMEC	Japan Oil, Gas, and Metals Corporation
KfW	Kreditanstalt fuer Wiederaufbau (German Reconstruction Credit Institute)
LCD	Liquid-crystal display
LED	Light-emitting diode
M&As	Mergers and acquisitions
MEP	Ministry of Environmental Protection
METI	Ministry of Economy, Trade and Industry
MIIT	Ministry of Industry and Information Technology
MJ	Mega joule
MLR	Ministry of Land Resources
MOFCOM	Ministry of Commerce
NdFeB	magnets Neodymium-iron-boron permanent magnets
NDRC	National Development and Reform Commission
NEDO	New Energy and Industrial Technology Development Organization
NiMh	batteries Nickel-metal hydride batteries
NRC	U.S. National Research Council
OPEC	Organization of Petroleum Exporting Countries
PBOC	People's Bank of China

PPM	Parts per million
PRC	People's Republic of China
R&D	Research and development
REEs	Rare Earth Elements
REMs	Rare Earth Metals
REO	Rare Earth Oxides
RMB	Renminbi
RoW	Rest of the world
SOC	Marginal social opportunity cost of capital
SOE	State-owned enterprise(s)
SPC	Shadow price of capital
SRTP	Social rate of time preference
USGS	United States Geological Survey
VOC	Volatile organic compounds
WTO	World Trade Organization

1 Introduction

On 7 September 2010, a Chinese fishing trawler rammed two Japan Cost Guard vessels in the waters around the disputed Senkaku/ Diaoyu islands in the East China Sea, which are claimed by both the People's Republic of China[1] and Japan to be in their exclusive zones at least since the discovery of potentially large oil and natural gas reserves located around the islands at the end of the 1960s. As a consequence of their provocative and dangerous behavior, the crew of the Chinese trawler was arrested and detained by the Japanese coast guard (Lackner & McEwen-Fial, 2011, p. 7; Smith, 2014; "Bare anger", 2010). While this event has led to increasing concerns that future peace in East Asia might be threatened by both arising, ever-fiercer territorial conflicts and by the revision of geostrategic analyses and strategies, this event also turned out to be of great importance for the discipline of resource economics and the strategic natural resources policies[2] of highly industrialized countries that were not even involved in the dispute. As a reaction on the detainment of Chinese citizens, the Chinese government not only arrested four Japanese businesspersons but also informally embargoed the exports of the natural resource "Rare Earths" to Japan (Mazza et al., 2013, p. 4; Smith, 2014).

Rare Earths[3] are a group of 15, respectively 17, metals with the atomic numbers 57 through 71, which form the lanthanide series in the periodic table. The metallic elements of Scandium and Yttrium do not belong to the lanthanide series but are incorporated in the REE group in many studies because they have very similar physical-chemical properties (Hurst, 2010, p. 3; Jordens et al., 2013, p. 98). Due to their increasing use, these metals are also called "technology metals", "vitamins of technology" or "seeds of technology". Although the deposits of Rare Earths are globally dispersed and have been extracted in several countries since their commercialization in the mid-1880s, over 90% of the global demand is provided by the production of Chinese mines since the late 1990s (Humphries, 2013, pp. 1–4). This situation is the "Chinese Rare Earths virtual monopoly".

In microeconomic theory, a monopoly is a market situation in which there is only one supplier of a specific good so that this supplier has a market share of 100% and the market power to set prices due to the lack of competition. When compared to the idealistic, welfare-maximizing market structure of perfect competition,[4] the price is set higher by the monopolist in order to maximize his/her profits, and the resulting supplied quantity is lower. Due to its history of Soviet-style economic planning, the existence of State-owned enterprises in many key sectors and industries still today, the ongoing issuance of Five-Year-Plans[5] as a basis for an active, all-embracing industrial policy and its status as a non-market economy in international trade,[6] the PRC is often assumed to be a unitary, strategically planning economic actor. Therefore, the high concentration of global REEs production in China is sometimes seen as a monopolistic situation (Lackner & McEwen-Fial, 2011, p. 12; Ting & Seaman, 2013, p. 235). However, the market structure of the Chinese REEs mining sector was not as highly concentrated as in the standard definition of a monopolist market or of even an oligopolistic market[7] at the time of the embargo. The concentration of production in China was achieved by the domestic location advantages of low Chinese wages and lax environmental standards in combination with active governmental promoting measures. One of these measures was the policy of "easy access" so that new mining permits were granted without large requirements. As a consequence, mining companies of all ownership types – privately owned, State-owned and joint-stock companies – and of all operational sizes have been established. Consequently, the prices of Rare Earths steadily declined as the Chinese REEs mining sector expanded (Ting & Seaman, 2013, p. 239). Therefore, the virtual monopoly of China is not a monopoly by definition and has no intrinsic pricing power. However, for REEs consumers outside of China, the virtual monopoly poses an uncertain threat to supply security. While the potential risks of the concentration of REEs production in China was overlooked or ignored before September 2010, and consumers believed in the security of REEs supply through free markets, the issue gained a lot of international attention when the Chinese government enforced the acting of China as a unitary economic agent in the form of an embargo. In addition to the embargo of REEs exports to Japan, exports to both the European Union and the USA were stopped in October 2010. The embargo to the USA is predominantly explained as a Chinese counteraction against the opening of an investigation of the U.S. Trade Representative against Chinese policies in the green energy sector that violated WTO rules on 15 October 2010. These violations included export subsidies, restriction of domestic market access for foreign firms and also the preferential treatment of domestic companies in the access to Rare Earths as required material for green technologies. The export ban to the EU is mainly explained by the attempts of Japanese companies to bypass the embargo to Japan by purchasing Rare Earths from European companies. As a consequence, all major REEs consuming countries outside of China were embargoed at the same time from 18–28 October (Lackner & McEwen-Fial, 2011, pp. 8–10).

There were two major immediate impacts of this total embargo. First, prices for REEs skyrocketed due to the restriction of their physical availability on the world market. The price of some REMs increased tenfold as a consequence of short supply (Lackner & McEwen-Fial, 2011, p. 10). Second, Rare Earths came under the spotlight of the media, governments and economists that previously neglected the role of REEs as a strategic natural resource that is indispensable for the development and expansion of new technologies but whose production is highly concentrated in a country that might not be fully considered a secure supplier. The majority of scientific articles on Rare Earths published before 2010 were in the fields of geology, metallurgy and theoretical and practical applications. The geological articles mainly provide information on global stocks of reserves and resources and specific deposits that are dispersed in several countries around the world, and describe the special geological characteristics of REEs-bearing minerals (Castor, 2008; Kanazawa & Kamitani, 2006; Long et al., 2010; Olson et al., 1954). The articles on REEs metallurgy mainly cover the techniques that are required to process REEs into refined and pure metals, such as separation through electrolysis. The articles on application fields include the research in the fields of superconductors, batteries, phosphors and catalysts (Adachi et al., 2010) but also fields of medical and biological research, such as the effects of using Rare Earths as feed additives in the fattening of pigs and calves (Miller, 2006). The only publications that acknowledged Rare Earths as strategic natural resources prior to the embargo were the studies of Papp et al. (2008), who identify the factors that influence the price determination of REEs, and the U.S. National Research Council (2008) and Angerer et al. (2009), who identify REEs as critical resources for the USA and Germany, respectively. As a consequence of the embargo, not only prices but also the number of published articles and studies that deal with REEs as strategic and potentially scarce natural resources increased significantly. Studies on behalf of different governments or from private research institutes mainly try to cover the whole spectrum of assumingly relevant aspects of Rare Earths: the summary of geological information on deposits, the current market concentration in China and its impact on prices, the fields of application in which REMs are used, the possibility to secure or diversify supply, the impact of REEs mining on the environment and human health and the exploration of possibilities to recycle REEs (Grasso, 2013; Hilpert & Kröger, 2011; Hilpert & Mildner, 2013; Humphries, 2013; Hurst, 2010; Schueler et al., 2011; United Nations Conference on Trade and Development, 2014). Scientific journal articles and working papers predominantly focus more specifically on one of these aspects, or on the assessment of the scarcity or criticality of Rare Earths (Alonso et al., 2012; Binnemans & Jones, 2015; Boer & Lammertsma, 2013; Bradshaw et al., 2013; Erdmann et al., 2011; Graedel et al., 2012; Nassar et al., 2015; Ruettinger & Feil, 2011; Silberglitt et al., 2013), or on the benefitting factors in China and the rest of the world that fostered the establishment of the Chinese virtual monopoly (Biedermann, 2014; Butler, 2014; Clagett, 2013; Goldman, 2014; He, 2014). Because China did not only embargo REEs exports for the short term but also announced the adjustment of its general trade regime for REEs in order to limit the volumes of future exports, several papers especially focus on the economic implications of these trade-restricting measures and/or on the analysis of whether these restrictions might violate WTO law (He, 2014; Jebe et al., 2012; Lackner & McEwen-Fial, 2011; Mancheri, 2015; Morrison & Tang, 2012; Ribeiro, 2014; Van Calster, 2013; Zhang, 2013; Zhang et al., 2015). However, the current number of papers with empirical-quantitative approaches is low. Those papers have been published in the period from 2013 on so that there was a distinct time delay between the publication of qualitative and quantitative literature. Pothen (2013b) utilizes the METRO model that has been formalized in Pothen (2013a) in order to measure the market power of China gained through its restrictive trade policies and to simulate the future developments of supply, demand and prices on the REEs market. Sanyal et al. (2013) investigates the impact of trade costs on Rare Earths exports based on a stochastic frontier model. Mueller et al. (2014) analyzes the wealth effects of Rare Earths prices and China's REEs policy for listed companies that are involved in the REEs industry in China or the USA. Wang et al. (2015) utilizes the curve-fitting "Generalized Weng model" in order to forecast the date of the production peaks of Chinese mines. Zhang et al. (2015) measure the effectiveness of China's restrictive measures by carrying out a price sensitivity analysis of Chinese REEs products on the Japanese and U.S. markets in different periods.

This study will expand the relatively small economic literature of Rare Earths as a strategic natural resource. It will use both an eclectic approach based on the existing literature and a qualitative analysis as well as a quantitative analysis based on the Hotelling rule for optimal paths of natural resource extraction. The main research goal is to analyze the explicit impacts and implicit implications of the Chinese virtual monopoly in the Rare Earth Metals sector for China itself and the REEs consuming countries in the rest of the world. The Chinese view of its virtual monopoly is best described by the "three narratives of reinventing an industry" of Wuebbeke (2013). According to the Chinese government, the short-term embargo and the longer-term restrictive adjustments in the trade regime of REEs were not based on international, geopolitical issues but were imperative due to the situation of the domestic Rare Earths industry. First, the extracted amount of REEs is seen to be excessive, while the prices are deemed to be too low for a natural resource that is both exhaustible and indispensable for the development of emerging high technologies. The intrinsic value of REEs is assumedly not reflected by their prices on the global market. In the industrial structure before 2010, neither the Chinese government nor individual companies had the price-setting power that a pure monopolist possesses. Therefore, REMs as strategic resources would be "squandered" at low prices while China is threatened to run out of natural resources rapidly due to excessive extraction of REEs for exports. Thus, the adjustments in the trade regime and the overall regulatory framework are seen as measures that should not only restrict exports but also limit the overall production of REEs. This should lead to an upward revision of prices and to the conservation of natural resources for future Chinese generations. These goals are also supported by policies of industrial reorganization that aim to reduce the number of mining companies as well as prevent cases of occurring illegal mining. Second, the Chinese government stresses the importance of the restriction of REEs mining and exportation for environmental protection. REEs mines were not environmentally regulated until 2010 so that the lax Chinese environmental standards even constituted a competitive advantage. This has led to a severe impact on the environment and human health in the surroundings of REEs mines. Thus, the restriction of exports and production, the reorganization of the industry and the close monitoring of the compliance of companies to new standards in the long term are also seen as necessary for the implementation of stricter environmental regulations of REEs mining (Wuebbeke, 2013, pp. 387–392). From the view of the Chinese government, the virtual monopoly is therefore more a burden for the country than an advantage because it implicates a high concentration of the environmental impact of REEs mining in China while China lacks the monopolistic benefit of price-setting power. The government officially explained the embargo as necessary for an inspection of REEs companies in order to monitor which firms would violate the existing regulations or would even operate without permits (Lackner & McEwen-Fial, 2011, p. 4f.). However, the embargoed economies saw the issue differently. There were suggestions that China would use its virtual monopoly in order to achieve geopolitical objectives, for example, to pressure Japan to make political concessions in the island dispute. Thus, the embargo and the general restriction of trade were partly seen as a sign of emerging neomercantilism (Lackner & McEwen-Fial, 2011, p. 10ff.). A second, purely economic explanatory approach is based on the view that export restrictions and taxes on Rare Earths should give Chinese companies in REEs-dependent production sectors an important competitive advantage. The adjustments of the trade regime would be only another stone in the Chinese mosaic of industrial policy consisting of State subsidies, pressure on foreign companies to invest in China and the exchange-rate policy of undervaluing the Chinese currency Renminbi (Krugman, 2010). Both explanatory approaches have led to efforts to break the Chinese virtual monopoly. These efforts include the diversification and securing of supply by the exploration and development of new REEs deposits, the promoting and carrying out of research for substitutes for Rare Earths, the research to find possibilities to reuse or recycle REMs and, last but not least, a WTO complaint that was jointly filed by the EU, Japan and the USA in 2012.

The research questions that can be derived from these narratives are as follows: (1) Is there an adequate methodical approach to assess the Chinese thesis that Rare Earths have been underpriced in past periods? Can this hypothesis either be supported, or should it rather be rejected? (2) What does an optimal future path of extraction, which eliminates excessive mining and the problem that Chinese Rare Earths would be depleted faster than desired by the current Chinese government and future generations, look like? (3) What are the reasons for adjustments in the regulatory framework of the Chinese Rare Earths industry in addition to the aforementioned narratives? Which specific measures did the Chinese government implement? What are the impacts of these measures on the Chinese market and price-setting power? What are the implications for the Chinese optimal path of future extraction? (4) Which specific measures did the major REEs consuming countries in the rest of the world take in order to break the Chinese virtual monopoly? What are the impacts of these measures on the Chinese market power? What are the implications for the Chinese optimal path of future extraction?

The book is organized as follows: after the Introduction, Chapter 2 first gives an overall introduction of the physical-chemical and geological properties of REEs and their global stock of resources and reserves. Then, the processing route from REEs-bearing minerals to refined and pure metals is reviewed in order to highlight the impacts of REEs production on the environment and human health, which are the basis for the Chinese environmental narrative. The historical development trends in the REEs production are discussed in order to analyze the factors that benefitted the development of the Chinese virtual monopoly. Finally, the subsection about their current fields of application and the future growth potential of these fields will highlight the commercial and developmental importance of REMs. Chapter 3 assesses the scarcity of Rare Earths. This is necessary because it is sometimes stated that REEs are neither scarce nor rare. This hypothesis is mainly based on simple geological indicators, which are in turn based on the concept of physical availability. Therefore, different indicators for natural resource scarcity from the fields of geology, thermoeconomics and economics will be discussed and applied to Rare Earths in order to test this hypothesis. Chapter 4 will first discuss and review the Hotelling rule as an adequate methodical approach to answer research questions (1) and (2). Then, the historical optimal paths of extraction and price development are modeled in order to test the thesis that Rare Earths were underpriced in the past. Finally, four scenarios for the optimal future path of extraction are modeled in order to answer research question (2). Chapter 5 first reviews additional reasons for the adjustments in the regulatory framework of the Chinese REEs sector and the impacts of implemented measures on the Chinese market and price-setting power. It then discusses the counteractions of the major REEs consuming countries in the rest of the world and their effectiveness in breaking the Chinese virtual monopoly. Finally, the implications of measures of both China and the rest of the world for the Chinese optimal future path of extraction are analyzed. The study ends with a conclusion in Chapter 6.

Notes

1 In the course of this study, the People's Republic of China will be abbreviated as "China" and will refer only to Mainland China. The Special Administrative Regions of Hong Kong and Macau are excluded.

2 Natural resources policies are all government measures that intervene in the natural resources allocation, use or supply. It is justified by the needs to secure the supply with specific resources at an adequate price, to reduce the environmental impact of resource use or to compensate for market failures.

3 In the course of this study, the terms "Rare Earths", "Rare Earths Oxides", "Rare Earth Elements" and "Rare Earth Metals" will be used. The terms "Rare Earths", "Rare Earth Elements" and "Rare Earth Metals" are also interchangeable. The term "Rare Earth Oxides" specifically refers to Rare Earths in their oxidized form.

4 Perfect competition is fulfilled when the market has the following characteristics: an atomistic market structure with a large number of buyers and sellers and absence of individual market power to influence prices, freely mobile resources, the absence of barriers to enter and exit the market and a perfect distribution of information and homogenous productions.

5 In Chinese, the national programs are referred as "guidelines" since the Eleventh Five-Year program in 2006 and not as "plans" anymore. This choice of words should emphasize that the targets in the programs are not as binding as in the periods of economic planning anymore. Because the term "plan" is still internationally used in the vast majority of publications, this study will also use the term "plan" instead of "guideline" in order to prevent misunderstandings.

6 "A national economy in which the government seeks to determine economic activity largely through a mechanism of central planning, as in the former Soviet Union, in

contrast to a market economy which depends heavily upon market forces to allocate productive resources. In a 'non-market' economy, production targets, prices, costs, investment, allocations, raw materials, labour, international trade and most other economic aggregates are manipulated within a national economic plan drawn up by a central planning authority; hence, the public sector makes the major decisions affecting demand and supply within the national economy" (United Nations Conference on Trade and Development, n.d.).

7 An oligopolistic market is characterized by a supply side with only a few suppliers that have some market power and could either cooperate in a cartel in order to set monopolistic prices or compete with each other.

Bibliography

Adachi, G., Imanaka, N., & Tamura, S. (2010). Research trends in rare earths: A preliminary analysis. *Journal of Rare Earths*, *28*(6), 843–846.

Alonso, E., Sherman, A. M., Wallington, T. J., Everson, M. P., Field, F. R., Roth, R., & Kirchain, R. E. (2012). Evaluating rare earth availability: A case with revolutionary demand from clean technologies. *Environmental Science & Technology*, *46*(6), 3406–3414.

Angerer, G., Erdmann, L., Marscheider-Weidemann, F., Scharp, M., Luellmann, A., Handke, V., & Marwede, M. (2009). *Rohstoffe für Zukunftstechnologien: Einfluss des branchenspezifischen Rohstoffbedarfs in rohstoffintensiven Zukunftstechnologien auf die zukuenftige Rohstoffnachfrage* [Raw materials for future technologies: The influence of branch-specific natural resource consumption in material-intensive and resource-sensitive future technologies on the future demand for raw materials]. Stuttgart: Fraunhofer IRB Verlag.

Bare anger. (2010, November 10). *The Economist*. Retrieved from www.economist.com/node/17416850.

Biedermann, R. P. (2014). China's rare earth sector: Between domestic consolidation and global hegemony. *International Journal of Emerging Markets*, *9*(2), 276–293.

Binnemans, K., & Jones, P. T. (2015). Rare earths and the balance problem. *Journal of Sustainable Metallurgy*, *1*(1), 29–38.

Boer, H., & Lammertsma, K. (2013). Scarcity of Rare Earth Elements. *ChemSusChem*, *6*(11), 2045–2055.

Bradshaw, A. M., Reuter, B., & Hamacher, T. (2013). The potential scarcity of rare elements for the Energiewende. *Green*, *3*(2), 93–111.

Butler, C. J. (2014). Rare Earth Elements: China's monopoly and implications for U.S. national security. *The Fletcher Forum of World Affairs*, *38*(1), 23–39.

Castor, S. B. (2008). Rare earth deposits of North America. *Resource Geology*, *58*(4), 337–347.

Clagett, N. (2013). A rare opportunity: Streamlining permitting for rare earth materials within the United States. *Journal of Energy and Environmental Law*, *4*(2), 123–138.

Erdmann, L., Behrendt, S., & Feil, M. (2011). *Kritische Rohstoffe für Deutschland: Identifikation aus Sicht deutscher Unternehmen wirtschaftlich bedeutsamer mineralischer Rohstoffe, deren Versorgungslage sich mittel- bis langfristig als kritisch erweisen könnte* [Critical raw materials for Germany: Identification of economically significant mineral resources, whose supply situation could prove critical in the medium to long term, from the perspective of German companies]. Berlin: Institut für Zukunftstechnologien, Adelphi.

Goldman, J. A. (2014). The U.S. rare earth industry: Its growth and decline. *The Journal of Policy History, 26*(2), 139–166.

Graedel, T. E., Barr, R., Chandler, C., Chase, T., Choi, J., Christoffersen, L., . . . Zhu, C. (2012). Methodology of metal criticality determination. *Environmental Science & Technology, 46*(2), 1063–1070.

Grasso, V. B. (2013). *Rare Earth Elements in national defense: Background, oversight issues, and options for congress* (CRS Report for Congress R41744). Retrieved from www.fas.org/sgp/crs/natsec/R41744.pdf.

He, Y. (2014). Reregulation of China's rare earth production and export. *International Journal of Emerging Markets, 9*(2), 236–256.

Hilpert, H. G., & Kröger, A. E. (2011). Seltene Erden: Die Vitamine der Industrie [Rare earths: Industrial vitamins]. In S.-A. Mildner (Ed.), *Konfliktrisiko Rohstoffe?: Herausforderungen und Chancen im Umgang mit knappen Ressourcen* [Conflict risk: Raw materials? Challenges and opportunities in handling with scarce resources] (pp. 159–167). Berlin: German Institute for International and Security Affairs.

Hilpert, H. G., & Mildner, S.-A. (2013). *Fragmentation or cooperation in global resource governance? A comparative analysis of the raw materials strategies of the G20* (German Institute for International and Security Affairs Research Paper 1/2013). Retrieved from www.swp-berlin.org/fileadmin/contents/products/research_papers/2013_RP01_hlp_mdn.pdf.

Humphries, M. (2013). *Rare Earth Elements: The global supply chain* (CRS Report for Congress 41347). Retrieved from www.fas.org/sgp/crs/natsec/R41347.pdf.

Hurst, C. (2010). *China's Rare Earth Elements industry: What can the west learn?* Washington, DC: Institute for the Analysis of Global Security. Retrieved from www.iags.org/rareearth0310hurst.pdf.

Jebe, R., Mayer, D., & Lee, Y.-S. (2012). China's export restrictions of raw materials and rare earths: A new balance between free trade and environmental protection? *The George Washington International Law Review, 44*(4), 579–642.

Jordens, A., Cheng, Y. P., & Waters, K. E. (2013). A review of the beneficiation of Rare Earth Element bearing minerals. *Minerals Engineering, 41*, 97–114.

Kanazawa, Y., & Kamitani, M. (2006). Rare earth minerals and resources in the world. *Journal of Alloys and Compounds, 408–412*, 1339–1343.

Krugman, P. (2010, October 17). Rare and foolish. *The New York Times*. Retrieved from www.nytimes.com/2010/10/18/opinion/18krugman.html?_r=0.

Lackner, D., & McEwen-Fial, S. (2011). *From resource advantage to economic superiority: Development and implications of China's rare earth policy* (Frankfurt Working Papers on East Asia 06/2011). Retrieved from www.izo.uni-frankfurt.de/Veroeffentlichungen/Frankfurt-Working-Papers-on-East-Asia/WP_6-2011_Lackner_and_McEwen_Rare_earth_China.pdf.

Long, K. R., Van Gosen, B. S., Foley, N. K., & Cordier, D. J. (2010). *The principal Rare Earth Elements deposits of the United States: A summary of domestic deposits and a global perspective* (U.S. Geological Survey Scientific Investigations Report 2010–5220). Retrieved from https://pubs.usgs.gov/sir/2010/5220/.

Mancheri, N. A. (2015). World trade in rare earths, Chinese export restrictions, and implications. *Resources Policy, 46*(2), 262–271.

Mazza, M., Blumenthal, D., & Schmitt, G. J. (2013). *Ensuring Japan's critical resource security: Case studies in Rare Earth Element and natural gas supplies*. Washington, DC: American Enterprise Institute. Retrieved from www.aei.org/papers/foreign-and-defense-policy/regional/asia/ensuring-japans-critical-resource-security-case-studies-in-rare-earth-element-and-natural-gas-supplies/.

Miller, T. (2006). *Einfluss Seltener Erden in der Schweine- und Kälbermast* [Influence of Rare Earth Elements on fattening pigs and calves] (Doctoral dissertation). Retrieved from https://edoc.ub.uni-muenchen.de/5202/.

Morrison, W. M., & Tang, R. (2012). *China's rare earth industry and export regime: Economic and trade implications for the United States* (CRS Report for Congress 42510). Retrieved from www.fas.org/sgp/crs/row/R42510.pdf.

Mueller, M., Schweizer, D., & Seiler, V. (2014). *Wealth effects of rare earth prices and China's Rare Earth Elements policy* (Center for International Economics Working Paper Series No. 2014–13). Retrieved from http://groups.uni-paderborn.de/wp-wiwi/RePEc/pdf/ciepap/WP88.pdf.

Nassar, N. T., Du, X., & Graedel, T. E. (2015). Criticality of the Rare Earth Elements. *Journal of Industrial Ecology*, *19*(6), 1044–1054.

National Research Council. (2008). *Minerals, critical minerals, and the U.S. economy*. Washington, DC: The National Academies Press.

Olson, J. C., Shawe, D. R., Pray, L. C., & Sharp, W. N. (1954). *Rare-earth mineral deposits of the Mountain Pass District San Bernadino County California* (Geological Survey Professional Paper 261). Washington, DC: United States Government Printing Office.

Papp, J. F., Bray, E. L., Edelstein, D. L., Fenton, M. D., Guberman, D. E., Hedrick, J. B., . . . Tolcin, A. C. (2008). *Factors that influence the price of Al, Cd, Co, Cu, Fe, Ni, Pb, Rare Earth Elements, and Zn* (U.S. Geological Survey Open-File Report 2008–1356). Retrieved from https://pubs.er.usgs.gov/publication/ofr20081356.

Pothen, F. (2013a). *Dynamic market power in an exhaustible resource industry: The case of Rare Earth Elements* (ZEW Discussion Paper No. 14–005). Retrieved from http://ftp.zew.de/pub/zew-docs/dp/dp14005.pdf.

Pothen, F. (2013b). *The metal resources (METRO) model: A dynamic partial equilibrium model for metal markets applied to Rare Earth Elements* (ZEW Discussion Paper No. 13–112). Retrieved from http://ftp.zew.de/pub/zew-docs/dp/dp13112.pdf. 22.11.2014.

Ribeiro, G. F. (2014). Export controls as industrial policy on natural resources regulatory limitations on China-raw materials and China-rare earths cases. *Brazilian Journal of International Law*, *12*(2), 78–92.

Ruettinger, L., & Feil, M. (2011). *Sustainable prevention of resource conflicts: New risks raw materials for the future? Case study and scenarios for China and rare earths* (Report 3.4). Berlin: Adelphi.

Sanyal, P., Brady, P. V., & Vugrin, E. D. (2013). *The impact of trade costs on rare earth exports: A stochastic frontier estimation approach* (Sandia Report SAND2013–7751). Retrieved from http://prod.sandia.gov/techlib/access-control.cgi/2013/137751.pdf.

Schueler, D., Liu, R., Buchert, M., Dittrich, S., & Merz, C. (2011). *Study on rare earths and their recycling* (Oeko-Institut e.V. Final Report for the Greens/EFA Group in the European Parliament). Retrieved from www.oeko.de/oekodoc/1112/2011-003-en.pdf.

Silberglitt, R., Bartis, J. T., Chow, B. G., An, D. L., & Brady, K. (2013). *Critical materials present danger to US manufacturing*. Santa Monica: RAND Corporation.

Smith, S. A. (2014, October 29). The Senkaku islands and Japan's evolving diplomacy. *The Council on Foreign Relations*. Retrieved from www.cfr.org/territorial-disputes/senkaku-islands-japans-evolving-diplomacy/p33698.

Ting, M. H., & Seaman, J. (2013). Rare earths: Future elements of conflict in Asia? *Asian Studies Review*, *37*(2), 234–252.

United Nations Conference on Trade and Development. (n.d.). *Glossary of customs terms: Non-market economy*. Retrieved from www.asycuda.org/cuglossa.asp?term=market+economy.

United Nations Conference on Trade and Development. (2014). *Commodities at a glance: Special issue on rare earths*. Geneva: UNCTAD.

Van Calster, G. (2013). China, minerals export, raw and rare earth materials: A perfect storm for World Trade Organization dispute settlement. *Review of European, Comparative & International Environmental Law*, *22*(1), 117–122.

Wang, X., Lei, Y., Ge, J., & Wu, S. (2015). Production forecast of China's rare earths based on the Generalized Weng model and policy recommendations. *Resource Policy*, *43*, 11–18.

Wuebbeke, J. (2013). Rare Earth Elements in China: Policies and narratives of reinventing an industry. *Resources Policy*, *38*(3), 384–394.

Zhang, L., Guo, Q., Zhang, J., Huang, Y., & Xiong, T. (2015). Did China's rare earth export policies work? Empirical evidence from USA and Japan. *Resources Policy*, *43*, 82–90.

Zhang, S. (2013). On problems in rare earth exports of China and countermeasures. *International Business and Management*, *6*(1), 21–25.

2 Introduction to Rare Earth Metals

Chapter 2 gives an overall introduction to Rare Earth Metals as an exhaustible natural resource. First, the special physical-chemical properties of REMs and geological aspects of their deposits are highlighted. Second, an overview of the global stocks of resources and reserves and a review of the mining and processing process are given. Third, the historical development trends in the extraction of Rare Earths are examined. Finally, the subsection about the fields of REEs application explains their commercial and non-commercial importance.

Physical-chemical and geological properties

The REMs group consists of 15 metals with the atomic numbers 57 through 71 in the narrow definition. This group is also called the lanthanide series because it compromises lanthanum as well as the elements from cerium through lutetium, which share chemical similarities with lanthanum. In the broad definition, the group additionally includes the elements scandium (atomic number 21) and yttrium (atomic number 39) as the sixteenth and seventeenth REMs (Hurst, 2010, p. 3; Jordens et al., 2013, p. 98). While Scandium and Yttrium do not belong to the lanthanide group, they are commonly found in the same mineral assemblages (U.S. Environmental Protection Agency, 2012, pp. 2–1). In the following, this study will refer to the broad definition of the REMs group. Figure 2.1 illustrates the location of the REMs group in the periodic table of elements.

The REMs group is further divided into two or three subgroups, respectively. Although this division is based on the atomic weight of the different Rare Earth Elements, the actual determination of the group boundaries is arbitrary. In the first classification, the REEs are divided into light and heavy Rare Earths. The light REMs are also called the cerium subgroup and consist of the first eight Rare Earths, from lanthanum to gadolinium. The heavy REMs are synonymously called the yttrium subgroup and incorporate the remaining nine REEs. The second classification divides the main group into the light Rare Earths or cerium subgroup, which consists of the elements from lanthanum to samarium; the middle Rare Earths or terbium subgroup, which consists of the metals from europium to dysprosium; and the heavy Rare Earths or yttrium subgroup, which incorporates the REMs from holmium to lutetium, and scandium and yttrium (British Geological

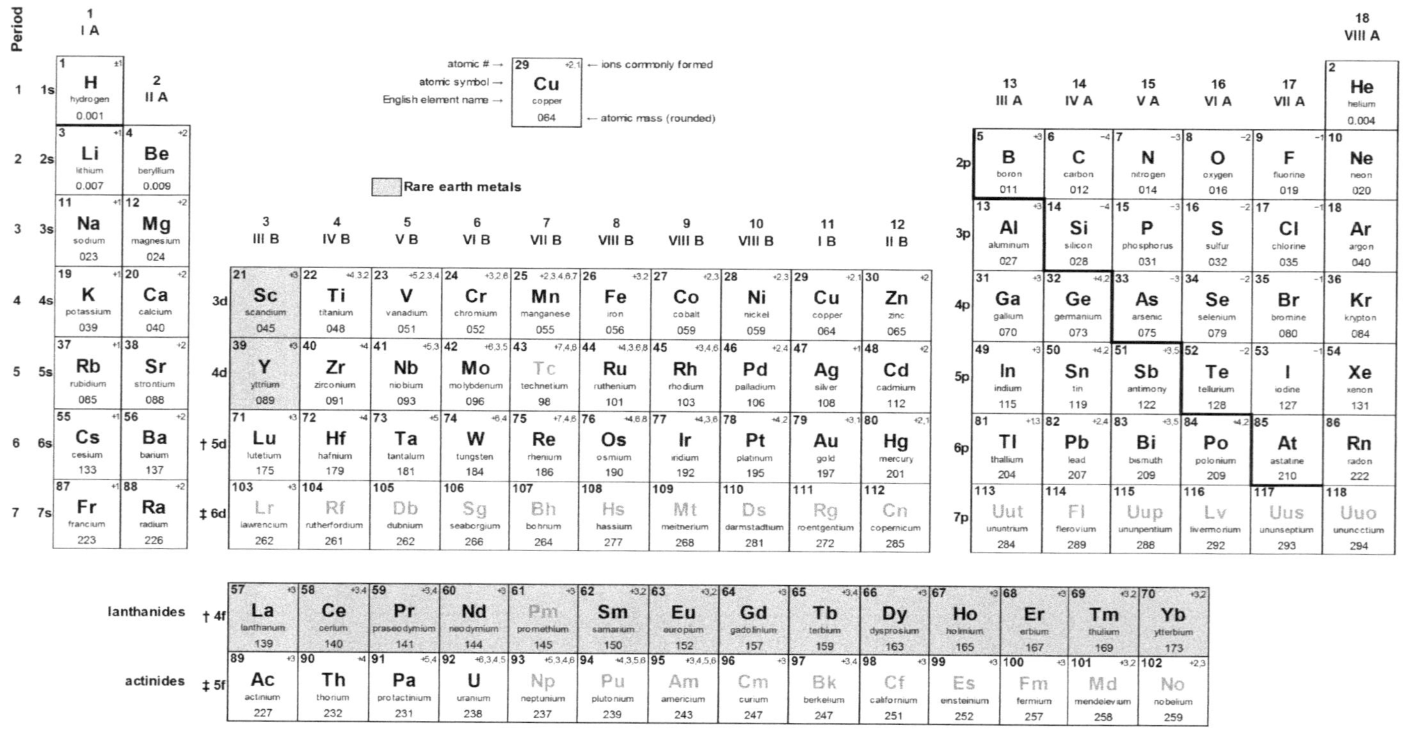

Figure 2.1 Periodic table of elements

Source: Adapted from Bigler, J. (2016). *Periodic Table and Element Data in spreadsheet form*. Retrieved from www.mrbigler.com/documents/Periodic-Table.xls. Copyright 2007–2017 Jeff Bigler.

Survey, 2011, p. 2; Gupta & Krishnamurthy, 2005, pp. 8–21). As the first classification is more widespread in the literature about Rare Earths, this study will also utilize this grouping.

The root for the close chemical similarity of all the REEs is the similar electronic configuration. REEs are highly electropositive and mostly form trivalent ionic mineral compounds. In addition, Rare Earths are highly reactive towards oxygen and form solid solution with it. Because of the similar chemical nature (ionic radii and oxidation states) of all REEs, they often substitute for one another in crystal structures so that multiple Rare Earths occur in one mineral (Gupta & Krishnamurthy, 2005, p. 61). Another feature is the "lanthanide contraction". This term describes a steady decrease in the size of atoms and ions with the increase in atomic numbers in the lanthanide series. As a result, lanthanum has the greatest and lutetium has the smallest radius. The basicity of each individual REEs is also related to this. While the basicity decreases from lanthanum to scandium, the variation in basicity of adjacent elements in the series is not large. A large variation simplifies the separation of metals from one another in the so-called classical separation procedures like fractional crystallization.[1] Therefore, the separation of adjacent REMs is most difficult and requires more complex separation procedures. Consequently, it took almost 160 years after the first discovery of a REM near the Swedish town of Ytterby[2] in 1787 and the research of several generations of mineralogists and chemists to isolate every individual REEs from their mineral compound and clearly identify them (Gupta & Krishnamurthy, 2005, pp. 3–17).

As mentioned before, individual REEs are not found in their metallic state in nature due to their high reactivity but form mineral compounds with other REMs and third elements. There are over 200 known REEs-bearing minerals. These minerals predominantly contain either light or heavy REEs. The light REEs-dominated minerals include bastnaesite, monazite, allanite, loparite, ancylite, parasite, lanthanite, chevinite, cerite, stillwellite, britholite, fluocerite and cerianite; the heavy REEs-dominated minerals include gadolinite, xenotime, samarskite, euxenite, fergusonite, yttrotantalite, yttrotungstite and yttrialite (Haque et al., 2014, p. 618). Despite this large variety of different mineral compounds containing REEs, only three types are considered commercially feasible and are predominantly mined at the current state of extraction technology: bastnaesite, xenotime and monazite (U.S. Environmental Protection Agency, 2012, pp. 2–3; Weng et al., 2015, p. 1929). These three types form about 95% of the global reserves for Rare Earths (Golev et al., 2014, p. 53).

Bastnaesite[3] is the most abundant of these three minerals. It occurs as veins or dissemination of carbonate-silicate rocks in the geological environments of contact metamorphic zones,[4] vein deposits[5] and pegmatites.[6] As a fluorcarbonate of the cerium group, it is especially enriched in light REO, which constitute 75% of the compound. Therefore, bastnaesite deposits are the primary sources of extracted light REMs (Gupta & Krishnamurthy, 2005, p. 61; U.S. Environmental Protection Agency, 2012, pp. 2–3).

Monazite[7] occurs in the pegmatites of acidic igneous rocks, metamorphic rocks, some vein deposits and placer deposits.[8] It is also generally enriched with light

REEs, especially cerium, lanthanum and neodymium. In comparison to bastnaesite, monazite incorporates lower shares of lanthanum but larger shares of neodymium and heavy REO. The overall share of REO approximately is 65%. Furthermore, it often contains the radioactive element thorium in various amounts and sometimes contains uranium (British Geological Survey, 2011, p. 3; Gupta & Krishnamurthy, 2005, p. 62f.; U.S. Environmental Protection Agency, 2012, pp. 2–4). This has an impact on mining and processing procedures and regulations, which is further discussed later.

Xenotime is comprised of around 60% of REO. It contains an even larger share of heavy REEs than monazite and is dominated by yttrium, dysprosium, erbium, ytterbium and holtum. This yttrium phosphate[9] is found as a minor constituent of granite or gneiss, or it co-occurs with monazite in placer deposits after having undergone a weathering, a transportation and a concentration process. Thorium and uranium are also sometimes found as impurities in xenotime but less often than they are found in monazite (British Geological Survey, 2011, p. 3; Gupta & Krishnamurthy, 2005, p. 63; U.S. Environmental Protection Agency, 2012, pp. 2–4).

Although not considered a major important source for REMs due to its low grade of only 0.05 to 0.2% REO content, the mineral type of ion adsorption clays is considered important in the course of this study. This type is extensively distributed mainly over the provinces of Jiangxi, Guangdong, Hunan and Fujian in southern China and was formed out of granites, which have gone through a strong chemical and biological weathering process due to the warm and moist weather in the subtropical zone of southern China. At the end of the weathering process, the REEs were absorbed in their ion state on the surface of clay minerals. The advantages of ion adsorption clays are the absence of radioactive impurities and simple mining opportunities due to the weathering process. Furthermore, this mineral type must not be omitted in this study because it accounts for more of the 80% of global, known heavy REMs reserves (Kanazawa & Kamitani, 2006, p. 1343; Yang et al., 2013, p. 133).

Overview of the global stocks of resources and reserves

There are different national and international approaches to assess the current stock of REMs. The USGS uses the term "resource" to describe "a concentration of naturally occurring solid, liquid, or gaseous materials in or on the Earth's crust in such form that economic extraction of a commodity is currently or potentially feasible" (U.S. Geological Survey, 1976, p. A2f.). Resources are further divided into identified or undiscovered resources. The term "identified resources" is hereby used to describe deposits whose locations, quality and quantity have been geologically measured. Undiscovered resources have not been geologically measured but are assumed to exist on the base of broad geologic knowledge and theory. This is further subdivided into hypothetical undiscovered resources in known mining districts with known geological conditions and speculative resources in areas with favorable geological conditions where no discoveries have been made yet (Ibid., p. A3f.).

The reserve is "the portion of the identified resource from which a usable mineral and energy commodity can be economically and legally extracted at the time of determination" (U.S. Geological Survey, 1976, p. A3f.), whereas identified subeconomic resources are resources which are not a part of the reserves due to current economic and legal conditions. This is further divided into paramarginal resources, which are on the brink of being economically extractable or are only not commercially practical due to legal or political conditions, and submarginal resources, which would need higher prices or progress in cost-reducing extraction technology to be economically feasible. Reserves are also subclassified in measured reserves, for which tonnage is computed based on extensive inspection, sampling and measurement, and indicated reserves, for which tonnage and grade are computed partly from inspection, sampling and measurement on a lesser scale. Measured and indicated reserves combined form the class of demonstrated reserves. Inferred reserves are the portion of reserves for which the quantitative estimates are only based on broad knowledge of the geologic character of the deposits and very few, if any, samples or measurements (U.S. Geological Survey, 1976, p. A3f.). Figure 2.2 summarizes the classification of minerals resources and their interconnections.

The problem of international comparison of resources and reserves is based on differences between national classification systems. The BGS used a different classification system in the past, and tried to create and establish a new, internationally adopted system in the early 1980s but did not succeed. Then, the BGS adopted the USGS system so that data on REMs reserves and resources from both geological surveys are compatible and comparable (Riddler, 1994, p. 8). The definitions of Chinese, Australian and Canadian geological institutions still differ in the definition of reserves and resources from the USGS/BGS system. Since 1994, the Committee for Mineral Reserves International Reporting Standards, which was founded by an

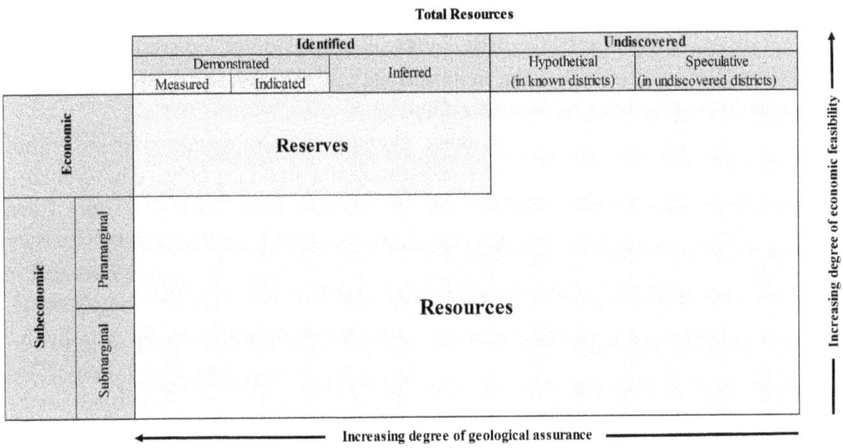

Figure 2.2 USGS classification of mineral resources

Source: Adapted from U.S. Geological Survey (1976, p. A2).

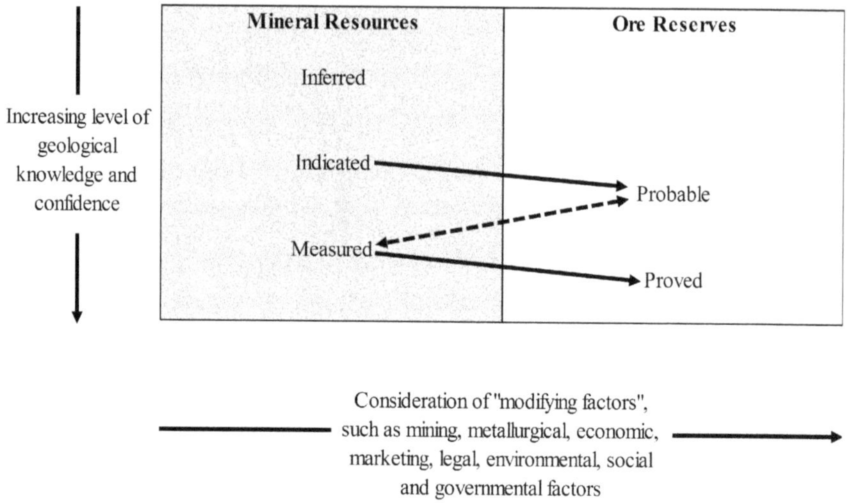

Figure 2.3 CRIRSCO standardized classification

alliance of national organizations for reporting mineral resources, is responsible for creating and establishing a unified standard on the international level. It is currently representing Australia, Canada, Chile, Mongolia, Russia, South Africa, Europe and the USA, and published the first unified template for reporting stocks of reserves and resources for mineral resources in 2006. This template is displayed in Figure 2.3. When compared with the USGS system, the most significant change is the elimination of the "undiscovered resources" category, which leads to a lower overall accounted resource base. The second divergence is the extension of factors that influence the accessibility and classification of deposits as part of the resource or reserve stocks. Whereas the USGS has only considered economic and legal conditions, the criteria of mining, metallurgical, marketing, environmental, social and governmental issues have been added.

Despite this unified available standard, some of the member countries still either report mineral resources according to their national standard or have not yet converted data from the old national system to the new international system. Even more, China is not a member country of the CRIRSCO and still uses its own standard. This standard is not comparable with the CRIRSCO standard and is "not regarded as particularly suitable for reporting in a market economy" by the CRIRSCO because it creates difficulties for both domestic and foreign companies operating in the Chinese resource sector (Stoker, 2009, p. 20). For example, the availability of credible and publicly accessible geological information is not on the same level in breadth and quality as in Western countries so that the mining potential of same districts and the tonnage of their reserves might be overstated (Vivoda, 2011, p. 52). Therefore, there are still discrepancies in the data and extreme caution is needed when national tonnages are directly compared.

Table 2.1 Reserves in 2015 (in percentage of total REO equivalent content)

China	42.31%
Other countries	31.54%
Brazil	16.92%
Australia	2.46%
India	2.38%
United States	1.38%
Malaysia	0.02%

Source: Data retrieved from U.S. Geological Survey (1996–2016).

A second deviation in data on reserves and stocks stems from different stated units. The USGS states reserves and resources of REEs in REO-equivalent content. Another used unit is the tonnage of the REEs-bearing minerals, which have at least a specified, minimum cut-off grade. The stated size of REEs reserves is larger when this measurement is used instead of the measurement of REO equivalent content. Table 2.1 illustrates the distribution of global reserves in 2015 as a percentage of total REO equivalent content based on USGS data.

The USGS estimated global reserves at 130 mil. tons in 2015 (U.S. Geological Survey, 1996–2016). With 42.31% or 55 million tons, China has the highest proportion of global reserves. However, in a white paper published by the State Council of the People's Republic of China in 2012, it is stated that China only possesses 23% of the total Rare Earth reserves (Information Office of the State Council, 2012, p. 3). It is unclear which unit of measurement has been used to indicate the size of Chinese reserves in this document. Another document of the Chinese Ministry of Environmental Protection reports 52 million tons of proven industrial reserves (Schueler et al., 2011, p. 8). The term "industrial reserves" still stems from the old mineral classification system of the former Union of Soviet Socialist Republics, which the PRC had once adopted. This classification system was actually replaced by the 1999 Chinese Mineral Resource/Reserve Classification but is still being used from time to time in official documents. Industrial reserves are here as the part of the resources that is economically exploitable (also called "balanced resources") less estimated losses through the mining process (Thomas, 2012, p. 194ff.). Although the deviation between the two different identifications of Chinese REEs reserves is relatively small and could be explained by application of estimated losses in the mining process, the resulting estimates of the global reserves differ greatly. The indication of 52 million tons as 23% of total global reserves implies a Chinese estimation of global reserves of over 226 million ton REO equivalent.

Another factor for differences in estimated and reported reserves is the base price. Downward and upward trends of resource prices have a significant impact on the commercial exploitability. A sharp, enduring decline in prices could lead to adjustments of stated reserves. Therefore, stated reserves could also differ when different base prices are used in different estimations, or could fluctuate with enduring changes in price trends. For example, the USGS reported 13 million tons of U.S. reserves in 2010. While the accumulated U.S. production was not higher than 14.000 tons from 2010 to 2014, the indicated reserves dramatically decreased to 1.8 million tons in the same period (U.S. Geological Survey, 1996–2016). This indicates an adjustment of reserves due to diminished commercial exploitability.

While the stock of resources is also changing over time due to ongoing mining, exploration and development of new deposits, and extensive inspection, sampling and measurement of hypothetical and speculative deposits, the fluctuations tend not to be as drastic as in the case of reserves. The EU Commission–funded project Polinares estimated total global resources of 311.3 million tons of REO equivalent in a 2012 fact sheet about Rare Earths (Polinares Consortium, 2012, p. 2).

The global resources are highly concentrated in only two countries that have a combined share of 81%. With 169.4 million tons REO or 54% of total global resources, Russia is estimated to have the highest stock of REO resources. Despite this large stock of resources, Russia only has a share of global reserves of 14%. On the other hand, China possesses only 27% of the global resource stock but had a share of 65% of the global reserves in 2011 according to the Polinares data (Polinares Consortium, 2012, p. 2). This indicates a relatively low level of commercial exploitability of Russian deposits and a relatively high level of commercial exploitability of Chinese deposits.

While the known deposits are scattered on all continents around the world, only the deposits of China, the Kvanefjeld deposit in Greenland, the Mountain Pass deposit in the USA and the Mountain Weld deposit in Australia are mainly discussed in the literature. These deposits either are currently mined or are in an advanced phase of development, and they contain such large contents of Rare Earths that they are regarded as the potential primary sources for current and future REEs demand.

The Bayan Obo deposit, which is located 135 km northwest of the city Baotou in Inner Mongol Autonomous Province, is the most important deposit in China. The

Table 2.2 Resources in 2011 (in percentage of total REO equivalent content)

Russia	54.0%
China	27.0%
South America	5.0%
Other Asia	4.0%
Greenland	3.0%
Australia	2.0%
USA	2.0%
Canada	1.0%
Africa	1.0%
Other Europe	0.4%

Source: Data retrieved from Polinares Consortium (2012, p. 2).

dolomite rock formation, which hosts the three ore bodies (main ore body, east ore body and east ore body), is 18 km in length from east to west and 2 km in width (Kanazawa & Kamitani, 2006, p. 1342). Around 48 to 50% of the total Chinese production of REO is extracted from the Bayan Obo mine (Ruettinger & Feil, 2011, p. 8), which approximately accounts for 95% of total Chinese REO reserves (Gupta & Krishnamurthy, 2005, p. 120). The deposit is a polymetallic ore mine and contains not only REEs but also iron ore and niobium. Bayan Obo was originally mainly mined for its iron reserves of circa 1.5 billion tons with an average grade of 35%, while REMs (at least 48 million tons with an average grade of 6% REO content) and niobium (around 1 million tons with an average grade of 0.13%) are only co-products of iron ore extraction (Kanazawa & Kamitani, 2006, p. 1342). For every kilogram of produced REO, 170 kilograms of iron ore are extracted and sold (Valero Capilla & Valero Delgado, 2015, p. 241). This co-production of different metals greatly enhances the economic exploitability of Bayan Obo as a source for Rare Earths. Furthermore, it assumedly is the largest Chinese deposit of thorium (Ruettinger et al., 2015, p. 2). Thorium is currently researched as radioactive fuel for nuclear plants. Uranium is used in all commercial nuclear plants in China, but the country has run short of domestic reserves and is therefore searching for possible substitutions (Chen, 2014). When thorium can be successfully utilized as a substitute, this will further strengthen the economic exploitability. While 15 different REEs-bearing minerals are to be found in the ore bodies of Bayan Obo, the most productive ones are bastnaesite and monazite, which are contained in the ratio 7:3 or 6:4 (Li & Yang, 2014, p. 27f.). As explained earlier, bastnaesite is predominantly rich in light REO. Monazite is also rich in light REO but also contains smaller amounts of heavy REO. Thus, the Bayan Obo is all in all rather rich in light and rather poor in heavy REO.

The ion adsorption clays of southern China of Xunwu and Longnan account for only 3% of China's total REO reserves. The single deposits are relatively small and in the range of 3 to 12 tons of REEs-bearing minerals with low grades of 0.03 to 0.35% REO content. They are between 5 and 30 meters in thickness. The REEs-enriched layer of these deposits are located 0–2 meters under the soil and range from 5 to 10 meters in thickness (BGS, 2011, p. 11). Despite their small size, low grade and high dispersion over a wide area of the remote Nanling mountain ranges that forms the border between Central China and South China, the REEs-bearing clay deposits are of global importance because they account for 80% (around 1 million ton of REO equivalent content) of the global, known reserves for heavy REO (Li & Yang, 2014, p. 33).

An alternative deposit that is a promising source for heavy REMs is the Kvanefjeld project located on the Kuannersuit Plateau of the Ilimaussaq complex in southern Greenland. While the start of mining is still unknown, the development is in an advanced phase. The necessary studies on economic feasibility and environmental and social impacts were conducted and the mining license application phase was started in December 2015 (Greenland Minerals and Energy Ltd., 2015b). The Kvanefjeld project is comprised of several multi-element deposits, which are especially enriched in REEs, uranium and zinc. The three main deposits (Kvanefjeld deposit,

Sorenson deposit and Zone 3 deposit) combined contain 1.01 billion tons of ore resources with around 268 million tons of uranium oxides and 11.13 million tons of REO. Fourteen percent of the total Rare Earths content of the deposits are heavy Rare Earths (Greenland Minerals and Energy Ltd., 2015a, p. 3ff.). Due to the co-occurrence[10] with uranium, these REEs deposits could not be developed and mined in the past. Both Denmark and the Greenlandic government, which semi-autonomously governs the country since the "Act on Greenland Self-Government" of July 2009, had a zero-tolerance policy regarding mining of radioactive elements that prevented an earlier development (Hansen et al., 2013, p. 213ff.). This ban was lifted in a parliamentary vote in 2013. The Danish government, which still determines Greenland's foreign and defense policies, could have been able to uphold the ban of uranium mining due to national security issues[11] but also made a historical U-turn in its policies towards uranium mining and the future utilization of nuclear power ("Greenland drops uranium", 2013; Jacobsen, 2013). When fully operating, the Kvanefjeld project should be able to cover 25% of the world's REEs demand for one decade and is therefore considered the largest REEs mine outside China (Charles et al., 2013, p. 3; United Nations Conference on Trade and Development, 2014, p. 14).

The Mountain Pass deposit and mine in California is the largest REEs resource in the USA and still holds 20 to 47 million tons of ore with an estimated average grade of 8.9% REO after being mined for 50 years. The deposit consists of a carbonatite body with an overall length of 730 meters and an average width of 120 meters. It hosts the REEs-bearing mineral bastnaesite (10–15% of the total ore body) as well as calcite or dolomite (65%) and barite (20–25%). The mine was mined from 1952 on, but the mining permit expired and was not renewed in 2002. The open pit resulting from the first period of mining covers about 22 hectares and is circa 122 meters deep (Long et al., 2010, p. 36ff.).

The Mount Weld deposit in Western Australia has been mined since 2012. The REEs-bearing minerals monazite and xenotime are found encapsulated in iron oxide minerals in the main ore body (Haque et al., 2014, p. 621f.). The average grade in the ore of 14.8% total REO makes Mount Weld the world's richest known deposit (Golev et al., 2014, p. 53). The resource base of the deposit is 1.1834 million tons of REO (United Nations Conference on Trade and Development, 2014, p. 33). Due to the predominant occurrence of monazite, 95% of all REMs are light REMs so that the deposit is not a major source of heavy REO despite its high enrichment in Rare Earths (Ibid., p. 14). Unlike other monazite deposits, Mount Weld is relatively low in thorium but unusually high in europium. The co-occurrence and co-production of niobium and tantalum furthermore enhances the possibility of commercial exploitation (Gupta & Krishnamurthy, 2005, p. 82). While the goal of Lynas Corporation Ltd., the mining company extracting the deposit, is to reach a final annual production of 20,000 tons REO per year, the mine has only reached a production of 700 tons out of the 11,000 tons planned for 2012 (Humphries, 2013, p. 4). Therefore, it seems that this deposit will take a longer time to unfold its potential as a principal REEs source.

In addition to the validated stocks of resources and reserves of REEs, there are several reports on potential but unproven stocks. The first announcement that could have a major impact on the world's supply with REO stems from

North Korea. In 2013, North Korea reported to have found a large deposit at Jongju in the southern North Pyongan province (Els, 2013), which would contain 664.9 million tons at 9% total REO, 634 million tons between 5.7% and 9.0%, some billion tons between 3.97% and 5.7% and 2.8 billion tons of lower grade ores. This indicated amount of REEs contents would embody the largest know deposit of the world and would double the current estimates of REO reserves. Due to ongoing international sanctions against North Korea and possible political implications, this deposit will not be likely to be developed in the future even if a feasibility study shows a positive prospect of commercial exploitability (Haque et al., 2014, p. 624). Furthermore, the truth content of this report needs to be questioned. Many reports and announcements allegedly coming from North Korea turned out to be either hoaxes especially from South Korean and Japanese journalists, or official claims of the North Korean leadership that were soon proven to be wrong (Alfred, 2014; Broinowski, 2015). The reported size of the deposit has not been validated through the standard procedures of further exploration, inspection, sampling and measurement necessary to classify the deposit as reserves. Instead, the North Korean administration has advertised the discovery and emphasized its enormous size several times in new reports so that a high level of skepticism is appropriate (Jamasmie, 2015).

A more reliable report about a new discovery of large REEs resource stocks come from the "Japan Agency for Marine-Earth Science and Technology", which announced finding large deposits in the sedimentary mud of the seabed of the Pacific Oceans. According to rough estimations, this source could contain up to 100 billion tons of REO, which is almost a thousand times the reserves on the dry land. Because these deposits are located 3,500 to 6,000 meters deep in the ocean, numerous technical and economic barriers render an extraction impossible in the near future (Massari & Ruberti, 2013, p. 37).

In summary, the factual stocks of REEs resources and reserves are difficult to quantify due to international differences in mineral resource classification and in choice of the basic price to assess commercial exploitability as well as incomplete or invalidated country-level data that deviates from source to source. Because the USGS provides the world's largest data bank on resources, reserves and prices of REEs, its classification system will be used in the following. Although resources, reserves and known deposits are scattered all around the world, the most important, principal reserves and currently mined deposits are highly concentrated in a small number of countries. This is especially true for heavy Rare Earths, for which the ion adsorption clays of the Nanling area currently comprise the only reliable source in the world. While an alternative deposit is in development in Kvanefjeld, it is unclear when the mine will be operational.

Review of the mining and processing routes

The generalized processing route from extracted ores to individual pure Rare Earth Metals is divided five steps: mining, physical beneficiation, chemical treatment, separation and the step of reduction, refining and purification. These stages are displayed in Figure 2.4.

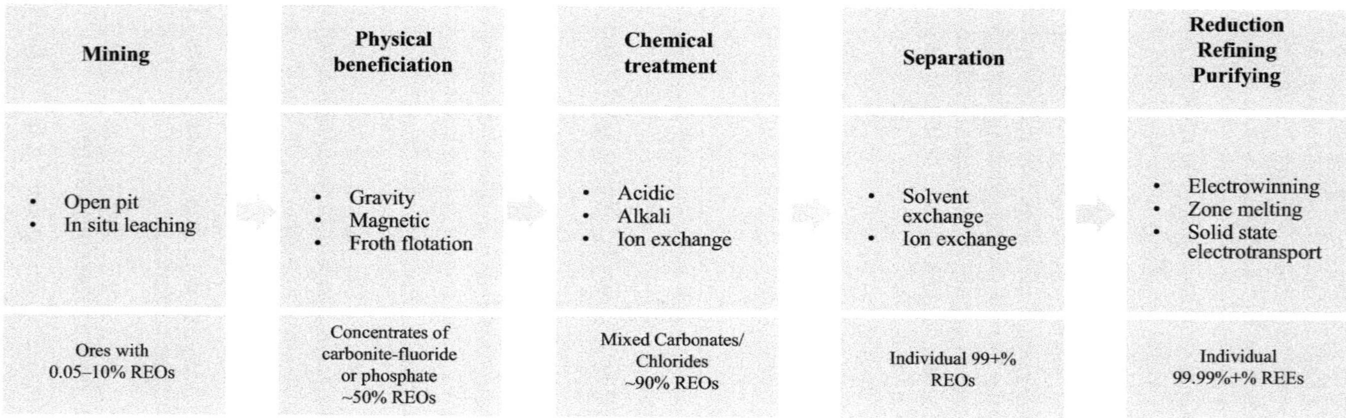

Figure 2.4 General processing routes for REE ores

Although these five steps are similar for most REEs-bearing deposits, the exact specifications of the process routes differ significantly depending on the exact mineral composition of each deposit. There is no standard procedure of REEs processing that could be applied to every Rare Earths mineral so that the mining techniques, the composition of chemical reagents, devices and the machinery used in the processing route have to be adjusted for each deposit. Treatment processes are affected by the type and nature of the deposit, the type and nature of other valuable minerals present with REO, the type and nature of gangue[12] minerals present in the deposit, the type and composition of the individual REO minerals and the social and environmental acceptability of the process (U.S. Environmental Protection Agency, 2012, pp. 4–1).

In the mining stage, the extraction techniques can be divided into surface and underground mining or in situ leach mining. Large open pit mines like in the case of Bayan Obo or Mountain Pass are typically used for surface mining of solid rock deposits. Drilling, earth-moving equipment and explosives are used to extract waste rock and ore. Underground mining, which is used to mine vein deposits, has the disadvantage of higher costs compared with surface mining but also has the advantage of producing smaller amounts of overburden and mineralized wastes, which have to be stored in stockpiles. While ratios of overburden to ore are between 1:1 to 1:20 for underground mines, they are between 10:1 to 80:1 for surface mines (U.S. Environmental Protection Agency, 2012, pp. 3–15). In situ leaching is an extraction technique predominantly used for the mining of soft rock deposits like the ion adsorption clays in south China. Hereby, one-third of the topsoil is removed, then holes of 0.8 meters in diameter and 1.5–3 meters in depth are drilled in a distance of 2–3 meters between holes. Then, a leaching solution is pumped into the deposit to dissolve the REEs-enriched layer. The slurry containing REO is finally driven out of the ground through injection of fresh water (Navarro & Zhao, 2014, p. 10). Due to lower required capital investment and low technology barriers, the extraction of heavy REO from clay deposits, which are not considered commercially feasible in general, takes place in decentralized, small and mobile plants (He, 2014, p. 241). The cost-related advantage of REMs-bearing clays manifest itself in the following steps of the processing route. Because the clays have already undergone a natural cracking procedure through weathering, their processing route only includes three stages (mining, separation and reduction, refining and purification) without the need of physical beneficiation and chemical treatment. The next required step, separation, is then undertaken in centralized facilities (Jordens et al., 2013, p. 102; Navarro & Zhao, 2014, p. 11).

The result of the mining stage is only the extraction of REMs-bearing, solid mineral compounds with low grades of 0.05% to 10% REO content, depending on the average grade of the individual deposit and the defined cut-off grade, from the ground. These mineral compounds have to be physically and chemically beneficiated, concentrated, separated and finally reduced, refined and purified into pure metals before they can be of any use for end-use applications. Due to this extensive processing route, only 50% of the final value of REMs is created in the mining stage, whereas it is 75% for most metals and over 90% for tin, silver and gold (Tyrer & Sykes, 2013, p. 14).

The next phase of processing, the physical beneficiation stage, aims to increase the REO content by separating the REMs from gangue minerals. The different techniques, which exploit differences in gravimetric, magnetizability and surface ionization potential, are gravity separation, magnetic separation and electrostatic separation and froth flotation. As the first step of all these procedures, the mineral compounds with REO content are crushed, grinded and milled into fine powder (U.S. Environmental Protection Agency, 2012, pp. 4–4).

The technique of wet gravity separation takes advantage of differences in density between REO and significantly less dense gangue materials (Jordens et al., 2013, p. 102). First, a pre-concentrate with a grade of 20 to 30% heavy minerals is produced by using a cone concentrator,[13] then a spiral concentrator is employed to achieve 80–90% of heavy minerals concentration. Afterwards, the concentrate will be further exposed to either gravity devices like shaking tables or operations of magnetic, electrostatic and froth flotation separation. In the process of magnetic separation, the difference in magnetic susceptibilities is exploited to initially extract strongly magnetic gangue minerals, for example iron, from the fine mineral powder, followed by extraction of the Rare Earths, which all show some degree of magnetic susceptibility due to their electronic configuration. Furthermore, xenotime, which has a higher magnetizability than monazite, can be isolated. Based on differences in conductivity, electrostatic separation is in general only used when other separation techniques will not suffice due to similar gravity and magnetic properties of the single minerals in the compound. Because the ground ore has to be completely dry, the energy costs associated with desiccation and electrostatic charging is seen as prohibitive (Jordens et al., 2013, p. 104). Froth flotation is used when the powder is too fine for other separation methods. It exploits the hydrophobicity of REEs and hydrophilicity of gangue materials. Hydrophobic materials are transported by air bubbles, on which they tend to stick, to the surface of the flotation pool, where they are skimmed (U.S. Environmental Protection Agency, 2012, pp. 4–5). The result of the beneficiation process are concentrated REMs-bearing minerals (bastnaesite, monazite or xenotime) with a grade of around 50% REO content.

These minerals are cracked in the stage of chemical treatment and converted to carbonates or chlorides, which can be then separated in the fifth stage under the use of process reagents such as inorganic acids (sulfuric acid, hydrochloric acid or nitric acid) and electrolytes such as ammonium chloride and thermal energy (Navarro & Zhao, 2014, p. 6). For example, the bastnaesite from Bayan Obo is cracked and converted into sulfates by roasting with 98% sulfuric acid at 500 degrees Celsius in a rotary kiln. In a leaching process with water and sodium chloride, the sulfates are then precipitated as a double sodium sulfate, converted to hydroxides in a strong caustic solution and finally dissolved in hydrochloride acid to obtain the chloride form required for the next stage (Peiro & Mendez, 2013, p. 1331f.).

In the fourth step, the chlorides or carbonates are separated into individual REO through solvent extraction or ion exchange. Solvent extraction utilizes the differences in basicity in order to obtain REO content of over 99%. Because the differences in basicity are only very small, the process is both time and cost intensive and is divided into several sub-steps: "separation of REO in trivalent stage, fractionation of REOs into three or four groups, separation of Y, extraction of Ce (Ce^{4+}) and Eu (Eu^{2+}), and separation of desired individual REO" (Navarro & Zhao, 2014, p. 5). Ion exchange as separation technique is also useable but in general less economical than solvent extraction in large-scale operations (Ibid.).

The achieved metal's purity grade of 99% and above is still not pure enough for many end-use applications. Thus, the goal of the last stage is to obtain individual Rare Earth Metals with purities of 99.99% and above by reduction, refining and purifying. The purpose of reduction, refining and purifying is the derivation of REEs from the REO compound through metallothermic reduction in molten salt or fused salt electrolysis (electrowinning) (Navarro & Zhao, 2014, p. 5). The utilized techniques, such as electrorefining or pyrovacuum treatment, depend on the specific impurities of the starting materials and the environment of the previous steps in the processing route (Gupta & Krishnamurthy, 2005, pp. 308–314).

The whole processing route is cost and input expensive. The facilities for the different subsequential steps of cracking and separation are more expansive than the other stages of REEs production (Tyrer & Sykes, 2013, p. 16), which significantly increases the level of required investments for a REEs project that includes all stages of the processing route and of the value chain. For example, the projected total cost of the development of the Kvanefjeld deposit are 1.36 billion USD. This is divided into major infrastructure costs of 240 million USD for the needed port, accommodation village and power plant; 315.5 million USD of indirect plan capital costs, for example for temporary construction facilities or engineering, procurement and construction; and 804.8 million of plant direct cost. Only 32.5 million of the plant direct cost is directly associated with mining, while 225.4 million are planned for the concentrator process plant and 371.2 million USD are required for the refinery process plant (Greenland Minerals and Energy Ltd., 2015a, p. 22). Therefore, besides the basic price, the pure tonnage is relevant to assess the economic exploitability of a deposit. Even if basic prices are high enough to offset mining costs, the high level of fixed investments for the whole processing chain needs to be considered. This is even truer due to the high loss of REEs in every stage as the result of inefficiency, technical inadequacies or barriers to physical-chemical possibilities. Even if relatively high recovery rates of 75% are assumed for each stage, the overall recovery rate will be only 23.7% for the whole process route from deposit to pure metals (Tyrer & Sykes, 2013, p. 16). In China, primary recovery rates of mining are in the range of 40 to 60% so that the overall recovery rate is indicated to be even below 23% (Schueler et al., 2011, p. 49). Therefore, the data on reserves would have to be adjusted for the global average recovery rate to assess potential global supply.

The input intensity is illustrated in Table 2.3 with the example of the mass balance of the chemical treatment stage of bastnaesite from Bayan Obo. For every ton of final Rare Earth Metals, 27.41 tons of inputs are needed. In the whole process, 5.97 tons of bastnaesite are first converted to 2.92 RE chlorides, which are

Table 2.3 Mass balance of the extraction of one ton of REMs from Bayan Obo (China)

	Chemical formula	*Input (tons)*	*Output (tons)*
Bastnaesite	$RECO_2F$	5.97	1.31
Sulfuric acid	H_2SO_4	4.41	0.97
Sodium chloride	NaCl	12.32	11.52
Sodium hydroxide	NaOH	1.64	0.36
Hydrochloric acid	HCl	1.17	0.26
Water	H_2O	1.90	3.47
Hydrofluoric acid	HF		0.47
Sodium sulfate	Na_2SO_4		3.03
RE sulfate	$RE(SO_4)_3$		1.36
RE disulfate	$RE_2(SO_4)_3*Na_2SO_4*12H_2O$		1.34
RE hydroxide	$RE(OH)_3$		0.40
RE chlorides	$RECl_3$		2.92
Total		**27.41**	**27.41**

Source: Data retrieved from Peiro and Mendez (2013, p. 1332).

then finally separated and converted to one ton of pure Rare Earth Metal. The use of 19.54 tons of chemical reagents in the cracking stage is a first indicator for the possible environmental impact of the processing route.

Each stage of the processing stage produces different wastes and emissions that pose a threat to the environment when not treated adequately. The wastes of the processing route and their corresponding waste management units and emissions are displayed in Figure 2.5 for the case of hard rock deposits. The first type of emission, dust, stems from the mining and drying processes or from the stockpiles of overburden materials, waste rocks or subeconomic ore. This dust contains fine particulate matter and, depending on the deposit type, metal and radioactive particles and volatile organic compounds. Wastewater as the second type of potential emissions is coming from the extraction process as mine water (also called neutral mine water), from the containment of surface or groundwater by stockpiled materials or from the tailings ponds[14] in the stages of beneficiation, chemical treatment and separation. The wastewater contains radioactive elements and metals from the deposit, acid mine drainage (acidic mine water), organic particles and turbidities (Schueler et al., 2011, pp. 42–46).

According to Schueler et al. (2011), the major short- and long-term risk source for potential environmental pollution are the tailings ponds, which are supposed to store huge amounts of wastes forever but are exposed to rainwater and winds. This bears the risks of groundwater and soil pollution from runoff water or leaking ponds, or even extensive containment of soil and major surface waters, for example rivers and lakes, in the case of collapsing dams due to poor construction, seismic events or storm waters (Schueler et al., 2011, p. 44f.). According to the Canadian Pembina Institute, which has been working to reduce the environmental

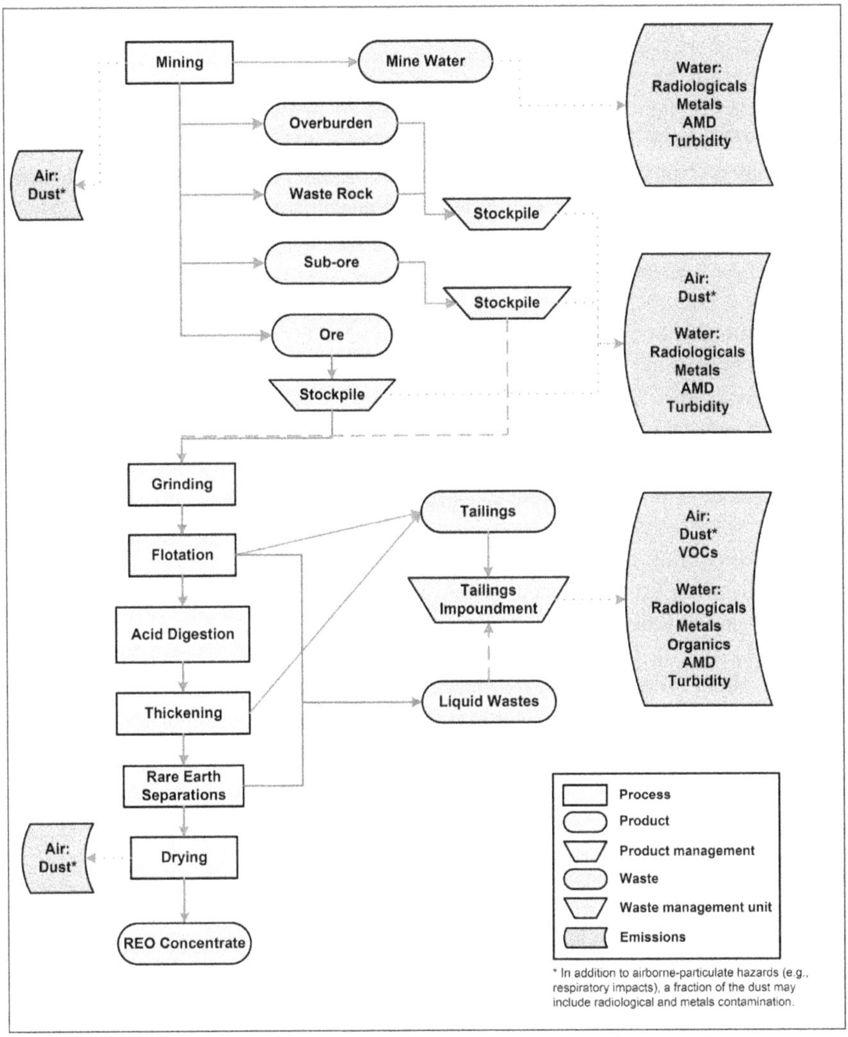

Figure 2.5 Hard rock resource processing and potential waste emissions

Source: U.S. Environmental Protection Agency (2012, pp. 4–3).

impacts of Canada's energy production since 1985, between two and five of the world's tailings dams experience major failures every year. Tailings dams are also "more than 10 times more likely to fail than conventional hydro or irrigation dams" (Lemphers, 2010). The collapse of the Samarco's Fundao tailings dam, which stored the wastes from iron ore extraction in southeast Brazil, in November 2015 contaminated 400 miles of rivers in the Rio Doce basin and parts of the southern Atlantic, killed 19 people and destroyed hundreds of houses. The parent companies of the mining company, Vale SA and BHP Billiton Ltd., concluded an agreement with the Brazilian government to pay around 2.45 billion USD, or 9.46 billon Brazilian reais, for environmental cleanup operations over the next 15 years. This only covered half of the estimated environmental damages of 20.2 billion reais and did not include private claims that might be raised by people who lost their homes or relatives (Boadle & Eisenhammer, 2016; Kiernan, 2016). This shows that tailings pounds are a source of serious risk for environmental pollution and human health, and potentially of high additional public and private costs.

Because Bayan Obo is the largest operating REEs mine in the world, its factual wastes and emissions, and their impact on the environment and human health, are the best documented. For every produced ton of Rare Earths, approximately 85 kg of fluorine and 13 kg of dust are produced: 9,600 to 12,000 cubic meters of waste gas containing dust concentrate, hydrofluoric acid, sulfur dioxide and sulfuric as well as one 75 cubic meters of acidic wastewater and one ton of radioactive waste are generated in the stage of chemical treatment. In the Baotou region, the annual generation of wastewater that is discharged without any treatment from all companies in the REEs industry amounts circa ten million tons (Hurst, 2010, p. 16). In a long-term study over 20 years, it has been shown that especially the thorium-containing dust of an annual 61.8 tons, which is produced in the crushing and grinding process, has a direct impact on the miners in Bayan Obo. The mortality rate of lung cancer has significantly increased for the workers (Schueler et al., 2011, p. 50). The main tailings pond of the State-owned enterprise Baotou Iron and Steel Group, which extracts ore at Bayan Obo, is the largest tailings impoundment in the world. It is around 12 km in length and holds over 230 million cubic meters of waste, while seven million tons of liquid waste is added every year. The pond is elevated 31.4 meters above the Huanghe (the Yellow River) and is only 10 km away from it (Kilby, 2014, p. 543). The river is the primary source of water for 150 million people (Hurst, 2010, p. 18). Due to the proximity to the river and the elevation above its basin, runoff water from the pond could easily contaminate the river in the case of leaks or even a dam collapse. There are some indications that groundwater pollution from leaks of the pond and emissions of thorium-containing dust have already affected the nearby villages, livestock and the agriculture. The measured radioactivity was 32 times higher in sampled plants and 1.7 times higher in tested soil than corresponding reference values (Schueler et al., 2011, p. 50). Around 4,000 hectares of farmland have been contaminated so that the harvest volumes of corn and wheat have decreased from 1,500 to 600 kg and from 800–1,000 kg to 400 kg, respectively, in the period from 2002 to 2006 (Ruettinger et al., 2015, p. 8). A radioactive contamination of the Baotou area and the Yellow River by untreated discharged water has been reported to dying fish in 2005 (Hurst, 2010, p. 17). In summary, the impact of unsafe production and missing emission treatment on the environment and human health of workers and inhabitants of the region is dramatic: "increase in cases of cancer, respiratory diseases, dental loss, pollution of drinking water sources, with a radioactive risk of pollution the water of the Yellow River" (Massari & Ruberti, 2013, p. 42). As a consequence, inhabitants of the village Xinguang Sancun have abandoned their homes so that the population of the village decreased from 2,000 to 300 within ten years. After an article by the French newspaper *Le Monde*, the Chinese government has committed four billion Yuan (around 600 million USD) to clean up mining damages in the Baotou region (Ali, 2014, p. 123f.).

The factual environmental effects of in situ leaching of ion adsorption clays is less documented but in general consist of underground water contamination, mining collapses and landslides. Ammonium sulfate contaminations of 3,500 to 4,000 mg/l in the groundwater, and pH values increased by 11% in surface water and by 17.8% in groundwater were measured near mines in Ganzhou, where also 100 landslides were reported. Between 2004 and 2010, 2,620 landslides because of in situ leaching of REEs and other resources were reported in China. These landslides have led to 32,322 recorded fatalities (Yang et al., 2013, p. 134).

These potential environmental risks also affect the availability of stocks of resources as reserves. From a strategic viewpoint of resource policy, a country should have the goal to internalize all stages of the process route to ensure supply security (Tyrer & Sykes, 2013, p. 14). However, from the viewpoint of environmental policy, an outsourcing of process stages with a high risk of severe environmental impact is preferable. Resulting strict environmental regulations could then lead to high investments in abatement technologies that aim to reduce and prevent emissions or to ruling out domestic production absolutely.

Due to Australian regulations, Lynas, the company mining at Mount Weld, decided to offshore the stages three to five. After extraction in Australia, the minerals are concentrated in Australia but then shipped to Kuantan, Malaysia, for further processing. After Lynas had started to develop the Mountain Weld mine in 2007, it also obtained approval from the Malaysian government to build a processing plant in 2008 (Schueler et al., 2011, p. 58). Chemical treatment, separation and reduction, refining and purification would then be undertaken in the Malaysian facility called Lynas Advanced Materials Plant. Besides other factors such as low labor costs, the lax environmental regulations of Malaysia are a major factor that increases the cost-efficiency of the plant. For example, the Malaysian Air Quality Guidelines, which are used to regulate emissions of fine particulate matter, stem from 1978 and do not reflect the current state of knowledge about adverse health effects of fine particulate air pollution and corresponding recommendations of the World Health Organization. Therefore, the abatement technology applied to air emissions was planned to comply only with Malaysian law, which is simply too old and inappropriate, but not with the best environmental practices. In addition to fine particulate matter, the emissions of dust, acidic gasses and acids are not treated with the utilization of state-of-the art or the best-available technology[15] so the sulfuric acid emissions are too high by a factor of two (Schmidt, 2013, p. 92). One of the numerous risk sources identified in a study from the German environmental research and consultancy institute Oeko-Institut e.V. are the residue storage facilities that were not conceived after state-of-the-art design and will leak even under normal operating conditions. They are also too limited in capacity and not designed to safeguard against heavy rain and especially the monsoon season (Schmidt, 2013, p. 94).

The permitting system for the development of a new mine in the USA is complex and lengthy, especially when resources are co-located with radioactive materials as Rare Earths are. Mining companies have to comply with federal, state and sometimes local laws so that they have to apply for overall 60 to 70 separate permits (Clagett, 2013, p. 128). The bottlenecks of fast mine permitting are most notably the environmental impact studies. The National Environmental Policy Act requires federal agencies to assess the environmental impact of mining operations that are either federally funded or take place on federal land. In the past, the preparation process of these studies took up to three years, while the following review process took up to an additional six years. After the impact study according to national regulations, an impact study according to State Environmental Policy Acts has to be carried out. Until 2013, 18 states, the District of Columbia and Guam had enacted state regulations modeled after the National Act. Resulting from this, a second impact study is required for mine permitting in these states even if this leads to duplicative research. As a consequence, the whole mine development takes at least seven years in the USA but can also take up to 15 years in individual cases (Clagett, 2013, p. 131). Therefore, deposits of REO are not available as reserves in the short run. Sharply increasing prices will ensure economic exploitability but will not eradicate regulatory barriers to exploitability.

In summary, the processing route is time, cost and input intensive. Low overall recovery rates reduce effective total supply so that unadjusted data on stocks of reserves alone is not a sufficient indicator for potential REEs availability. Because the mining stage itself adds only a minor proportion to the final value of REEs, the assessment of economic exploitability of deposits would have to include the costs of processing in the following stages. Furthermore, the processing route entails many sources of potential risks for the environment and human health. This has three different implications for REEs mining and processing. Either potential risks are neglected, like in the case of China, so that the environmental and social impact is drastic; or potential risks are regulated so that the establishment of a domestic processing route is not possible in the short term or some stages have to be offshored to safe pollution havens; or potential risks are so strictly regulated that mine development is effectively prevented or prohibited, like in Greenland before the U-turn in its policies towards uranium mining.

Historical development of Rare Earths production

The first discovery of Rare Earth minerals was in Ytterby, a Swedish village, in 1787 when Carl Axel Arrhenius, an amateur mineralogist, found an unrecorded, unknown black mineral. The Finnish chemist Johan Gadolin then analyzed this mineral in 1794 and concluded that it consisted of iron, silicate and 30% of a "new earth". In the following year, the Swedish chemist Anders Gustaf Ekeberg confirmed the discovery of a new mineral. He named the new earth "yttria", after the location of its discovery, and the new mineral "gadolinite", after its discoverer. As mentioned before, the discovery of Rare Earth elements went on for about 160 years until the 1940s, when the last REE promethium, named after the Greek mythological figure Prometheus, was proven to exist. Promethium does not occur in nature but was obtained from the products of the fission of uranium and of the neutron bombardment of neodymium in an ion-exchange chromatography (Gupta & Krishnamurthy, 2005, pp. 3–7).

Due to their long discovery history and complex physical-chemical nature that hampers the recovery of pure metals, commercial usage and extraction of REEs did not begin before the mid-1880s. At that time, the Austrian chemist Carl Auer von Welsbach developed a gas mantle lamp based on the combination of thorium and lanthanides obtained from monazite. He then founded the Treibacher Chemische Werke in Vienna to manufacture his novel lamps, whose light was superior and cheaper than the electric light of that time. From 1891 to 1935, around five billion units were produced and sold (Goldman, 2014, p. 141f.; Gupta & Krishnamurthy, 2005, p. 27). In 1902, the U.S.-American company Lindsay Light adopted Welsbach's manufacturing process to domestically produce gas mantle lamps. The required thorium was imported from Germany. When Germany cut the supply during World War I, Indian monazite sands became the global primary source while demand steadily increased as the result of newly researched application possibilities (Goldman, 2014, p. 142). In 1903, von Welsbach himself invented a pyrophoric alloy called flintstone in the search of an ignition system for his lamps. The flintstone was composed of 70% misch metal, a term created by von Welsbach for an alloy containing lanthanum, cerium, didymium and 30% iron, which became the first large-scale use for REMs (Gupta & Krishnamurthy, 2005, p. 27). Besides gas mantle lamps, they also started to be used as ignition system in cigarette lighters. The other new major field of application was enhancing the intensity of light, especially of searchlights, motion-picture projects and therapy-lamp carbons (Goldman, 2014, p. 142).

Initially, REEs were also mined from placer deposits in the USA from the late 1800s to mid-1900s. For example, around 5,000 tons of monazite were extracted from the monazite belt in California between 1885 and 1917 (Castor, 2008, p. 338). However, this production could barely reduce the increasing importance of India as REEs supplier. By 1941, 80% of the monazite consumption of the U.S. industry relied on imports from India. By 1944, 100% of consumption was covered by imports from India. This position of India as a major REEs supplier for the world and sole supplier for the USA finally resulted in the First Rare Earth Crisis. After gaining independence from the British Empire in 1947, the new Indian government stopped shipments of materials, which were considered critical for the development of the domestic market and a flourishing economy. The embargo of monazite was therefore seen as necessary for the development of a domestic processing industry (Goldman, 2014, p. 142f.). As a consequence for the USA and all other REEs consuming countries, the need to explore and develop new sources for Rare Earths arose. The major new source was found by accident in April 1949 when prospectors searched for uranium deposits in southern Nevada and adjacent parts of California under the use of Geiger counters. On this occasion, they found a radioactive mineral consisting of a considerable share of REO, fluorine and carbon dioxide on the South Clark Mountain Range near the community Mountain Pass, which later was confirmed to be bastnaesite by the U.S. Geological Survey. After extensive inspection, exploration and sample drillings, large and economically valuable deposits containing REEs-bearing minerals were proven to exist. The Molybdenum Corporation of America (renamed to Molycorp in 1974) purchased the mining rights in 1950 and began mining in 1952 (Olson et al., 1954, pp. III–VI). This gave an impetus to shifting global production shares of REO, which is displayed in Figure 2.6.

The period until the mid-1960s is also called "the Monazite period" because REEs were primarily produced from monazite deposits, whereas the period from the mid-1960s on is equivalently named "the Bastnaesite period". As result of more new application fields, especially the use of europium for red phosphors in color television sets and computers, and of cerium for glass polishing, the overall demand and production expanded (Clagett, 2013, p. 124). From 1965 to 1995, significant amounts of REEs were mined from the Mountain Pass mine, which enabled the USA to supersede India as the major global supplier of REO. At the climax of production, the Mountain Pass Mine covered 100% of the U.S. demand and around 33% of the demand in the rest of the world (Clagett, 2013, p. 124; Howanietz, 2015, p. 7). These dominant positions of the USA in general and the Mountain Pass mine in particular were achieved by several amplifying factors. First, the Mountain Pass mine deposit had the advantage of a high ore grade, while the ore grades of previous mined monazite deposits were relatively low. High ore grades led to lower extraction costs and thus ensured preferred production in this mine (Howanietz, 2015, p. 7; Humphries, 2013, p. 14). Second, the U.S. government actively promoted the development of the domestic REEs mining sector as a consequence of the Indian embargo. In the year 1947, the Ames Laboratory was established on the campus of the Iowa State University by the Atomic Energy Commission, which subsequently supported the research institute financially. The main mission of the Ames Laboratory was to conduct research in REEs production and application technology. The new technology was then transferred to the private sector, while the basic research in the public and private sector was supported by supplying high-purity Rare Earths (Goldman, 2014, p. 143f; Howanietz, 2015, p. 7). The technological breakthroughs of the laboratory include improvements and scaling-up of separation techniques. Researchers of the Manhattan Project found out that the lanthanide metals could be separated on a laboratory scale of some grams by ion exchange. In the Ames laboratory, techniques for separation on commercial scale of kilogram quantities were developed. Furthermore, the techniques to produce REMs of above 99% purity were developed and successfully tested (Gschneidner, 1987, pp. 24–27). As a result of these breakthroughs, the production and commercial usability of REEs sharply increased. As seen in Figure 2.6, the total production of REO doubled in the mid-60s due to U.S. extraction and processing activities. In 1966, the foundation of the Rare Earth Information Center as an Ames subdivision, which published research results in its own quarterly newsletter, RIC News, and consulted REEs companies, further strengthened the bonds of the private-public cooperation and finally consolidated the dominant roles of Ames Laboratory and the USA for the

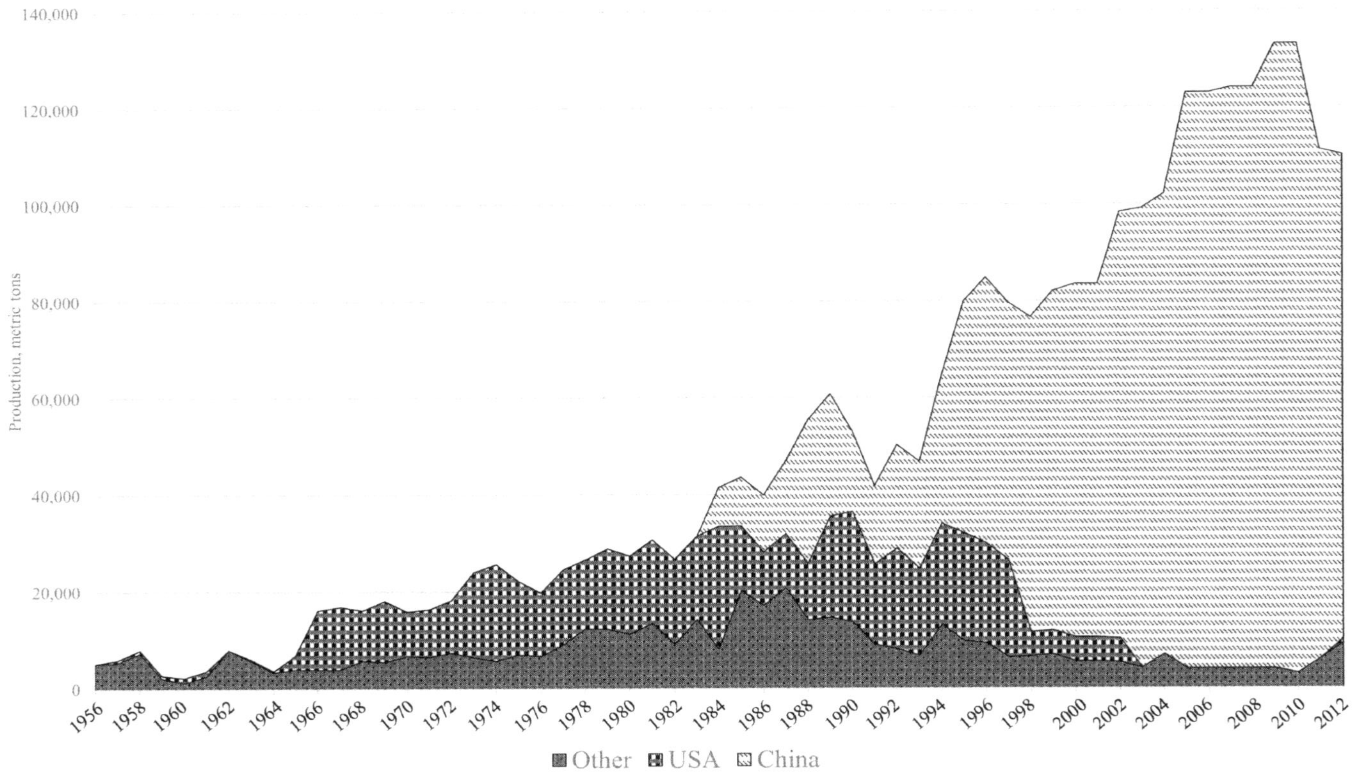

Figure 2.6 Global Rare Earth Oxides production, 1956–2012

Source: Data retrieved from British Geological Survey, 1986–1995, U.S. Geological Survey, 1994–2012, and U.S. Geological Survey, 2014.

global REEs industry (Goldman, 2014, p. 143f; Howanietz, 2015, p. 7). "Indeed, by 1965, Ames Laboratory became known as the 'birthplace of the modern rare-earth industry' and Chemical and Engineering News proclaimed it the 'Mecca of rare earths'" (Goldman, 2014, p. 144). While initially financed by the Atomic Energy Commission in the early years, 50 companies stepped in as major supporters of the laboratory, which had proven to be extremely important for the private REEs sector, when government support for the information center was suspended in 1968 (Gschneidner, 1987, p. 26).

As seen in Figure 2.6, a second shift of the dominant production location from the USA to China started in the mid-1980s. In 1927, the Bayan Obo deposits as source for iron ore were discovered, while the co-occurrence of bastnaesite and monazite was only found seven years later. The development of the mine for extraction of iron ore began in the 1950s. The recovery of REMs in small quantities as a side product then began in the late 1950s (Hurst, 2010, p. 11). However, the rapid development of the Chinese REEs industry did not begin before 1978, the year of emerging reintegration of China into the global markets in the course of Deng Xiaoping's Open Door Policy. Figure 2.7 illustrates China's increasing production of Rare Earths in REO equivalent metric tons and the resulting global market share in the following years: 1984–2012.[16]

In 1984, the PRC produced 8,000 metric tons of Rare Earth Oxides and had a share of just under 20% on the global market. Both the amount of produced REO and the market share increased rapidly. Between 1978 and 1989, the production increased by annual rates of 40% (Humphries, 2013, p. 17). On the climax in the year 2010, China had a global market share of 97.75% with a production of 130,000 metric tons REO. Due to the combined market share of over 90% since 2002, China is said to have a virtual monopoly. This second shift of production was driven by both U.S. domestic factors that hampered the further development of the industry and Chinese domestic factors that advantaged Chinese mining companies. The first factor was a U.S. paradigm shift in environmental regulation initiated by President Richard Nixon in 1970 with the establishment of the Environmental Protection Agency. The EPA issued stricter pollution standards that put economic pressure on domestic REEs industries because of its high pollution and emission intensity. Due to this pressure, the oldest REEs firm, Lindsay Chemical Company, shut down in 1973. The Michigan Chemical Corporation, which produced high-purity REMs in its ion-exchange facility, closed down in 1978 after several lawsuits and investigations of the EPA and the U.S. Department of Natural Resources. In 1985, a new regulation that limited the amount of lead in gasoline led to a sharp decline of demand of REEs, which were used as petroleum cracking catalysts (Goldman, 2014, p. 153). The Mountain Pass Mine, the dominant global Rare Earths source in the period from 1965 to 1985, was also negatively affected by stricter regulations. The pipeline system that transported the tailings to evaporation ponds suffered 60 spills between 1984 and 1998. This resulted in surface soil contamination with radiological and metallic constituents, and subsequently high fines and costs for cleaning up (Ali, 2014, p. 125; Howanietz, 2015, p. 8). In 2002, the Mountain Pass Mine failed to obtain a permit to build a new waste storage

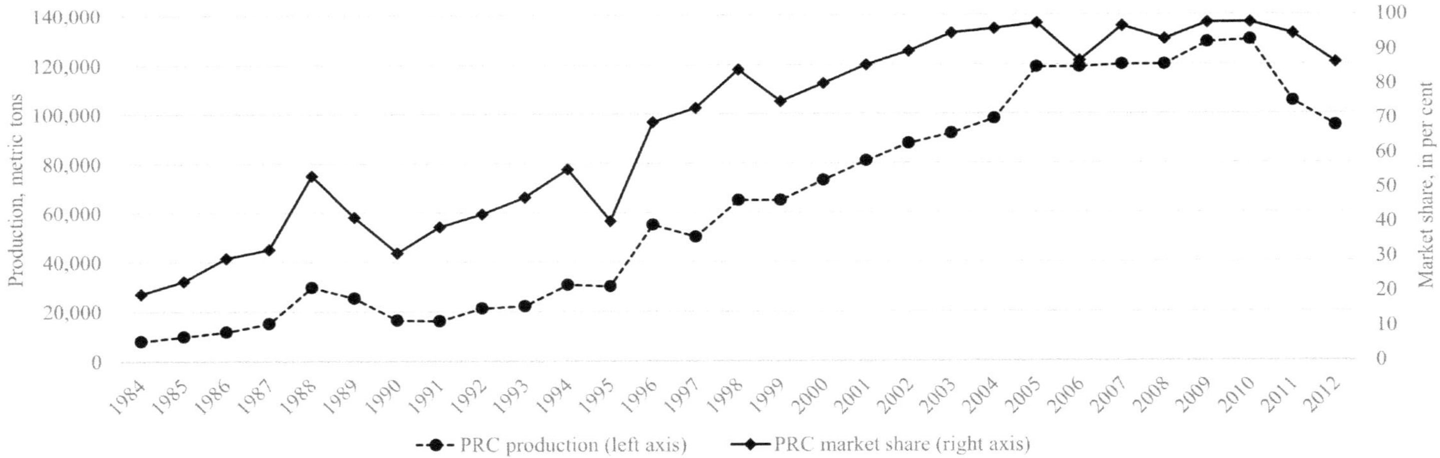

Figure 2.7 PRC production of REO and global market share, 1984–2012

Source: Data Retrieved from British Geological Survey, 1986–1995, U.S. Geological Survey, 1994–2012, and U.S. Geological Survey, 2014.

while the existing storages were running out of space. This drastically impeded the operative ability of the mine. Molycorp then decided to shut down the mine completely (Morrison & Tang, 2012, p. 3). At the same time, emission standards were low in China and the whole industry was almost completely unregulated with regard to environmental issues until 2010 (Clagett, 2013, p. 124).

The second factor for the shift comes from the trade regimes of both countries. In 1979, the USA and China reestablished official diplomatic relations in January, signed a bilateral trade agreement in July and finally provided mutual most favored nation treatment. Without high barriers to trade, Chinese REEs companies could fully benefit from their comparative advantage in total labor costs, which resulted from low wages and low labor standards. This advantage was further enhanced by Chinese trade policies. Until 2004, 70% of the REMs were solely produced for the export, which was utilized to acquire foreign currency and to establish strategic ties with Western countries with the purpose to gain access to advanced technology. Beginning in 1986, the ad valorem tax of 16% was fully rebated to foster REEs exports (He, 2014, p. 242; Howanietz, 2015, p. 8f.).

The third factor, the shift of production, was also a result of a shift of REEs-related research and development activities. The private support of the Ames Laboratory steadily declined due to deterioration of the financial situation of the supportive domestic REEs industry as a result of competitive pressure from Chinese REEs companies. In 2002, the Rare Earth Information Center was finally closed (Goldman, 2014, p. 154). At the same time, domestic innovations in the field of REE production and application were promoted in China. Despite low domestic demand and export-oriented production, REEs were seen as a strategic resource to develop domestic high-tech capacities in the mid to long run. This became especially clear in Deng Xiaoping's statement during his visit of the Baotou mining district in 1992: "There is oil in the Middle East; there are rare earths in China." This statement is regarded as evidence that the Chinese leaders were aware that Rare Earths would become increasingly relevant as resource in the future (Ting & Seaman, 2013, p. 238). As strategic resource, they were first included in the "National High Technology Research and Development Program" (Program 863) in 1986, which aimed to enhance China's international competitiveness and improve its overall capability in research and high technology in 19 selected fields (including information technology, biotechnology, agriculture, environment, resources and energy technologies, new materials, advance manufacturing and automation technology). The "National Program on Key Basic Research Projects" of 1997 (Program 973), which had the objective to mobilize scientists to conduct basic research in selected projects, also included REEs. The focus field of materials science that received 12% of the total budget was directly connected to develop new technologies in the field of REEs mining and processing (OECD, 2008, p. 460). Furthermore, specialized research institutions like the State Key Laboratory of Rare Earth Materials Chemistry and Applications were founded to conduct basic or applied research related to REEs. Because of increasing promotion of research activities in China and ceased support in the USA, the world's only two scientific journals that solely focus on REEs-related research topics, the

Journal of Rare Earth and the *China Rare Earth Information* journal, are Chinese run (Howanietz, 2015, p. 9; Hurst, 2010, pp. 8–10)

Based on patent data as a proxy of innovative activity, Fifarek et al. (2008) and Fifarek and Veloso (2010) investigated the adverse effects of offshoring REEs production on innovation at the national home base. Due to the growing Chinese dominance of REEs production, promotion of REEs technology and lower wage rates, U.S. firms began to offshore REEs-related activities to Asia in the mid-1980s in order to improve their individual competitiveness and began to purchase Rare Earth Materials and REEs-containing components from offshore providers (Fifarek et al., 2008, p. 226). For example, the technology leading company in REEs magnet powder metallurgy, Magnequench, established a powder plant in Tianjin in 2000 in order to be geographically near to REO suppliers and downstream users. In 2003, its technology center was relocated from the USA to Singapore (Fifarek et al., 2008, p. 227). Due to this offshoring, the USA has also lost its leadership in REEs technology innovation so that high technology downstream sectors, which utilize Rare Earths as inputs, have already relocated or are expected to relocate their plants to Asia (Fifarek et al., 2008, p. 234). For example, the PRC has not only successfully developed new technologies for extraction and refining of REEs but has also overtaken the former dominant productive and innovative role of the USA in the field of neodymium-iron-boron permanent magnets, which are used in electric generators and electric motors (Fifarek & Veloso, 2010, p. 565).

To summarize, the REO market size grew from only a few hundred mined tons in the mid-1880s to over 100,000 tons in the 2000s. The factors for this growth are the constant improvements in extraction and processing technology on the supply side and the development of new end-use applications on the demand side. There have been two major shifts of the dominant production location of REEs in the twentieth century: the production first shifted from India to the USA. Driving factors were the Indian embargo as well as the discovery of the Mountain Pass deposit, which was the world's largest and richest known REEs deposit at the time, and the active public promotion of REEs research and development. When public support ceased and production costs increased due to new, strict environmental regulations in the USA, production began to shift from the USA to China. This shift was further supported by Chinese favorable conditions such as low regulation costs, low wages, supportive trade policies and the State's promotion to seek a productive and innovative superiority in a strategic resource sector. Since 2002, China has a market share of over 90%, which embodies a virtual monopoly.

Fields of application

In addition to their traditional use in applications such as metallurgical additives and alloys, petroleum refining and glass additives, the use of Rare Earths in emerging technologies such as high-tech consumer goods, green technologies, industrial and medical appliances and national defense has steadily increased since 2002. Therefore, REEs are also called "technology metals" or "seeds of technology" (Du & Graedel, 2013, p. 783; Humphries, 2013, p. 2). Table 2.4 displays examples

Table 2.4 Applications fields of Rare Earths

Catalysts	*Electronics*	*Glass*	*Ceramics*	*Metal Alloys*	*Magnets*	*Other*
Petroleum refining	Display phosphors (CRT, PDP, LCD)	Polishing compounds	Capacitors	Hydrogen storage (NiMH batteries, Fuel cells)	Motors	Water treatment
Chemical processing	Medical imaging phosphors	Optical glass	Sensors	Steel	Disk drives & disk drive motors	Fluorescent lightning
Catalytic converter	Fiber optics	UV resistant glass	Colorants	Lighter flints	Actuators	Figments
Diesel additives	Optical temperature sensors	Thermal control mirrors	Scintillators	Aluminum/ Magnesium	Microphones & speakers	Fertilizer
Industrial pollution scrubber		Colorizers/ De-colorizers		Cast iron	Magnetic Resonance Imaging	Medical tracers
				Superalloys	Anti-lock brake systems	coatings
					Automotive parts	
					Communication systems	
					Electric drive & propulsion	
					Frictionless bearings	
					Magnetic storage disk	
					Microwave power tubes	
					Magnetic refrigeration	
					Magnetostrictive alloys	

Source: Data retrieved from Morrison and Tang (2012, p. 4).

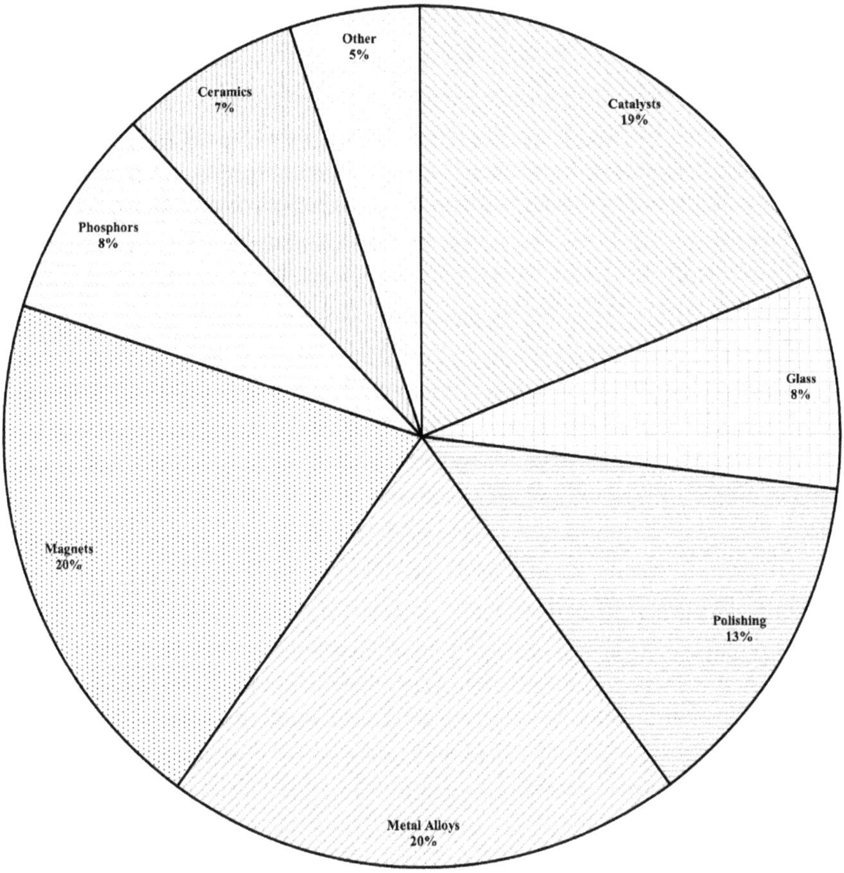

Figure 2.8 Market share of end-use applications, 2011

Source: Data retrieved from Kingsnorth (2012, p. 9).

for specific applications in the current major REEs end-use categories while Figure 2.8 illustrates the market shares of the major categories in the year 2011.

Measured by volume, the use in magnets and metal alloys are the largest application fields. Both fields had a market share of around 20% in 2011. Measured by economic volume, REEs magnets, which have a share of 37% of value, is by far the largest application field (Schueler et al., 2011, p. 67). Especially neodymium-iron boron permanent magnets are highly demanded due to their high magnetic flux density. NdFeB magnets are more powerful,[17] weigh less and can be miniaturized at a higher degree than conventional magnets (U.S. Environmental Protection Agency, 2012, pp. 2–3). Small NdFeB magnet-based servomotors power are used in hard disk drives in computers, in electric window openers in automobiles and in other everyday applications (Goonan, 2011, p. 9).

In the field of e-mobility, REEs magnets are used in electric motors in hybrid electric vehicles, plug-in hybrid electric vehicles and electric vehicles. Permanent magnet synchronous motors have the highest power-to-weight and power-to-volume ratios and are therefore the most efficient electric motors (Bradshaw et al., 2013, p. 100). Taking into account other automobile parts, typical hybrid vehicles contain up to 12 kg of REMs (Angerer et al., 2009, p. 37). NdFeB magnets are also used in gearless turbines for wind energy generation. Gearless turbines have a higher reliability and efficiency and require less maintenance than gear drive turbines. Although gearless turbines only have a market share of 14%, they have a high growth potential especially due to the construction of offshore wind power farms as part of the global drive towards green energy use. The offshore wind potential is higher than the onshore potential, and gearless turbines are more suitable for high-sea power generation than turbines with gears due to their reliability and robustness (Schueler et al., 2011, p. 69). Wind turbines contain up to one ton of neodymium per megawatt of electric capacity generated (Goonan, 2011, p. 9).

Metal alloys have a market share of 14% by value. The oldest application field in this category is the use in flintstone. Misch metal or cerium are mixed as minor alloys in casted steel or casted iron to improve their stability. Yttrium, lanthanum and cerium improve the performance when added to heat-resistant superalloys. Misch metal is also used in NiMh batteries used in hybrid electric vehicles and portable appliances. For example, 2.9 kg of REO are used per Toyota Prius II battery (Schueler et al., 2011, p. 78).

Nineteen percent of all REEs are used in automotive catalysts and as diesel additives, but the value share of this field is only 5% due to the low prices of the mainly used REMs cerium and lanthanum. Nevertheless, this field of end-use is of significant importance for emission reduction and improvement of the clean combustion of fuels. Polishing has a market share of 13% by volume and of 9% by value (Schueler et al., 2011, p. 79ff.). Applications include all high-valued and high-quality glass products, such as mirrors and lenses (Angerer et al., 2009, p. 311). In ceramics, REEs are added for color control in ceramic glaze or for modification of the properties of titanate in barium titanate powder, which is used in electronic applications. In the field of glass applications, REEs are added to glass to perform special functions like ultraviolet light absorbing (Goonan, 2011, p. 6ff.). Although only 8% of the total volume of demanded REEs are used in the phosphor category, this field has a share of 32% measured by value. Almost all energy saving lighting and display technologies, such as LEDs, LCDs, plasma displays and fluorescent tubes, utilize REMs as phosphors due to their high-energy efficiency and high color quality (Schueler et al., 2011, p. 76.). In addition to these commercial fields, REMs are also used in high-tech military systems. The military applications include precision-guided missiles, smart bombs, aircraft and targeting or weaponized lasers. Although the market volume of these applications is relatively small, the REEs' supply security is of special interest in the national defense planning of several countries with modern or currently modernizing armies (Grasso, 2013, pp. 10–14).

In summary, REEs are utilized in many different fields of applications. While applications in the fields of alloys have existed since the beginning of REEs commercialization, other fields related to high technologies have emerged since the early 2000s. Figures 2.9 and 2.10 display two different scenarios for the projected

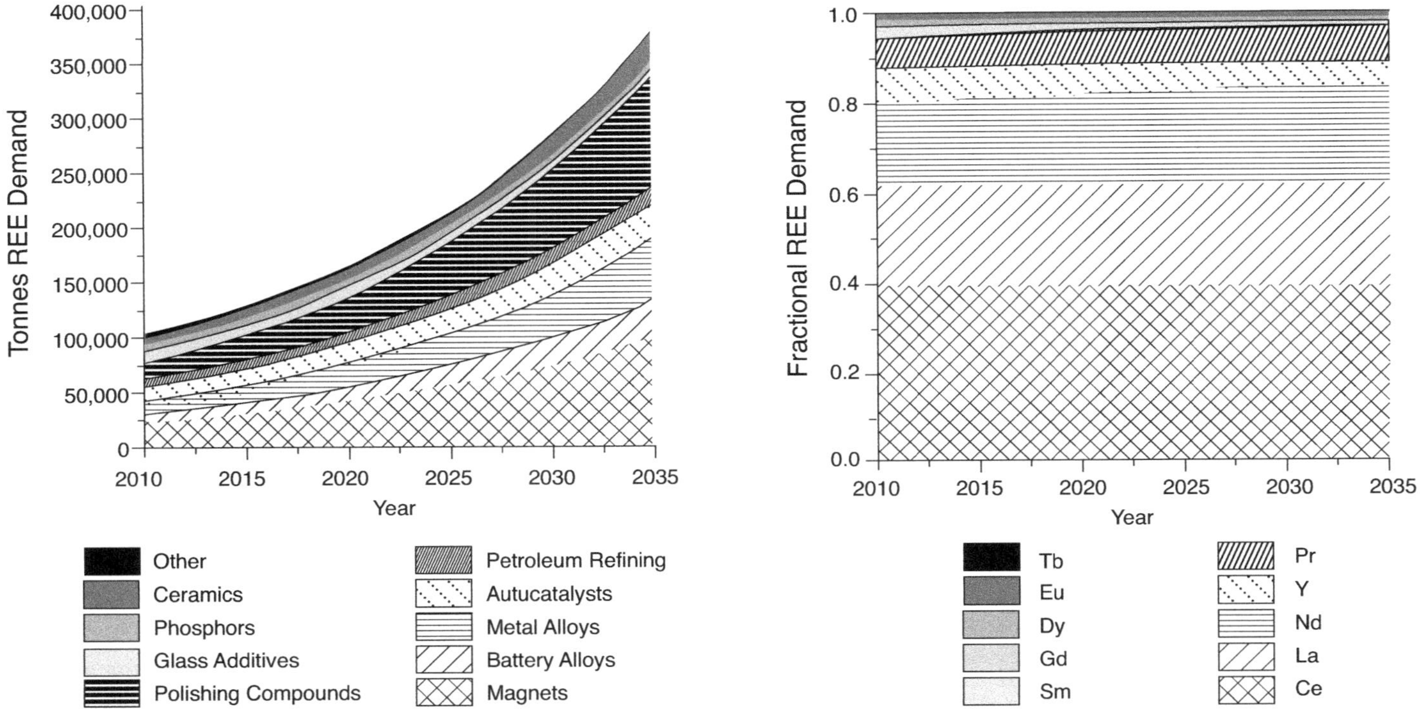

Figure 2.9 Projected volumes and market shares of REEs end-use fields, 2010–2035, Scenario 1

Source: Reprinted with permission Alonso, E., Sherman, A. M., Wallington, T. J., Everson, M. P., Field, F. R., Roth, R., & Kirchain, R. E. (2012). Evaluating rare earth availability: A case with revolutionary demand from clean technologies. *Environmental Science & Technology*, *46*(6), 3406–3414. Copyright 2012 American Chemical Society.

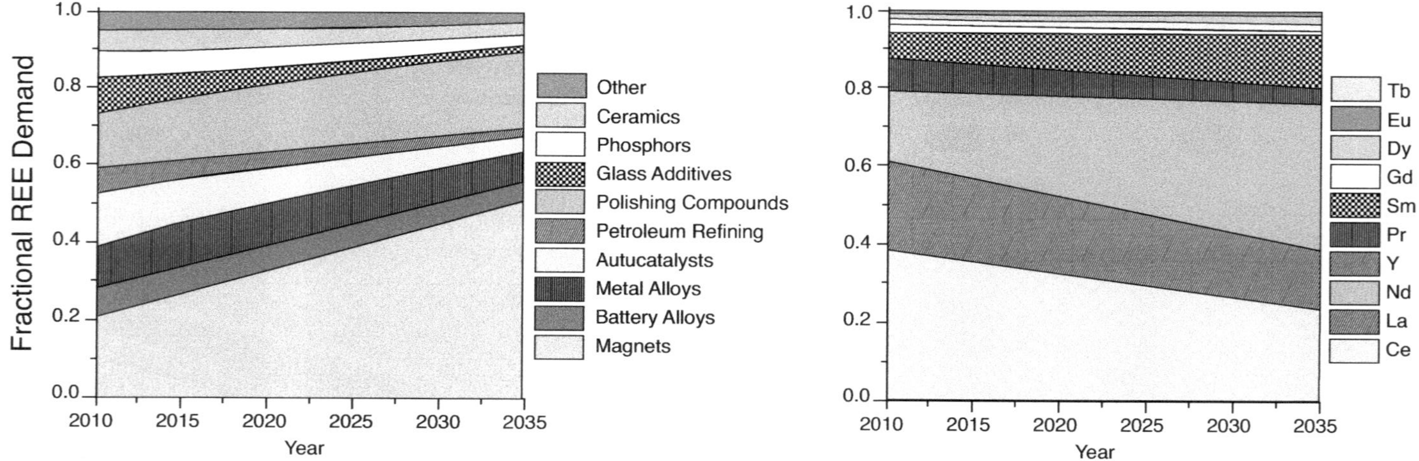

Figure 2.10 Projected volumes and market shares of REEs end-use fields, 2010–2035, Scenario 2

Source: Reprinted with permission from Alonso, E., Sherman, A. M., Wallington, T. J., Everson, M. P., Field, F. R., Roth, R., & Kirchain, R. E. (2012). Evaluating rare earth availability: A case with revolutionary demand from clean technologies. *Environmental Science & Technology*, *46*(6), 3406–3414. Copyright 2015 American Chemical Society.

future REEs demand. Scenario 1 is based on disaggregated evolutionary demand so that all applications grow at their historical rates. The average annual growth rate of all applications combined is 5.3%. This scenario leads to the clear extension in the fields of magnets, metal and battery alloys and polishing while the demand in the fields of phosphors and glass is assumed to decrease. Scenario 2 is based on implicit revolutionary demand. Industry sector-level growth rates were derived from reported expectations of industry experts (Alonso et al., 2012, p. 3408ff.). In this scenario, the increasing significance of the end uses of magnets, which are expected to obtain a market share of 40% until 2035, is even clearer than in scenario 1. This development is mainly driven by the expected drive for greener technologies, especially electric mobility and wind power generation. As projections, both scenarios have to be considered with care. Forecasts based on historical growth rates tend to neglect dynamic effects such as technology progress. New research and development activities could lead to new fields of REEs applications while existing fields could cease to exist as the gas mantle lamps did. On the other hand, the projection based on expert expectations could include an industry bias. In past projections for the period from 2006 to 2010, the realized growth rates were below the expected growth rates in six of the eight reported sectors (Alonso et al., 2012, p. 3409). In general, the overall REEs demand, however, is expected to grow in all scenarios.

Notes

1 "A process by which a chemical compound is separated into components by crystallization. In fractional crystallization the compound is mixed with a solvent, heated, and then gradually cooled so that, as each of its constituent components crystallizes, it can be removed in its pure form from the solution" (American Heritage Science Dictionary. [n.d.]. *Fractional crystallization*. Retrieved from Dictionary.com website, http://dictionary.reference.com/browse/fractional crystallization).

2 Erbium, Yttrium and Terbium were all named after Ytterby as the place of their discovery.

3 Chemical: Cerium lanthanum yttrium carbonate fluoride, or (Ce, La, Y) CO3F. The notion of Ce, La or Y used inside the parentheses states if the minerals is either especially enriched in cerium, lanthanum or yttrium.

4 "Type of metamorphism of local extent that affects the country rocks around magma bodies emplaced in a variety of environments from volcanic to upper mantle depths, in both continental and oceanic settings" (Callegari & Persev, 2007, p. 3).

5 "A vein-type deposit is a fairly well defined zone of mineralization, usually inclined and discordant, which is typically narrow compared to its length and depth. Most vein deposits occur in fault or fissure openings or in shear zones within country rock" (Schroeter, n.d., p. 1).

6 "Any of various coarse-grained igneous rocks that often occur as wide veins cutting across other types of rock. Pegmatites form from water-rich magmas or lavas that cool slowly, allowing the crystals to grow to large sizes. Although pegmatites can be compositionally similar to a number of rocks, they most often have the composition of granite" (The American Heritage Science Dictionary. [n.d.]. *Pegmatite*. Retrieved from Dictionary.com website, http://dictionary.reference.com/browse/pegmatite).

7 Chemical: (Ce, La, Nd, Th)PO_4, (La, Ce, Nd)PO_4, (Nd, La, Ce)PO_4 or (Sm, Gd, Ce, Th) PO_4, whereas the first composition is the most common.

8 "Natural concentration of heavy minerals caused by the effect of gravity on moving particles. When heavy, stable minerals are freed from their matrix by weathering processes, they are slowly washed downslope into streams that quickly winnow the lighter matrix. Thus the heavy minerals become concentrated in stream, beach, and lag (residual) gravels and constitute workable ore deposits" (Encyclopædia Britannica Online. [2016]. *Placer deposit*. Retrieved from www.britannica.com/science/placer-deposit).
9 Chemical: YPO_4.
10 The term "co-occurrence" means that some natural resources are regularly found together in the same mineral, mineral phase or deposit type.
11 For example, the potential use of Greenlandic uranium in nuclear weapons.
12 "The worthless rock or vein matter in which valuable metals or minerals occur." (Merriam-Webster. [n.d.]. *Gangue*. Retrieved from www.merriam-webster.com/dictionary/gangue).
13 The technical details and specifications of mineral concentrators will not be discussed in this study. For a detailed description of wet gravity concentrators, see Wills (2005, pp. 225–245).
14 Tailings are all materials that remain as waste of the processing route. These are gangue rock powders, chemical reagents, particle of different metals occurring in the deposit, radioactive elements, liquid wastes and wastewater. Tailings are transported to impoundments surrounded by dams (Schueler et al., 2011, pp. 42f.).
15 "The term best available technology is taken to mean the latest stage of development (state of the art) of processes, of facilities or of methods of operation which indicate the practical suitability of a particular measure for limiting discharges."(OECD. [2005]. *Glossary of statistical terms: Best available technology*. Retrieved from https://stats.oecd.org/glossary/detail.asp?ID=6358).
16 The year 1984 is the first for which detailed data on the Chinese production is available.
17 "Neodymium magnets are the strongest available magnets and exceed other permanent magnets such as samarium cobalt magnets by the factor 2.5 and other aluminum and iron based magnets by the factor 7–12" (Schueler et al., 2011, p. 66).

Bibliography

Alfred, C. (2014, April 28). 10 of the craziest rumors from North Korea, fact-checked. *The Huffington Post*. Retrieved from www.huffingtonpost.com/2014/04/28/north-korea-rumors_n_5160797.html.

Ali, S. H. (2014). Social and environmental impact of the rare earth industries. *Resources*, *3*(3), 123–134.

Alonso, E., Sherman, A. M., Wallington, T. J., Everson, M. P., Field, F. R., Roth, R., & Kirchain, R. E. (2012). Evaluating rare earth availability: A case with revolutionary demand from clean technologies. *Environmental Science & Technology*, *46*(6), 3406–3414.

Angerer, G., Erdmann, L., Marscheider-Weidemann, F., Scharp, M., Luellmann, A., Handke, V., & Marwede, M. (2009). *Rohstoffe für Zukunftstechnologien: Einfluss des branchenspezifischen Rohstoffbedarfs in rohstoffintensiven Zukunftstechnologien auf die zukuenftige Rohstoffnachfrage* [Raw materials for future technologies: The influence of branch-specific natural resource consumption in material-intensive and resource-sensitive future technologies on the future demand for raw materials]. Stuttgart: Fraunhofer IRB Verlag.

Bigler, J. (2016). *Periodic table and element data in spreadsheet form*. Retrieved from www.mrbigler.com/documents/Periodic-Table.xls.

Boadle, A., & Eisenhammer, S. (2016, March 2). Vale/BHP's Samarco to pay $5.1 billion in damages for dam disaster. *Reuters*. Retrieved from http://www.reuters.com/article/us-brazil-damburst-deal-idUSKCN0W42WP.

Bradshaw, A. M., Reuter, B., & Hamacher, T. (2013). The potential scarcity of rare elements for the Energiewende. *Green, 3*(2), 93–111.
British Geological Survey. (2011). *Mineral profile: Rare Earth Elements*. Retrieved from www.bgs.ac.uk/downloads/start.cfm?id=1638.
Broinowski, A. (2015, June 1). True or false: The "kooky" North Korea stories they couldn't make up-but did. *The Guardian*. Retrieved from www.theguardian.com/books/2015/jun/01/true-or-false-kooky-north-korea-stories.
Callegari, E., & Persev, N. N. (2007). *A systematic nomenclature for metamorphic rocks: 10 contact metamorphic rocks: Recommendations by the IUGS subcommission on the systematics of metamorphic rocks*. Retrieved from www.bgs.ac.uk/scmr/docs/papers/paper_10.pdf.
Castor, S. B. (2008). Rare earth deposits of North America. *Resource Geology, 58*(4), 337–347.
Charles, N., Tuduri, J., Guyonnet, D., Melleton, J., & Pourret, O. (2013). Rare Earth Elements in Europe and Greenland: A geological potential? An overview. In E. Jonsson (Ed.), *Mineral deposit research for a high-tech world: Proceedings of the 12th Biennial SGA meeting* (pp. 1698–1701). Uppsala Sweden: Society for Geology Applied to Mineral Deposits.
Chen, S. (2014, March 19). Chinese scientists urged to develop new thorium nuclear reactors by 2024. *South China Morning Post*. Retrieved from www.scmp.com/news/china/article/1452011/chinese-scientists-urged-develop-new-thorium-nuclear-reactors-2024?page=all.
Clagett, N. (2013). A rare opportunity: Streamlining permitting for rare earth materials within the United States. *Journal of Energy and Environmental Law, 4*(2), 123–138.
Committee for Mineral Reserves International Reporting Standards. (2013). *International reporting template for the public reporting of exploration results, mineral resources and mineral reserves*. Retrieved from www.crirsco.com/templates/international_reporting_template_november_2013.pdf.
Dictionary.com. (n.d.). Retrieved from www.dictionary.com/.
Du, X., & Graedel, T. E. (2013). Uncovering the end uses of the Rare Earth Elements. *Science of the Total Environment, 461–462*, 781–784.
Els, F. (2013, December 5). Largest known rare earth deposit discovered in North Korea. *Mining.com*. Retrieved from www.mining.com/largest-known-rare-earth-deposit-discovered-in-north-korea-86139/.
Encyclopædia Britannica Online. (2016). Retrieved from www.britannica.com/.
Fifarek, B. J., & Veloso, F. M. (2010). Offshoring and the global geography of innovation. *Journal of Economic Geography, 10*, 559–578.
Fifarek, B. J., Veloso, F. M., & Davidson, C. I. (2008). Offshoring technology innovation: A cause study of rare-earth technology. *Journal of Operations Management, 26*, 222–238.
Goldman, J. A. (2014). The U.S. rare earth industry: Its growth and decline. *The Journal of Policy History, 26*(2), 139–166.
Golev, A., Scott, M., Erskine, P. D., Ali, S. H., & Ballantyne, G. R. (2014). Rare earths supply chains: Current status, constraints and opportunities. *Resources Policy, 41*, 52–59.
Goonan, T. G. (2011). *Rare Earth Elements: End use and recyclability* (USGS Scientific Investigation Report 2011–5094). Retrieved from http://pubs.usgs.gov/sir/2011/5094/pdf/sir2011-5094.pdf.
Grasso, V. B. (2013). *Rare Earth Elements in national defense: Background, oversight issues, and options for congress* (CRS Report for Congress R41744). Retrieved from www.fas.org/sgp/crs/natsec/R41744.pdf.

Greenland drops uranium mining ban. (2013, October 23). *World Nuclear News*. Retrieved from www.world-nuclear-news.org/NP-Greenland_drops_uranium_mining_ban-2510134.html.

Greenland Minerals and Energy Ltd. (2015a). *Kvanefjeld feasibility study completed, company announcement, May 25, 2015*. Retrieved from www.ggg.gl/docs/ASX-announcements/Kvanefjeld-Feasibility.pdf.

Greenland Minerals and Energy Ltd. (2015b). *Kvanefjeld update: Mining license application guidance phase to commence, company announcement, December 2, 2015*. Retrieved from ww.ggg.gl/docs/ASX-announcements/progressing-to-permitting_1504869.pdf.

Gschneidner, K. A. (1987). Past, present and future of rare-earth metallurgy. In K. A. Gschneidner, & J. Capellen (Eds.), *1787–1987: Two hundred years of rare earths* (pp. 23–32). Ames: Rare-Earth Information Center.

Gupta, C. K., & Krishnamurthy, N. (2005). *Extractive metallurgy of rare earths* (Taylor & Francis e-library ed.). Boca Raton, FL: CRC Press.

Hansen, S. H., Pedersen, L. C., Vilsgaard, K. D., Elbaek Nielsen, I., & Hansen, S. F. (2013). Environmental and ethical aspects of sustainable mining in Greenland. *Journal of Earth Science and Engineering, 3*(4), 213–224.

Haque, N., Hughes, A., Lim, S., & Vernon, C. (2014). Rare Earth Elements: Overview of mining, mineralogy, uses, sustainability and environmental impact. *Resources, 3*(4), 614–635.

He, Y. (2014). Reregulation of China's rare earth production and export. *International Journal of Emerging Markets, 9*(2), 236–256.

Howanietz, R. (2015). *Changes to the regulatory framework of the Chinese rare earth industry after the Global Financial Crisis*. Paper presented at the 20th Euro-Asia International Research Seminar, Bochum, Germany.

Humphries, M. (2013). *Rare Earth Elements: The global supply chain* (CRS Report for Congress 41347). Retrieved from www.fas.org/sgp/crs/natsec/R41347.pdf.

Hurst, C. (2010). *China's Rare Earth Elements industry: What can the west learn?* Washington, DC: Institute for the Analysis of Global Security. Retrieved from www.iags.org/rareearth0310hurst.pdf.

Information Office of the State Council. (2012). *Situation and policies of China's rare earth industry*. Beijing: Foreign Languages Press.

Jacobsen, H. (2013, January 29). Danish U-turn clears way for uranium mining in Greenland. *Euractiv*. Retrieved from www.euractiv.com/section/sustainable-dev/news/danish-u-turn-clears-way-for-uranium-mining-in-greenland/.

Jamasmie, C. (2015, March 27). Skepticism grows over North Korea's massive rare earth discovery. *Mining.com*. Retrieved from www.mining.com/scepticism-grows-north-koreas-massive-rare-earth-discovery/.

Jordens, A., Cheng, Y. P., & Waters, K. E. (2013). A review of the beneficiation of Rare Earth Element bearing minerals. *Minerals Engineering, 41*, 97–114.

Kanazawa, Y., & Kamitani, M. (2006). Rare earth minerals and resources in the world. *Journal of Alloys and Compounds, 408–412*, 1339–1343.

Kiernan, P. (2016, March 2). Mining firms Samarco, Vale and BHP Billiton settle with Brazil over dam disaster. *The Wall Street Journal*. Retrieved from http://www.wsj.com/articles/mining-firms-samarco-vale-and-bhp-billiton-settle-with-brazil-over-dam-disaster-1456960073.

Kilby, C. (2014). China's rare earth trade: Health and the environment. *The China Quarterly, 218*, 540–550.

Kingsnorth, D. J. (2012). *The global rare earths industry: A delicate balancing act*. Presentation at the German Mineral Resources Agency, 16 April 2012, Berlin. Retrieved from www.deutsche-rohstoffagentur.de/DERA/DE/Downloads/RD_kingsnorth_2012.pdf?__blob=publicationFile.

Lemphers, N. (2010, October 12). Could the Hungarian tailings dam tragedy happen in Alberta? *Pembina Institute*. Retrieved from www.pembina.org/blog/417.

Li, L. Z., & Yang, X. (2014). China's rare earth ore deposits and beneficiation techniques. In *ERES 2014: Proceedings of the first European rare earth resources conference* (pp. 28–39). Milos Island, Greece: European Rare Earth Resources.

Long, K. R., Van Gosen, B. S., Foley, N. K., & Cordier, D. J. (2010). *The principal Rare Earth Elements deposits of the United States: A summary of domestic deposits and a global perspective* (U.S. Geological Survey Scientific Investigations Report 2010–5220). Retrieved from https://pubs.usgs.gov/sir/2010/5220/.

Massari, S., & Ruberti, M. (2013). Rare Earth Elements as critical raw materials: Focus on international markets and future strategies. *Resources Policy, 38*(1), 36–43.

Merriam-Webster. (n.d.). *Dictionary*. Retrieved from www.merriam-webster.com/dictionary/dictionary.

Morrison, W. M., & Tang, R. (2012). *China's rare earth industry and export regime: Economic and trade implications for the United States* (CRS Report for Congress 42510). Retrieved from www.fas.org/sgp/crs/row/R42510.pdf.

Navarro, J., & Zhao, F. (2014). Life-cycle assessment of the production of Rare Earth Elements for energy applications: A review. *Frontiers in Energy Research, 2*(45), 1–17.

OECD. (2005). *Glossary of statistical terms*. Retrieved from https://stats.oecd.org/glossary.

OECD. (2008). *OECD reviews of innovation policy: China*. Paris: OECD Publishing.

Olson, J. C., Shawe, D. R., Pray, L. C., & Sharp, W. N. (1954). *Rare-earth mineral deposits of the Mountain Pass District San Bernardino County California* (Geological Survey Professional Paper 261). Washington, DC: United States Government Printing Office.

Peiro, T., & Mendez, V. (2013). Material and energy requirement for rare earth production. *JOM, 65*(10), 1327–1340.

Polinares Consortium. (2012). *Fact sheet: Rare Earths Oxides (REO)* (Polinares Working Paper No. 37). Retrieved from www.polinares.eu/docs/d2-1/polinares_wp2_annex2_factsheet3_v1_10.pdf.

Riddler, G. P. (1994). What is a mineral resource? In M. K. G. Whateley, & P. K. Harvey (Eds.), *Mineral resource evaluation II: Methods and case histories* (pp. 1–10). Bath: Geological Society Publishing House.

Ruettinger, L., & Feil, M. (2011). *Sustainable prevention of resource conflicts: New risks raw materials for the future? Case study and scenarios for China and rare earths* (Report 3.4). Berlin: Adelphi.

Ruettinger, L., Treimer, R., Tiess, G., Griestop, L., Schueler, F., & Wittrock, J. (2015). *Umwelt- und Sozialauswirkungen der Gewinnung Seltener Erden in Bayan Obo* [Environmental and social impacts of rare earths mining in Bayan Obo]. China and Berlin: Adelphi.

Schmidt, G. (2013). *Description and critical environmental evaluation of the REE refining plant LAMP near Kuantan/Malaysia: Radiological and non-radiological environmental consequences of the plant's operation and its wastes* (Oeko-Institut e.V. Report Prepared on Behalf of NGO "Save Malaysia, Stop Lynas"). Retrieved from www.oeko.de/oekodoc/1628/2013-001-en.pdf.

Schroeter, T. (n.d.). *Vein-type deposits*. Retrieved from http://it.geol.science.cmu.ac.th/gs/courseware/205363/TEXTS/Vein%20type%20deposits.doc.

Schueler, D., Liu, R., Buchert, M., Dittrich, S., & Merz, C. (2011). *Study on rare earths and their recycling* (Oeko-Institut e.V. Final Report for the Greens/EFA Group in the European Parliament). Retrieved from www.oeko.de/oekodoc/1112/2011-003-en.pdf.

Stoker, P. (2009). *Progress on the revision of the Chinese mineral resources and mineral reserves reporting standard*. Retrieved from www.crirsco.com/progress_revision_chinese_mineral1.pdf.

Thomas, L. (2012). *Coal geology* (2nd ed.). Oxford: Wiley-Blackwell.

Ting, M. H., & Seaman, J. (2013). Rare earths: Future elements of conflict in Asia? *Asian Studies Review*, *37*(2), 234–252.

Tyrer, M., & Sykes, J. P. (2013). The statistics of the rare earths industry. *Significance*, *10*(2), 12–16.

United Nations Conference on Trade and Development. (2014). *Commodities at a glance: Special issue on rare earths*. Geneva: UNCTAD.

U.S. Environmental Protection Agency. (2012). *Rare Earth Elements: A review of production, processing, recycling, and associated environmental issues*. Washington, DC: Office of Research and Development.

U.S. Geological Survey. (1976). *Principles of the mineral resource classification system of the U.S. Bureau of Mines and U.S. Geological Survey*. Washington, DC: U.S. Government Printing Office.

U.S. Geological Survey. (1994–2012). *Minerals yearbook, vols. 1994–2012*. Retrieved from https://minerals.usgs.gov/minerals/pubs/commodity/rare_earths/index.html#myb.

U.S. Geological Survey. (1996–2016). *Mineral commodity summaries, vols. 1996–2016*. Retrieved from https://minerals.usgs.gov/minerals/pubs/commodity/rare_earths/index.html#myb.

U.S. Geological Survey. (2014). *Historical statistics for mineral and material commodities in the United States*. Retrieved from http://minerals.usgs.gov/minerals/pubs/historical-statistics/.

Valero Capilla, A., & Valero Delgado, A. (2015). *Thanatia: The destiny of the earth's mineral resources: A thermodynamic cradle-to-cradle assessment*. Singapore: World Scientific Publishing.

Vivoda, V. (2011). Determinants of foreign direct investment in the mining sector in Asia: A comparison between China and India. *Resources Policy*, *36*(1), 49–59.

Weng, Z., Jowitt, S. M., Mudd, G. M., & Haque, N. (2015). A detailed assessment of global Rare Earth Element resources: Opportunities and challenges. *Economic Geology*, *110*(8), 1925–1952.

Wills, B. (2005). *Wills' mineral processing technology: An introduction to the practical aspects of ore treatment and mineral recovery* (7th ed.). Oxford: Butterworth Heinemann.

Yang, X. J., Lin, A., Li, X.-L., Wu, Y., Zhou, W., & Cheng, Z. (2013). China's ion-adsorption rare earth resources, mining consequences and preservation. *Environmental Development*, *8*, 131–136.

3 Assessment of Rare Earths scarcity

The concept of scarcity is a fundamental problem of all economic activities and economics as a discipline. Broadly speaking, goods that are "deficient in quantity or number compared with the demand" (Merriam-Webster, n.d.) are denoted as scarce goods. In economics, all goods that carry opportunity costs are scarce. To produce or consume one unit of a specific good, the opportunity to produce or consume another good has to be given up (Baumgaertner et al., 2006, p. 489). Furthermore, goods can be either relatively or absolutely scarce. Relative scarcity refers to the scarcity of one good or resource in relation to another good or resource or to a lower quality of the same good or resource. Consumers have the choice to substitute goods, which carry high opportunity costs and are therefore very scarce, with less scarce goods. The concept of absolute scarcity, on the other hand, refers to the scarcity of all goods and resources in relation to population and per capita consumption levels (Daly, 1974, p. 17). The concept of absolute scarcity dates back to Thomas Robert Malthus's work "An essay on the principle of population" of 1798. Malthus (1798) argued in his essay that the limitedness of farmland would be an absolute scarcity constraint on food production so that the population could only grow to a specific point, at which at least a minimum subsistence level of per capita food consumption is covered. Population growth beyond this point would then lead to the "Malthusian catastrophe" of hunger, disease and war that would push the population back to its subsistence level: 170 years later, the Club of Rome utilized this concept in its 1972 report "The limits to growth" to emphasize that economic growth is constrained by finite resource availability and growth-induced environmental degradation in the long run (Neumayer, 2010, p. 48).

As exhaustible resources, Rare Earths Elements are absolutely scarce per definition. While their availability is fixed and finite at any point in time, the wants they are able to satisfy are not. The "cake-eating problem", the decision how to temporally allocate the consumption of a finite stock of REEs over infinite time, leads to intertemporal opportunity costs (Asheim & Buchholz, 2000, p. 2; Perman et al., 2011, p. 533). To produce or consume one unit of REEs in the present, the opportunity to produce or consume one unit of REEs in the future is given up. However, many papers point out that REEs are not rare or scarce (Boer & Lammertsma, 2013, p. 2045; Chen, 2011, p. 1; Hilpert & Kröger, 2011, p. 3). If this statement were true, REEs would be of little interest from the perspective of economics. Therefore, this chapter will use different geological, thermodynamic and economic indicators to measure the scarcity of REEs beyond the pure definition as an absolutely scarce, exhaustible resource.

Geochemical scarcity

The notion that Rare Earths are not considered rare is mostly derived from the indicator of geochemical scarcity, which measures the relative geological availability of elements in the earth's crust in the unit of parts per million in mass. Figure 3.1 shows the abundance of Rare Earths in comparison to industrial metals (iron, copper, zinc and others) and precious metals (gold, silver, platinum and others). Promethium is not included in the figure because it does not occur in nature and therefore has an infinitesimal availability.

The availability of the REEs group is in the range of 62 to 0.46 ppm. In general, light REEs are more abundant than heavy REEs. The crust abundance of most available Rare Earth Metal, cerium, is 62 ppm, so that cerium is more abundant than the industrial metals lead (Pb), Copper (Cu) and Tin (Sn). The least abundant metal in the group, lutetium, is less available than all major industrial metals but still six times more available than silver, which is the precious

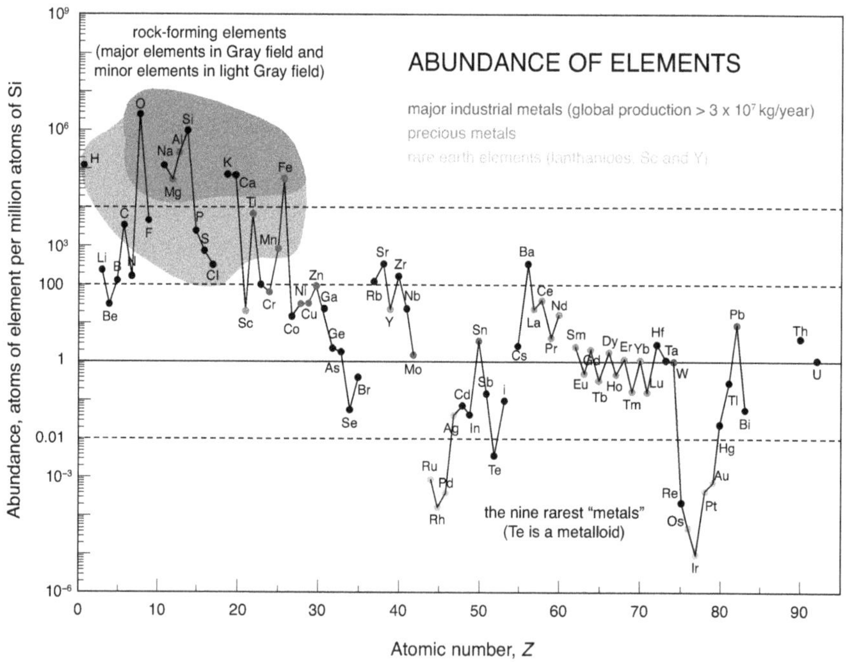

Figure 3.1 Abundance of REEs in the earth's crust

Source: Generalic, E. (n.d.). *Abundance of elements*. Retrieved from www.periodni.com/rare_earth_elements.html.

metal with the highest crust abundance (United Nations Conference on Trade and Development, 2014, p. 4).

Overall, the REEs group is rather relatively abundant. However, a high abundance in the earth's crust does not mean that large tonnages are commercially exploitable. Some industrial metals such as copper or tin are relatively geological scarce but can be mined in large tonnages from deposits at concentrations thousands of times greater than the crustal average (Ayres, 2001, p. 11). By contrast, REEs are relatively abundant in the earth's crust but are also globally highly dispersed so that they are rarely concentrated in deposits that can be economically exploited. Whereas many deposits of precious metals only have one mineral phase, REEs deposits often have several different mineral phases. Each mineral phase requires different technologies for extraction and processing so that single-mineral-phase deposits, such as Bayan Obo, are preferentially mined (Long et al., 2010, pp. 5–7). The scarcity in adequate deposits is even higher for heavy REMs, which are predominantly mined in southern China.

Thermodynamic scarcity

The indicator of thermodynamic scarcity is measured in terms of exergy replacement costs (Valero Capilla & Valero Delgado, 2015, p. 39). The concept of exergy stems from thermodynamics and describes the amount of energy that is available in a fuel for doing work. The amount of energy that is not used for doing work when the fuel is burnt to perform work is analogously called anergy (Ayres, 2001, p. 1). The exergy replacement costs is then defined as the exergy required to recover the deposit from the reference environment with the best available technology plus the environmental exergy costs for restoring the mining zone after extraction has ended (Mulvaney, 2011, p. 159). The higher the grade of mineral or metal ore, the greater is the so-called exergy content of the mineral or metal ore. The greater the exergy content of ore, the less exergy is required to extract, concentrate and refine it (Ayres, 2001, p. 2).

When this concept is applied to Rare Earths, their thermodynamic scarcity is determined by their physical-chemical and geological properties. As shown in the previous subsection, their crust abundance is relatively high, but they are highly dispersed so that high-grade deposits are rare. As explained in Chapter 2, their physical-chemical properties are very similar so that their separation is more complex and complicated in comparison to other metals or minerals. This leads to the multi-staged, input- and cost-intensive processing route explained in Chapter 2, which utilizes great amounts of exergy in the reduction process to pure REMs (Valero Capilla & Valero Delgado, 2015, p. 100). The environmental exergy costs to restore the mining zone are also high, especially when emissions are hardly treated or abated as in the case of Bayan Obo.

The exergy costs for producing one kilogram of REEs have been calculated for production in Bayan Obo. The exergy costs are 357.1 ± 4.35 Mega joule for lanthanum, 586.2 ± 116 MJ for cerium, 358.0 ± 72.1 MJ for praseodymium, 651.6 ± 128.4 MJ for neodymium, 3,657.0 ± 712.5 MJ for gadolinium and 1,253.1 ± 245.8 MJ for yttrium. The environmental exergy costs are not included in this estimation. Based on these values, the overall exergy consumption per kg of REEs is among the highest of all metal productions (Valero Capilla & Valero Delgado, 2015, p. 242ff.). Thus, REMs can be classified as thermodynamic scarce.

Static ranges of resources and reserves

Static ranges of resources and reserves are very simple indicators of the availability concept. They indicate whether there is an adequate supply of a specific natural resource in the long run by dividing the proved resource or reserve stock of a natural resource by its annual consumption or mined quantity (Siebert, 1979, p. 410). The mined quantity of REEs was 124,000 tons REO in the year 2015 (U.S. Geological Survey, 1996–2016). As listed in Chapter 2, the proved stock of global resources was 311.3 million tons of REO in the year 2011 and the proved stock of global reserves was 130 million tons of REO in 2015. Thus, the static resource range is around 2,510 years and the static reserve range is around 1,048 years. These two ranges do not reflect a high level of absolute scarcity for REEs. For example, a joint study of the German geological survey, "Bundesanstalt fuer Geowissenschaften und Rohstoffe", the institute for economic research and policy advice, "Rheinisch-Westfaelisches Institut fuer Wirtschaftsforschung", and the Fraunhofer institute listed reserves and resources ranges of 119 and of over 597 years of iron ore, of 32 and of over 158 years for copper, of 23 and of over 42 years for tin, and of 17 and of over 37 years for gold on the basis of data from 2004 (Bundesanstalt für Geowissenschaften und Rohstoffe, 2005, p. 17ff.) This indicates a very high physical availability of REEs in relation to industrial and precious metals.

The critique of this static concept is that it does not consider any dynamic adjustment effects such as increasing demand due to market growth, increasing stocks due to exploration activities or significant technological progress. Resource-augmenting technological progress increases the efficiency of resource use so that less production is required to satisfy the needs of the end-users. This could lead to lower annual extraction quantities and extended ranges. On the other hand, augmenting-resource technological progress creates new extraction techniques so that extraction costs either decrease or lower grade deposits can be exploited commercially (Neumayer, 2010, p. 70). One example for a potential groundbreaking augmenting-resource technique that is currently emerging is bio mining. In this technique, bacteria that feed through the decomposition of ore and excrete metal-containing liquids are used to recover metals from low-grade deposits from mines that have been regarded as fully depleted and shut down (Donner, 2011). As a consequence, the stock of reserves could increase significantly in the future. However, there is also the so-called Jevons paradox that the boost of use efficiency of natural resources could lead to an even higher demand as it was the case when coal demand increased due to the improvement of steam engines. While resource-augmenting technologies could lead to an increased real stock of resources, this rebound effect could lead to unchanged or even increased rates of resource depletion (Weiszaecker & Ayres, 2013, p. 52f.).

While exploration activities and technological progress are difficult to implement into the calculation of static ranges, an expected market growth can be implemented rather easily. Scenario 1 in Chapter 2 assumes annual market growth rates of 5.3%. When both ranges are adjusted by this growth rate, the reserve and resource ranges decrease to around 78 years and 94 years, respectively.[1] Other expectations for the growth of the market volume lie between 8 and 11% per year (Hilpert & Kröger, 2011, p. 160). Under the assumption of a market growth of 10%, the ranges further decrease to 48 years for reserves and 58 years for resources, which indicates a higher scarcity than the scarcity derived from the first and second calculation. This highlights the impact of different expected growth rates on this indicator and the suspected unreliability of static ranges as meaningful indicators. Nevertheless, this indicator is still meaningful to indicate how large future adjustment processes have to be to sustain resource supply security in the long run (Siebert, 1979, p. 410).

Unit costs, user costs and market prices

The indicators of market price, shadow prices and unit costs are based on further specification and subdivision of absolute scarcity into Malthusian stock scarcity and Malthusian flow scarcity. In Malthusian stock scarcity, the stock of resources is fixed and uniform in quality so that the marginal costs of extraction are constant within a period. In Malthusian flow scarcity, the stock of resources is also fixed but marginal costs are not constant and rise as output rises within a period due to decreasing resource quality. While average costs of mining are decreasing with an increasing extraction rate in the concept of stock scarcity, they are increasing with an increasing extraction rate in the concept of flow scarcity (Hall & Hall, 1984, p. 366; Hanley et al., 2007, p. 244).

The second specification is the differentiation between use value and exchange value. Both increasing exchange values and use values are indicators for the increasing scarcity of a natural resource. Exchange value is generally indicated by the market price and reflects the value spent by a private person to acquire one resource unit. On the other hand, the use value reflects the utility derived from the utilization of one unit of a resource. This utility is also referred to as happiness or satisfaction of the commodity use, which are two concepts that are very difficult to measure (Stern, 1996, p. 6f.). One approach to measure the use value was put forward by Barnett and Morse (1963), who developed the indicator of "unit costs" on the basis of the writings of David Ricardo. Ricardo (1817) explained that increasing resource prices are the result of increasing average costs of extraction due to differences of deposit sizes and deposit quality (i.e. the ore grade). Large, high-grade deposits have the lowest extraction costs and are therefore exploited first. If the demand increases or the mined deposit is depleted, a smaller deposit with lower ore quality has to be mined in order to secure resource supply. A larger quantity of labor, which is the required input factor to recover resources from nature in order to produce use value, is then needed to recover the same amount of resources from the lower qualitative deposit that was previously recovered from the high qualitative deposit. This leads to higher average costs of extraction due to increased labor inputs. The use value of a natural resource can be therefore derived from the labor cost to recover it from its deposit (Ricardo, 1817, p. 51ff.). Barnett and Morse further expanded Ricardo's approach on the basis of a neoclassical production function to include capital inputs. Unit costs do not reflect average costs of extraction anymore but reflect the multi-factor productivity of capital and labor in the extraction process (Cleveland & Stern, 2001, p. 240f.):

$$UC_t = \frac{\alpha\left(\frac{L_t}{L_b}\right) + \beta\left(\frac{K_t}{K_b}\right)}{\frac{Q_t}{Q_b}} \tag{3.1}$$

UC_t = unit cost of extraction at time t,
Q_t = net output (value-added) in constant dollars,
L_t = labor cost measured as number of persons employed,
K_t = capital cost measured as net fixed capital stock in constant dollars,
Q_b, L_b, K_b = output, labor and capital inputs in the base year b,
$\alpha_t = I^{Lt}/I^{Tt}$ where I^L is total labor compensation and I^T is value-added originating in the industry in question.

This approach was criticized for various reasons. First, unit costs do not include exchange value, which reflects changing consumer preferences. Therefore, scarcity is measured only from the supply side, while demand is faded out. Unit costs could be decreasing due to augmenting-resource technological progress while total demand is increasing at the same time. If the increase in demand is higher than the decrease in unit costs, then unit cost will falsely indicate decreasing scarcity (Krautkraemer, 2005, p. 16). Second, only capital and labor are included in the model, but other purchased inputs that are required for resource extraction such as water or fuels are not included. Furthermore, the possibility of input substitution is not taken into account (Cleveland & Stern, 2001, p. 242f.). Third, unit costs only reflect the current scarcity and opportunity costs, but not future scarcity and intertemporal opportunity costs, so the concept is not sufficient to indicate long-term scarcity. The indicator of user costs should accomplish this (Siebert, 1979, p. 412).

User costs, which are synonymously called scarcity rents or in situ shadow prices, measure the value of a resource in the deposit from the sight of individual miner owners. It is defined as the net marginal profit for resource owners, "that is the price of the resource for the marginal unit minus the marginal cost for extracting this unit" (Neumayer, 2000, p. 14). Foregone revenues of future resource extraction and future sale in favor of present extraction and present sale embody the intertemporal opportunity costs of the mine owners that is not included in the concept of unit costs. Increasing scarcity of resources is then indicated by scarcity rents that are rising over time (Hall & Hall, 1984, p. 365). Due to the inclusion of intertemporal opportunity costs and the demand side via the market price, user costs are seen as the perfect scarcity indicator. However, it is very difficult to measure user costs empirically (Siebert, 1979, p. 415). While Fisher suggested estimating user costs by marginal replacement costs, which is the exploration cost of discovering new deposits, it is more common to use real market prices as a proxy due to their availability (Fisher, 1977, p. 27). In some cases, prices are even considered a better scarcity indicator than user costs. In a scenario where the quality of deposits is degrading due to stock effects, the resource rents would decline if there were no available technical changes that could offset increasing extraction costs. While more inputs of capital and labor have to be used to obtain smaller amounts of the resource, the value and price of degraded, low-quality deposits is relatively low. While the market prices are increasing due to lower supply, the rents are decreasing and could even drop to zero. This is a false indication of decreasing scarcity (Stern, 1996, p. 5). Halvorsen and Smith (1984) show that shadow prices of unextracted ore in Canada fell substantially from 1956 to 1974, but the prices of processed ore increased in the same period. From the view of end-using industries, who need processed ore, prices are thereby a more meaningful indicator for scarcity.

According to Hall and Hall, prices should be equal to the average or unit costs plus user cost in the case of Malthusian stock scarcity and equal to average or unit costs "plus the present value of the increase in future average cost to be borne in perpetuity plus the user cost" in the case of Malthusian flow scarcity (Hall & Hall, 1984, p. 33). Fisher formulated a more general requirement for prices as a scarcity indicator. He deems a "price, which reflects both the direct and indirect sacrifices required to obtain a unit of the resource" to be the best measure for scarcity (Fisher, 1977, p. 9). The real price of a resource should increase when its average extraction costs rise, demand increases, long-term supply decreases or substitution becomes more difficult. Furthermore, the expected scarcity should be reflected by real prices. A resource owner, who is expecting higher future prices, would store units of the resource in order to sell them in the future. This leads to a decreased supply and resource shortages in the present, both of which induce rising present prices (Siebert, 1979, p. 412).

One limitation of real prices as a scarcity indicator stems from the distribution of information and information asymmetries. Only when resource allocators are informed that resources are scarce, then economic indicators will reflect this scarcity. Nevertheless, when allocators already know that resources are scarce, no indicators would be needed to measure resource scarcity. Instead, allocators could directly provide information about scarcity (Norgaard, 1990, p. 20f.). While resource owners have perfect information about the present and future demand, extraction costs and the global quantity of the resource stock in the neoclassical framework of perfect competition (so that prices can be fully functioning as an indicator), the acquisition of information is expensive for mining companies in the non-model reality. Exploration costs arise in order to find resources that are "hidden" in their subterranean deposits. With ongoing exploration, more information about the location of deposits and their sizes is available. This information effect leads to lower exploration costs and easier findings of new deposits. With further cumulative discovery, the depletion effect of exploration sets in. New discoveries are becoming less probable and exploration costs increase. At first, the information effect is able to dominate the depletion effect and the reserve base increases, leading to an increasing level of production and decreasing prices. When the depletion effects begins to dominate, it is realized that the resource is scarcer than believed, which leads to production cuts and rising prices. The climax of the production level, at which the shift in perceived scarcity happens, is also named Hubbert peak (Reynolds, 1999, pp. 157–165).

A second argument against real prices are price-affecting contortions. One potential major price contortion could stem from a highly concentrated market structure. On the supply side, a monopolistic mining company would extract lesser quantities of resources than mining companies in a free market would extract in order to influence prices and maximize its profit. This would lead to higher prices. When the market would be a monopsony, then the single resource-demanding company would utilize its market power in order to bring down prices. Therefore, the market structure is of importance for the price determination. In addition, cost-reducing progress in the transportation sector could lead to lower prices at the consumption level of end-users while the production prices are increasing at the same time (Siebert, 1979, p. 413). The choice of an adequate deflator is also critical in the analysis of a time series of real prices and can affect the indicated scarcity. Prices could also not only reflect pure scarcity but state intervention through resource taxes, production subsidies and exchange controls (Perman et al., 2011, p. 534f.). Especially because of growing international trade, the role of governments in setting restrictive or supportive trade policies (implementation or suspension of taxes, penalties and quotas) and regulative policies, which control the material flow by setting rules for the extraction and use of resources, could contort the prices of natural resources on the global market (Papp et al., 2008, p. 24). Furthermore, the financialization of resource commodities in the form of speculation with resource derivatives leads to a decoupling of resource prices from the fundamental price determinants of demand and supply. Resource speculations could lead to excessive price volatility that does not reflect changes in pure physical availability and scarcity (Bujis & Sievers, 2012, p. 16ff.). In addition to speculation, political instabilities in the major supplier countries will also lead to price fluctuations that reflect short-term shortages in physical availability but not long-term scarcity. This is especially observable for crude oil (Valero Capilla & Valero Delgado, 2015, p. 33). Overall, Papp et al. (2008) have identified six factors that directly, and four factors that might indirectly, affect the prices of different metals in a report for the U.S. Geological Survey. The six factors affecting prices are the scarcity of the resource; the balance between supply and demand; the stocks and rate of use; actual or anticipated supply disruptions; earnings, market performance and expectations and the investment level. The supply-demand balance includes not only levels of supply and consumption but also the geographical distribution of deposits and consuming countries. When the number of consuming countries is high and they are geographically distributed around the world, but one single country is the main resource supplier, this country or even political, social or economic events in this country might have a significant impact on the resource price. The size of existing stocks and the rate of use especially induce increasing prices when the rate of use is relatively high in relation to the stock size. Furthermore, expectations about possible supply disruptions and other relevant events affect prices. With regard to the investment level, a driving factor for rising prices is increased investment in resources on financial markets. The four factors that interact with the six factors are the globalization, the policy of governments, the geopolitics and the growth on different level. In the course of globalization, more and more countries play a role as producers and consumers of resources, which has an impact on the demand-supply balance. Geopolitical events like economic paradigm changes and armed conflicts are supposed to cause major price changes. Finally, the business growth and the growth of national economies influence the balance between the production and consumption of resources. If large new mines are explored and developed, the supply of resources could rise faster than the demand of downstream industries. This would lead to decreasing prices. On the other hand, emerging economies could temporarily have exorbitant demand levels to construct public and transportation infrastructure that lead to high prices.

The usage of unit costs, user costs and market prices in order to measure the scarcity of Rare Earth Elements is hampered due to poor data availability. There is no available data on average extraction costs, labor costs, capital costs and the other variables to measure the unit costs of the global REEs industry. It is similar concerning user costs. Due to the complicated process route, the low value-added of the mining stage, the high capital costs of the cracking and separation stage and general uncertainties, Tyrer and Sykes argue that the in situ value of one REEs unit could even be zero (Tyrer & Sykes, 2013, p. 16). The analysis based on real market prices is possible with some restrictions. There is no global REO price because REO are not traded through public exchanges and have no formal trading prices. A relatively small number of traders also marks a market structure that is far away from the neoclassical, atomistic market structure so that prices tend to be more speculative (Weng et al., 2015, p. 1947). For the analysis in this study, the market prices on the U.S. market will be used as a proxy for global market prices. The USGS provides data for REEs world production and real market prices based on the value of the USD in 1998 for the years from 1922 through 2014. The data from 1922 through 2009 are used to analyze the scarcity before the embargo year of 2010. In addition to data availability, U.S. real prices are the most adequate choice for a proxy. As explained before, the USA was a major producer of REEs from 1965 to 2002 so that domestic prices are not distorted by additional transport costs or restrictions of international trade. Price-affecting U.S. restrictions of REEs imports from China are also assumed minimal since the grant of mutual most favored nation treatment in 1979. Figure 3.2 illustrates the growth rates of REO real prices from 1922 to 2009. The growth rates have been calculated using logarithmic differences.

Overall, the growth rates of real prices do not indicate increasing scarcity. While there were relatively large price spikes and sharp declines in the 1930s and 1940s, growth rates have meandered around the zero growth line especially since the

Figure 3.2 Growth rates of REO real prices, 1922–2009

Source: Author's calculation based on data from USGS (2014).

beginning of large-scale mining in China in the 1990s. This indicates an unchanged level of scarcity for almost 20 years but might also reflect possible price distortions of government intervention. As described in Chapter 2, the Chinese government promoted the expansion and export of REO through its industrial policy so that the domestic production steadily increased to an excessive level and REO prices outside China steadily decreased. This is also shown in a comparison of price trends of REO and typical industrial metals such as iron, zinc and copper in the period of 1998 to 2006. In general, this period is marked by increasing resource prices due to the increasing demand of the large emerging economies of India and China. In 2007, resources prices sharply decreased due to the global economic downturn of the Global Financial Crisis (Papp et al., 2008, pp. 49–53). While the prices are generally highly and positively correlated in the group of industrial metals (iron ore and zinc: 0.82, iron ore and copper: 0.92, copper and zinc: 0.94), the prices of REO and industrial metals are negatively correlated (iron ore and REO: -0.41, copper and REO: -0.66, zinc and REO: -0.64).[2] While the prices of industrial metals and all other commodities that China demanded increased, the prices of REO and all other commodities that China produced and exported decreased. This is also the so-called China discount, which "is defined as lower prices that result from excessive and disordered exports and the economic and non-economic measures taken by importers to force down the prices" (Zhang et al., 2015, p. 82). The Chinese claim that the REO prices are too low so that a strategic resource is squandered mainly stems from this situation.

To summarize, it is doubtful that real prices are an adequate indicator to measure the scarcity of REEs due to the possibility of price contortions in China.

Temporal and structural imbalances of demand and supply

Temporal imbalances of demand and supply lead to increased scarcity especially in the short and medium term. Due to the cost and time intensity of mine development, the supply with natural resources does not adapt to increased demand as fast as the demand for other goods that do not require a high level of initial fixed investments. As a result, the supply is rigid especially in the short term. At the same time, the demand is relatively inelastic in the short and medium term due to a lack of substitution possibilities (Bundesamt fuer Umwelt, 2010, p. 24f.).

Figure 3.3 displays the consequence of rigid supply and inelastic demand. The starting point is the assumption of increased demand (the demand curve shifts from D_1 to D_2) due to, for example, development of new applications for a natural resource. However, the supply curve does not adapt to the increased demand. The production is only expanded until the capacity limits of existing mines are reached. Additional supply beyond that limit would require high investments in order to develop new mines. The supplied quantity moderately increases from q_1 to q_2 while the price sharply and disproportionately increases from p_1 to p_2 as the result of temporal deficiency of supply compared with the demand, which is the broad definition of scarcity. This has implications especially for the temporal management of REO extraction. As already explained, the development of new

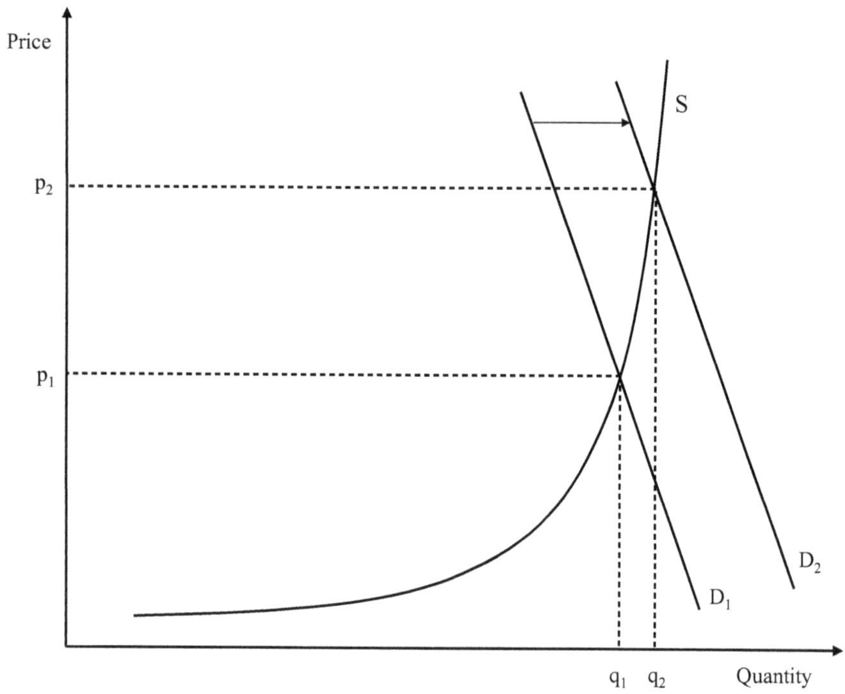

Figure 3.3 Temporal imbalances of supply and demand in the short and medium term

REO mines require high initial fixed investments. While the static range of REO reserves is relatively high, it is not guaranteed that newly developed mines will be ready to compensate the depletion of the major existing mines.

Wang et al. (2015) forecast the future Chinese REO production and the Hubbert peaks for the production from mixed REO mines, bastnaesite mines and ion adsorption clays based on the Generalized Weng model. The Generalized Weng is a variation of Hubbert's original curve-fitting forecasting model and is mainly used by Chinese scholars. According to their results, the production from mixed mines has already peaked in 2014, while the production from bastnaesite mines and ion adsorption clays will peak in 2018 and 2024, respectively (Wang et al., 2015, p. 15). The production quantities from all mines are estimated to decline by an annual rate of 4% after their peak (Wang et al., 2015, p. 16). The results of Wang et al. imply that new mines have to be developed in time to compensate the declines of Chinese production, which covers over 90% of the current demand, in order to prevent short- and medium-term scarcity. This is especially a challenge when major deposits are located in countries with high regulatory barriers for mining, such as the USA, where mine development takes 7 to 15 years. A second implication is related to the structure of supply. Ion adsorption clays are currently the major source for heavy REEs, which do not occur in the other major deposits of Bayan Obo or the Mountain Pass Mine. The decline in the supply of heavy REEs after 2024 makes it imperative to develop deposits that specifically contain heavy REO.

The structural imbalance between the demand and supply of specific REMs is an additional problem that has implications for scarcity. In the course of this chapter, REMs have been analyzed as one good because they are mined as mineral compounds and the availability of data is especially high for the aggregation level of REO equivalent tons. At the disaggregated level of demand and supply of specific REMs, there is the "balancing problem". The demand for individual elements and the natural abundance of REEs in their minerals compounds is difficult to balance. There is the tendency of an oversupply with the more abundant light REEs and the tendency of an undersupply with the less abundant heavy REEs. In the 1960s and 1970s, europium was especially highly demanded due its use in color television, which was the major driver for REO extraction. This period's major mine of Mountain Pass only has an europium content of 0.1 percentage by weight so that 300 tons lanthanum oxide, 450 tons cerium oxide, 38 tons praseodymium oxide, 118 tons neodymium oxide, 7.3 tons samarium oxide, 1.4 gadolinium oxide and 0.9 tons yttrium oxide are mined in the process of recovering one ton of europium oxide. At the moment, the demand for neodymium is especially difficult to balance. As illustrated in Chapter 2, the market growth rate in the application field of magnets is expected to be the highest so that the demand for neodymium will increase in the next years. Due to the low abundance of neodymium in the light REO group, cerium, praseodymium and samarium are extracted in excess (Binnemans & Jones, 2015, p. 30f.). This leads to extremely low prices for these REMs and to either unnecessary waste of resources or stockpiling costs.

Dudley Kingsnorth, who has an expertise of the REEs markets and REEs project development through his 22 years of association with the REEs industry (Curtin University, n.d.), estimates that there will be supply shortages of 25% of demand for neodymium, 23% of demand for dysprosium, 29% of demand for terbium and 39% of demand for erbium at least until 2020 (Rademaker et al., 2013, p. 10129). Boer and Lammertsma (2013) illustrate that there is a potential of short-term shortages and scarcity of dysprosium, terbium, europium, neodymium and yttrium in the European Union due to the "Strategic energy technology plan" that aims to enhance research, development and demonstration in REEs-dependent low-carbon technologies such as wind turbines, electric mobility, energy-efficient lighting system and automotive catalysts. Alonso et al. (2012) forecast the demand of individual REMs until 2035 based on expectations for "revolutionary demand", that is, the demand of new technologies like wind turbines and electric vehicles. They conclude that especially the supply with dysprosium, which is added to NdFeB magnets in order to improve their performance at high temperatures, will hardly keep up with increasing demand. In order to meet the forecast demand of 2035, the annual growth rate of dysprosium supply would have to be between 9 and 14%. If there were an aggressive push towards automotive electrification and use of wind energy, the annual growth rate of production and supply would have to be double the historic supply growth rate (Alonso et al., 2012, p. 3412). The view that dysprosium will be increasingly scarce in the future is supported by Seo and Morimoto (2014), who analyzed the supply security for the Japanese magnet industry.

Overall, there is the risk that the supply of REEs, and especially of specific REEs, will grow at a lower rate than the demand. This indicates increasing scarcity according to the broad definition. When temporal and structural imbalances are considered at the same time, this is most notably the case for the less abundant heavy REEs, which are predominantly extracted in southern China. After the Hubbert peak of the clay deposits in 2024, their supply will decline by an annual rate of 4%, while it should annually increase by 9–14% to meet the forecast demand in 2035. Therefore, it can be summarized that there is an increasing scarcity of heavy REEs until new deposits are developed that are not only able to compensate for the depletion of the major source for heavy REEs but also satisfy steadily increasing demand. The Kvanefjeld project, which will be the largest mine outside China and will also provide heavy REEs, will not solely be able to secure supply because it is expected to only cover 25% of the demand for one decade.

Criticality assessment

The concept of the criticality matrix[3] was originally developed by the U.S. National Research Council of the National Academies to assess the impact of the potential restrictions of the supply of nonfuel minerals on the U.S. economy (National Research Council, 2008, p. 1f.). The term of "criticality" is hereby vaguely defined. According to the NRC, critical materials are "any material – from metals to alloys to composites – upon which the economic health and national security of the nation resided". Critical materials have to perform an essential economic, social or other function for which no satisfactory substitute exists so that there are severe consequences if the supply is restricted (National Research Council, 2008, p. 20f.).

As illustrated in Figure 3.4, the NRC matrix is based on the two axes of "supply risk", which reflects the probability that the supply is partially or wholly restricted and therefore embodies increasing scarcity, and of "impact of supply restrictions", which measures the importance of use and the economic impact of restrictions on the U.S. economy. It could also be said that the importance of use reflects the use value of a mineral. In the example in Figure 3.4, mineral A has a higher supply risk and impact of supply restriction than mineral B, and is therefore considered more critical (National Research Council, 2008, p. 22).

Nine dimensions, five dimensions of primary availability and four dimensions of secondary availability, are used to evaluate the position of a mineral resource on the horizontal axis in the long term. The first of the five dimensions of primary availability is the geologic availability, which measures the pure existence or the natural abundance of the mineral. The second dimension of technical availability refers to the technological ability to extract and process the mineral. The social and environmental availability as the third dimension factors the impacts of extraction on the local environment and communities located in mining districts into the supply risk (National Research Council, 2008, pp. 50–55). The state influence on extraction is evaluated in the fourth dimension of political availability. The

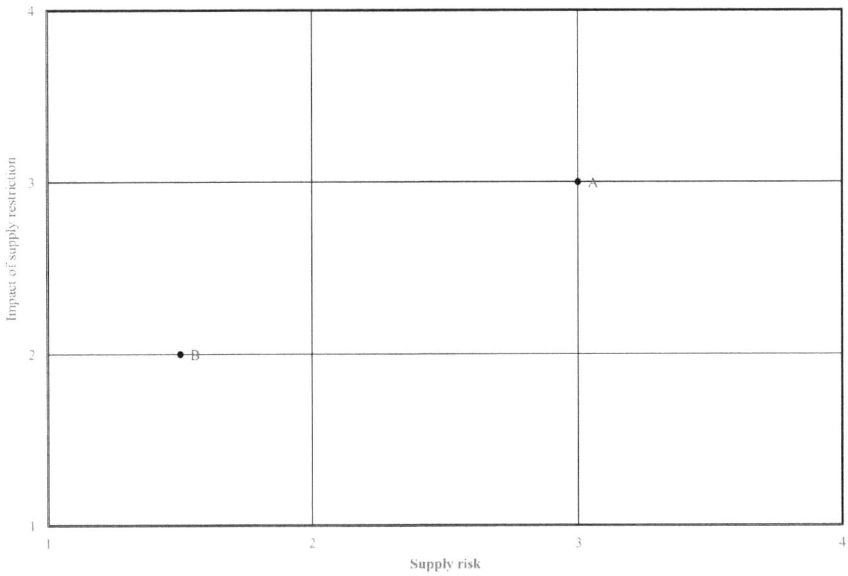

Figure 3.4 Criticality matrix concept of the U.S. National Research Council

state influence "encompasses (a) legislation, rules, and regulations that influence investment in mineral exploration and mine development and (b) the risks and results of change in these policies" (National Research Council, 2008, p. 56). The economic availability as the last dimension evaluates the availability of the mineral at a required time, quantity and purity at a price users are willing to pay (National Research Council, 2008, p. 57). The four dimensions of secondary supply are the technical availability, social and environmental availability, political availability and economic availability and relate on the possibility to recycle or reuse a nonfuel mineral resource (National Research Council, 2008, pp. 61–66).

In the short to medium term,[4] the supply risk for the USA is measured by the indicators of U.S. import dependence (net import reliance as a percent of apparent consumption), the world reserve to production ratio, the world reserve base[5] to production ratio, the world byproduct production as a percentage of the total world primary production and the U.S. secondary production from scrap as a percentage of U.S. apparent consumption (National Research Council, 2008, p. 78). In order to calculate the composite weighted score of the axis, each application group that requires the analyzed mineral is first assigned an impact score from 1 (low impact) to 4 (high impact) according to their proportion of the total U.S. use of that mineral. For example, the group of emission control, magnets and electronics consumes 44% of all Rare Earths in the USA so that the impact of a supply shock is expected to be high and scored a 4. The group of petroleum refining only consumes 8% of the total U.S. demand and is therefore scored a 1. Then, the proportion of each group is multiplied with its impact score to calculate weighted scores that can be finally aggregated to a composite weighted score (National Research Council, 2008, p. 86f.).

The vertical axis of economic impact is based on the idea of substantiality. Restricted mineral supply will only have a significant impact on the US economy when no substitutes exist. The time dimensions for substantiality are either the short to medium term or the long term. In the long term, substitutes can be developed so that the impact will be dampened. Furthermore, the industries that heavily rely on nonfuel minerals and their value added to the GDP have to be identified in order to assess the impact for the whole economy. Only if there are mineral consuming sectors that also have a significant share of the GDP, the impact on the overall U.S. production and domestic employment will be significant (National Research Council, 2008, p. 42ff.) The indicators that are used to measure the economic impact of supply restriction in the short to medium term are the U.S. consumption of a mineral in million USD, the percentage of U.S. consumption in existing uses for which substitution is difficult or impossible and the importance of growth in emerging uses that could overwhelm existing global production (National Research Council, 2008, p. 78). The placement of a mineral on the axis is then based on a judgment by the National Research Council assisted by the values of each indicator instead of a quantitative method (National Research Council, 2008, p. 76).

Due to the high import dependency of 100% in 2006, small U.S. secondary production and predominant production of REEs as co-products, the composite supply risk of REEs is evaluated as high despite large ratios of world reserve in relation to annual production and of world reserve base in relation to annual production. The composite economic impact is also high (weighted score of 3.15) because there are either no or only less-effective substitutes for REEs in their fields of application. REEs are the most critical for the fields of emission controls, magnets and electronics (National Research Council, 2008, pp. 85–89).

The U.S. Department of Energy adopted this methodology in 2011 to assess the criticality of individual REMs and other minerals especially for the application fields of wind turbines, electric vehicles, photovoltaic thin films and energy-efficient lighting in the clean energy economy. The importance to clean energy in the short (2011–2015) and medium (2015–2025) terms is computed from the clean energy demand for minerals (weighting factor of 75%) and substitutability limitations (weighting factor of 25%). The supply risk is calculated based on five categories: basic availability (40%); competing technology demand (10%); political, regulatory and social factors (20%); codependence on other markets (10%) and producer diversity (20%). The basic availability in the short term is based on the current production from mines and other sources to meet demand, while the potential for new mines to begin producing is considered in the medium term. The indicator of competing technology demand estimates the consumption rivalry from other sectors. Political, social and regulatory factors in the major producer countries are, for example, the risk of political instability, trade restrictions, or all social, administrative or regulatory processes that prevent or delay mining. When a mineral is only produced as a byproduct or coproduct, its supply is codependent on the demand for the mainly extracted mineral. When the coproduced mineral has a lower revenue stream than the main mineral, the supply is considered less secure so that a higher score is assigned. Furthermore, when the production of a mineral is concentrated in a small number of companies, the supply security is seen as more critical due to the lack of producer diversity (U.S. Department of Energy, 2011, p. 114). Figure 3.5 illustrates the overall assessment in the short term on the left and in the medium term in the right based on data from 2010.

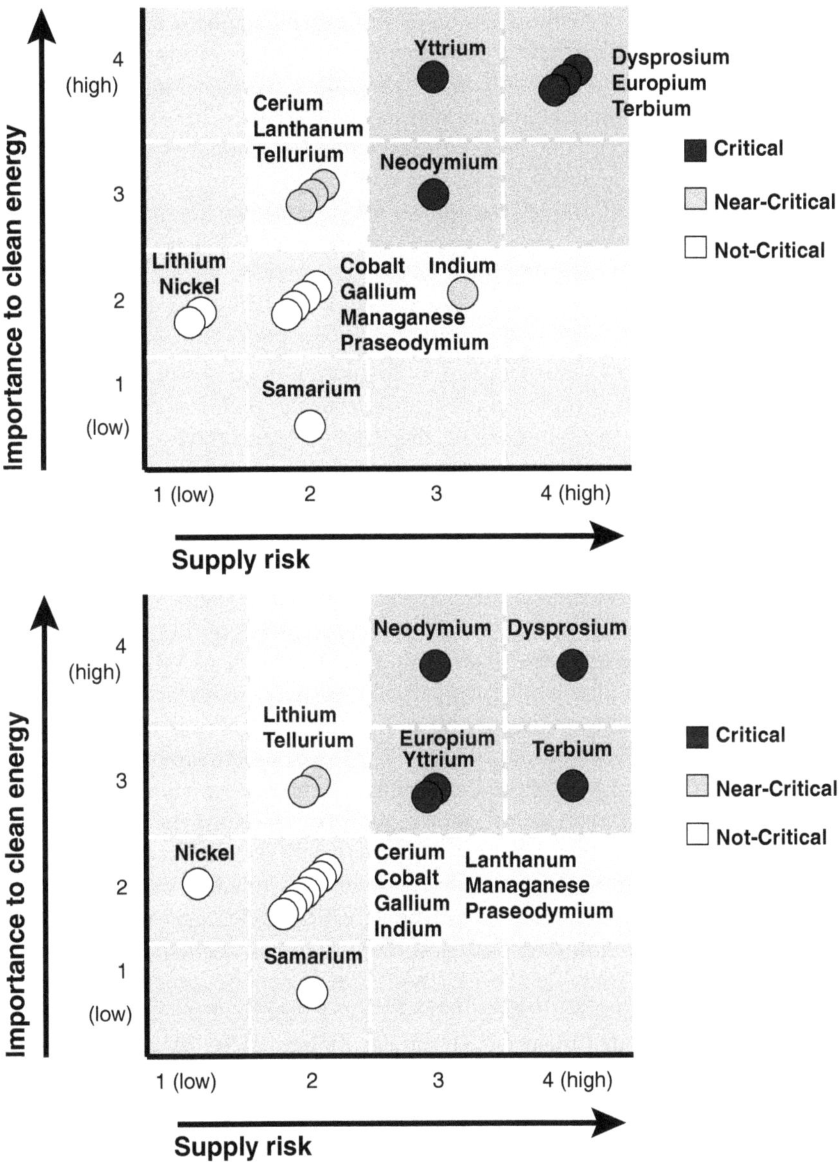

Figure 3.5 Criticality assessment of the U.S. Department of Energy

Source: U.S. Department of Energy (2011, p. 115).

In the short term, dysprosium, europium and terbium have the highest criticality, while neodymium and yttrium are also considered critical. Cerium and lanthanum are near-critical, which means that small changes in one of the categories of supply risk or importance could put them at the level of criticality (U.S. Department of Energy, 2011, p. 115). In the medium term, the criticality of some REMs is expected to decrease due to the anticipated start of production from new mines (U.S. Department of Energy, 2011, p. 82). Lanthanum is expected to become a non-critical mineral in the medium term, while terbium, europium and yttrium will stay critical because their improvement in the factors of supply risk and/or importance to clean energy is only minimal. On the other hand, neodymium will increase in criticality and dysprosium will stay very critical. These two REMs will be increasingly important due to their use in permanent magnets, while the supply is not secured in the medium or even long term.

The European Commission's "Ad-hoc working group on defining critical raw materials" adopted the matrix concept in a 2010 report to identify minerals that are critical for the EU within a time period of ten years. In order to measure the economic importance, the value-added chains of defined mega sectors (e.g. construction material, metals, mechanical equipment, electronics and ICT, road transport etc.) were evaluated. A supply disruption in an upstream industry is supposed to disrupt the whole value chain (European Commission, 2010, p. 24). In order to evaluate the supply risks, the level of concentration of worldwide production, the political and economic stability of producing countries, the potential to substitute the raw material by another one, the recycling rate and the environmental country risk are taken into account. The level of concentration is measured by the HHI[6] and then linked to the political and economic stability indicated by the World Bank's "Worldwide Governance Indicator". Increasing concentration of world production in a country with low political and economic stability is indicating an increasing supply risk. The grade of substitutability is based on the expert opinion of the Fraunhofer institute, while the recycling rate is based on the percentage of new metal and mineral content from secondary production (European Commission, 2010, p. 26). The environmental country risk is measured by the "Environmental Performance Indexes", which was developed by the EU Joint Research Centre" and aggregates 25 performance indicators in ten policy categories of environmental public health and ecosystem vitality. It is assumed that countries with a poor environmental situation might get under pressure to adjust environmental regulations, which could negatively affect the supply (European Commission, 2010, p. 29). The report concludes that REEs are critical raw materials for the EU. While the economic importance is only scored around 6.0 on a scale from 0.0 to 10.0, REEs have the highest supply risk among all included materials (European Commission, 2010, p. 33). This criticality assessment was updated based on data from 2013. The REEs group is divided in the subgroups of light and heavy REEs for this updated assessment. The results in the new report do not differ much from the results from 2010. Both light and heavy REEs are considered critical materials. While both subgroups only have a moderate economic importance for the EU, the supply risk of heavy

REEs is the highest and the supply risk of lights REEs is the second highest among all included materials (European Commission, 2014, p. 24).

The criticality of REEs and other materials for Germany in the short to medium term was evaluated in a 2011 report on behalf of the German government–owned development bank "Kreditanstalt fuer Wiederaufbau". In this report, the economic importance is measured by volume relevance (Germany's share on global consumption for a specific resource, the changes in the share on global consumption in the years 2004–2008, the changes in the import volume in the years 2004–2008) and strategic relevance (sensitivity of the German value-added chains, global increase in demand due to emerging technologies until 2030, substitutability). The supply risk is measured by country risk (country risk of Germany's imports, country risk of the global production and country concentration of global reserves in the base year of 2008), market risk (company concentration in the global production and the ratio of global reserve to global production in 2008) and structural risk (proportions of primary and secondary production in 2008 and recyclability) (Erdmann et al., 2011, p. 42). The matrix is based on a scale of 0.0 to 0.8 for the supply risk and 0.0 to 1.0 for the economic importance. The grade of indicated criticality is evaluated in six zones, from zone I with low criticality to zone VI with highest criticality. REEs are evaluated as being of high criticality (zone V) due to the high dependency of Germany in REO imports from China and the alarmingly high global company concentration. The economic importance is seen as high due to an increase of imports and consumption of 50% between 2004 and 2008, especially due to the demand of emerging future technologies (electric mobility, wind energy, catalysts and miniaturized information and communication technologies) (Erdmann et al., 2011, p. 43ff.). When the EC reports and the German reports are compared, Germany is more sensitive to a supply disruption than the EU as a composite. This indicates that Germany is more engaged in industries with REEs-dependent value chains than the EU countries are on average.

The matrix approach has been further developed since its first conceptualization. Silberglitt et al. (2013) suggest measuring the supply risk for the USA with an adjusted HHI, which is built upon the three criteria that the dominant producer of a specific mineral has to be outside the USA, that the USA has sizable net imports and that the dominant producers have a low quality of governance. The criterion of sizable net imports is met when 10% of the U.S. consumption is net imported. Shortfalls in governance are measured by using the average values of the six dimensions of the "World Governance Indicators". The adjusted HHI is then formalized as follows:

$$\text{Adjusted HHI} = \sum (100\text{-average WGI})^{*}(\text{market share}) \tag{3.2}$$

When the adjusted HHI is applied to REEs, the evaluated concentration decreases from 0.95 (on a scale from 0 to 1) to 62 (on a scale from 0 to 100). This indicates a high concentration of REEs production in countries with shortfalls in governance and a high country risk for the U.S. supply security (Silberglitt et al., 2013, pp. 5–9).

A second suggestion for methodical adjustment comes from Graedel et al. (2012), who introduce environmental implications as a third axis in the matrix so that environmental risks for supply security are considered with a higher weight than in other studies. In order to evaluate the environmental impact on human health and ecosystems, inventory data from the ecoinvent database is weighted according to the ReCiPe end point method (Graedel et al., 2012, p. 1066). This adjusted approach of a criticality space was used by Nassar et al. (2015) in order to assess the criticality of REEs on the national levels of China and the USA, and on the global level in the medium and long terms based on data from 2008. The medium-term supply risk is measured by six indicators: depletion time, companion metal fraction (i.e. the percentage of mineral that is mined as byproduct), policy potential index, human development index, political stability indicator of the World Governance Indicators and global supply concentration. The long-term risk only consists of depletion time and companion metal fraction (Nassar et al., 2015, p. 1045). The vulnerability to supply restriction is measured by importance and substitutability on the global level. On the national level, the component of substitutability is added, which is comprised of the net import reliance and the ability to innovate based on INSEAD's country-level global innovation index, which should reflect the ability of a country to develop substitutes for critical materials (Nassar et al., 2015, p. 1046). Figure 3.6 displays the results of criticality assessment in the long term on the global level (a), in the medium term on the U.S. level (b) and in the medium term on the Chinese level (c). The criticality of each REE is illustrated as a cloud. Every point in this cloud embodies one of 10,000 iterations of a Monte Carlo simulation to reflect each variable's uncertainty and provide confidence intervals. Nassar et al. (2015) explain that the lack of significant overlapping of clouds in (a) suggest that each REM has its own unique criticality. However, on the country-specific national level, there is a significant overlap, for example, of praseodymium and neodymium on the U.S. level.

Overall, the indicated criticality is lower than in other studies. In the long term, the indicated criticality on the global level is moderate and lower than the criticality of other metals such as silver, indium or niobium, which the authors attribute to the high natural abundance of REO in the earth's crust and to the elemental and geographic specificity of their analysis. According to the authors, most studies choose to assess the criticality only on the national or regional level for the short or medium term in order to emphasize the urgency of adjustments in the resource policy as a means of securing resource supply. However, they also add that no clear benchmark values to separate between criticality and non-criticality exist (Nassar et al., 2015, pp. 1047–1052).

Although the approach of a criticality matrix or space was widely used to assess REEs since 2008, the approach has flaws like all other scarcity indicators. Achzet and Helbig (2013) point out that the selection of indicators and their weights largely vary from study to study but in no paper is the reason why specific indicators and weights are chosen given. Furthermore, the weighting of indicators seems to be arbitrary in all studies due to missing empiric evidence about the influence of each indicator on the supply risk. There are also uncertainties of dynamic factors of

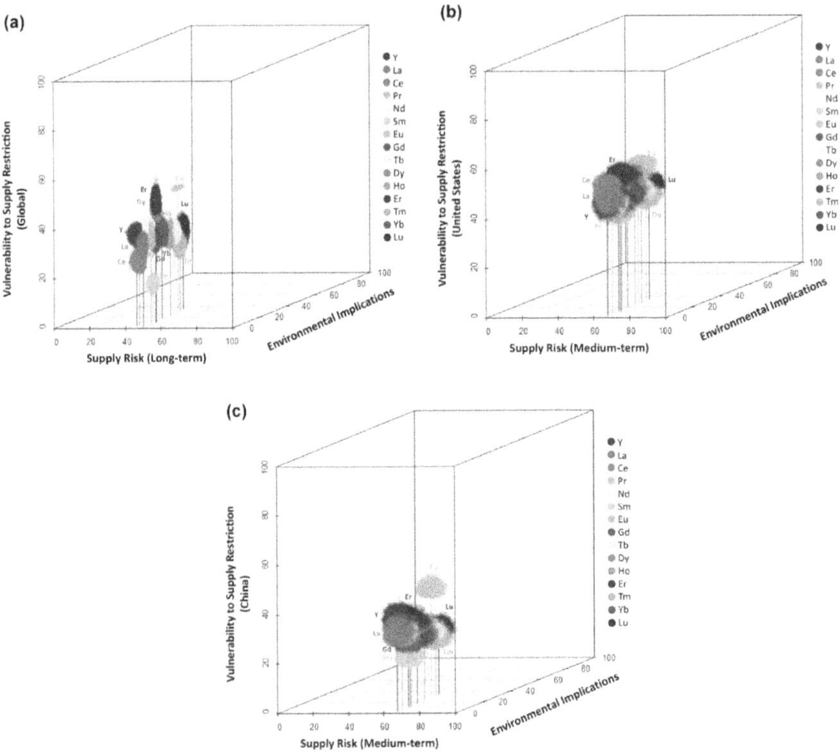

Figure 3.6 Assessment of REEs in the criticality space

Source: Reprinted with permission from Nassar, N. T; Du, X.; & Graedel, T. E. (2015). Criticality of the Rare Earth Elements. *Journal of Industrial Ecology*, *19*(6), 1044–1054. Published by Wiley-Blackwell for Yale University on behalf of the School of Forestry and Environmental Studies. Copyright 2015 Yale University.

supply risk assessment, for example the development of substitutability in the used time horizon (Achzet & Helbig, 2013, p. 446f.). Knoeri et al. (2013) especially criticize both the use of static indicators that produce only a snapshot of criticality at one point in time and the lack of feedback routes between demand and supply so that activities on the demand side do not affect the activities on the supply side. They propose using a material flow model to measure the environmental impacts along the production chain and an agent-based model to simulate the dynamic interrelation between substitution decisions and the underlying material flow system (Knoeri et al., 2013, pp. 809–812). However, the formalization of these models and the application on REEs is not carried out in their paper.

In summary, the approach of the criticality matrix does not only aim to measure the probability of supply disruptions that lead to temporary or permanent increasing scarcity but also evaluates the impact of scarcity on the economy. The results of most studies confirm the results of the previous subsections that especially neodymium and dysprosium, which are used in emerging technologies (permanent magnets, emission control and electronics) are expected to be critical in the short and medium terms. Nassar et al. (2015) expand the matrix to a third-dimensional criticality space and are the only authors that extend the time horizon of the assessment to include the long term. In the long term, the criticality is evaluated to be only moderate.

Intermediate conclusion on Rare Earths scarcity

Table 3.1 summarizes the results of all scarcity indicators used to assess the scarcity of REEs in this study in order verify the hypothesis that REEs are not rare or scarce. Overall, the results are not clear in the sense that all indicators show a similar level of scarcity at first glance. The widely used geological indicator of geochemically scarcity as well as the availability approach of static ranges

Table 3.1 Summary of the assessment of Rare Earths scarcity

Scarcity Indicator	*Level of indicated scarcity*
Geochemical scarcity	Low level of scarcity of the REE group, high level of deposit scarcity
Thermodynamic scarcity	High level
Static ranges of reserves and resources	Low level
Adjusted ranges of reserves and resources	Level of scarcity is depending on the expected market growth
Real market price	Low level
Temporal and structural imbalances of demand and supply	High risk level of increasing scarcity of heavy REEs after 2024
NRC criticality matrix	U.S. national level: high supply risk, high composite criticality of the REE group and of REEs used in emission controls, magnets, electronics, metallurgical, optimals and ceramics in the short to medium term
U.S. DoE criticality matrix	U.S. national level: high level of criticality of dysprosium, europium, terbium, yttrium and neodymium in the short and medium terms, near-criticality of cerium and lanthanum in the short term
EC criticality matrix	EU level: high level of criticality for both light and heavy REEs from 2010 to 2024
KfW criticality matrix	German national level: high criticality of the REE group in the short to medium term
Criticality space of Nassar et al. (2015)	U.S. national level: lower level of criticality in the medium term than in other studies Global level: moderate level of scarcity in the long term

of reserves and resources indicate a low level of REEs scarcity. The real market price, which is seen as a precise scarcity indicator in the neoclassical theory, has been stagnating for REEs since the 1990s so that there is no indication of increasing REO scarcity. This could be attributed to governmental policies and other factors like the China discount that have a disruptive influence on prices, on the one hand, but also to the expansion of supply along with the increase of demand on the other hand.

The indicator of adjusted ranges of reserves and resource could indicate all levels of scarcity depending on the expected market growth. Its reliability depends on the reliability of demand forecasts. As mentioned in Chapter 2, expert opinions overestimated market growth rates in some past cases. Thus, the significance of adjusted ranges should be interpreted with caution. High levels of scarcity are shown in the indicators of thermodynamic scarcity and deposit scarcity, which reflects the rarity of high-grade deposits. The approach of the criticality matrix was originally developed by the U.S. NRC in 2008 but was widely adopted to evaluate the criticality on different regional or national levels mainly in the short to medium terms. All studies show high levels of criticality of either the REEs group, the subgroups of light and heavy REEs or specific individual REEs on the U.S., EU and German levels. Overall, there is the commonly shared indication of high criticality of all REEs that are used in emerging technologies in the short and medium terms. The study of Nassar et al. (2015) stands out due to the introduction of the third dimension of environmental impact and its long-term assessment of REEs' criticality on the global level. The indicated criticality only shows a moderate level. This can be mainly attributed to the composition of the supply risk dimension that is only based on the two indicators of depletion time and companion metal fraction in the long-term evaluation. Both indicators are also more strongly weighted than in the medium-term assessment. However, the long depletion time is based on the overall natural abundance of REEs in the earth's crust but not on the abundance in high-grade deposits. Due to neglecting the dispersed nature of REO, the results of Nassar et al. (2015) underestimate the long-term availability.

Temporal and structural imbalances between demand and supply also have an indication for REEs scarcity beyond the medium term. Due to the peak of Chinese mines until 2024, there is extreme pressure for the rest of the world to explore and develop new mines outside of China in order to prevent temporary shortages and sharply increasing prices. Especially the supply with heavy REEs, which have the highest expected growth rates in demand, is at risk. The production from Chinese mines is expected to decrease by an annual rate of 4% after 2024 while demand will increase by annual rates of up to 14%. The Kvanefjeld project, which is still in the process of development, will not be able to sustain current levels of supply. Therefore, this indicator is in line with the results of the NRC, U.S. DoE, EC and KfW studies that see special criticality in the case of heavy REEs.

In summary, all indicators have some shortcomings or flaws that diminish their significance as single-use indicators to measure REE scarcity. In the overall picture, the hypothesis that Rare Earths are not rare or scarce cannot be validated. All of the indicators except real market prices and geological abundance show at least a moderate level of scarcity for the REE group, and most indicators show a high level of scarcity at least for heavy REEs.

Notes

1 Author's calculation is based on the formula:

$$\text{Range in years} = \text{Stock}_t - \sum_{t=1}^{n}(\text{Extraction rate}_t * (1 + \text{Grow rate})^{t-1}) \equiv 0$$

2 Author's calculation is based on data from U.S. Geological Survey (2014).

3 While other studies (for example: Behrendt et al., 2007; Bundesanstalt für Geowissenschaften und Rohstoffe, 2005; Angerer et al., 2009) also measure the criticality of natural resources, these studies will not be considered in the course of this study because they only aggregate selected indicators into one target value.

4 "A few months to a few years, but less than a decade" (National Research Council, 2008, p. 3).

5 The reserve base includes reserves, paramarginal resources and submarginal resources.

6 The Herfindahl-Hirschman-Index is used to measure the market concentration. It is calculated by adding the square of each firm's market share and has values between 0.00 in the case of perfect competition and 1.00 in the case of a pure monopoly. See Weinstock (1982) and Weinstock (1984).

Bibliography

Achzet, B., & Helbig, C. (2013). How to evaluate raw material supply risks: An overview. *Resources Policy*, *38*(4), 435–447.

Alonso, E., Sherman, A. M., Wallington, T. J., Everson, M. P., Field, F. R., Roth, R., & Kirchain, R. E. (2012). Evaluating rare earth availability: A case with revolutionary demand from clean technologies. *Environmental Science & Technology*, *46*(6), 3406–3414.

Angerer, G., Erdmann, L., Marscheider-Weidemann, F., Scharp, M., Luellmann, A., . . . Marwede, M. (2009). *Rohstoffe für Zukunftstechnologien: Einfluss des branchenspezifischen Rohstoffbedarfs in rohstoffintensiven Zukunftstechnologien auf die zukuenftige Rohstoffnachfrage* [Raw materials for future technologies: The influence of branch-specific natural resource consumption in material-intensive and resource-sensitive future technologies on the future demand for raw materials]. Stuttgart: Fraunhofer IRB Verlag.

Asheim, G. B., & Buchholz, W. (2000). *The Hartwick rule: Myths and facts* (CESifo Working Paper No. 299). Retrieved from www.cesifo-group.de/DocDL/cesifo_wp299.pdf.

Ayres, R. U. (2001). *Resources, scarcity, growth and the environment* (INSEAD Centre for Management of Environmental Resources Working Paper 2000/31/EPS/CMER). Retrieved from www.insead.edu/faculty-research/publications/working-papers/resources-scarcity-growth-and-the-environment-8893.

Barnett, H. J., & Morse, C. (1963). *Scarcity and growth: The economics of natural resource availability*. Baltimore: Hopkins Press.

Baumgaertner, S., Becker, C., Faber, M., & Manstetten, R. (2006). Relative and absolute scarcity of nature: Assessing the roles of economics and ecology for biodiversity conservation. *Ecological Economics*, *59*(4), 487–498.

Behrendt, S., Kahlenborn, W., Feil, M., Dereje, C., Bleischwitz, R., Delzeit, R., & Scharp, M. (2007). *Seltene Metalle: Maßnahmen und Konzepte zur Loesung des Problems konfliktverschaerfender Rohstoffausbeutung am Beispiel Coltan* [Rare metals: Measures and concepts for the solution of the problem of conflict-aggravating raw material extraction: The example of coltan]. Berlin: Umweltbundesamt.

Binnemans, K., & Jones, P. T. (2015). Rare earths and the balance problem. *Journal of Sustainable Metallurgy*, *1*(1), 29–38.

Boer, H., & Lammertsma, K. (2013). Scarcity of Rare Earth Elements. *ChemSusChem*, *6*(11), 2045–2055.

Bujis, B., & Sievers, H. (2012). *Resource security risks in perspective: Complexity and nuance* (Polinares Working Paper No. 33). Retrieved from www.polinares.eu/docs/d2-1/polinares_wp2_annex1b.pdf.

Bundesamt fuer Umwelt. (2010). *Preisentwicklung bei natuerlichen Ressourcen: Vergleich von Theorie und Empirie* [Price development for natural resources: Comparison of theory and empirical evidence]. Retrieved from www.bafu.admin.ch/bafu/de/home/themen/wirtschaft-konsum/publikationen-studien/publikationen/preisentwicklungen-natuerlichen-ressourcen.html.

Bundesanstalt für Geowissenschaften und Rohstoffe. (2005). *Trends der Angebots- und Nachfragesituation bei mineralischen Rohstoffen* (Forschungsprojekt Nr. 09/05 des Bundesministeriums für Wirtschaft und Technologie) [Trends in the supply and demand situations for mineral raw materials (Research Project No. 09/05 of the German Federal Ministry of Economics and Technology)]. Hannover: BGR.

Chen, Z. (2011). Global rare earth resources and scenarios of future rare earth industry. *Journal of Rare Earths*, *29*(1), 1–6.

Cleveland, C. J., & Stern, D. I. (2001). Natural resource scarcity indicators: An ecological economic synthesis. In C. J. Cleveland, D. I. Stern, & R. Constanza (Eds.), *The economics of nature and the nature of economics* (pp. 238–261). Cheltenham, Northampton: Edward Elgar.

Curtin University. (n.d.). *Staff profile of Professor Dudley Kingsnorth*. Retrieved from http://oasisapps.curtin.edu.au/staff/profile/view/Dudley.Kingsnorth.

Daly, H. E. (1974). The economics of the steady state. *The American Economic Review*, *64*(2), 15–21.

Donner, S. (2011, February 10). Biomining: Bakterien als Goldgräber [Biomining: Bacteria as gold diggers]. *Wirtschaftswoche*. Retrieved from www.wiwo.de/technologie/biomining-bakterien-als-goldgraeber/5241056.html.

Erdmann, L., Behrendt, S., & Feil, M. (2011). *Kritische Rohstoffe für Deutschland: Identifikation aus Sicht deutscher Unternehmen wirtschaftlich bedeutsamer mineralischer Rohstoffe, deren Versorgungslage sich mittel- bis langfristig als kritisch erweisen könnte* [Critical raw materials for Germany: Identification of economically significant mineral resources, whose supply situation could prove critical in the medium to long term, from the perspective of German companies]. Berlin: Institut für Zukunftstechnologien, Adelphi.

European Commission. (2010). *Critical raw materials for the EU: Report of the ad-hoc working group on defining critical raw materials*. Brussels: European Commission.

European Commission. (2014). *Critical raw materials for the EU: Report of the ad-hoc working group on defining critical raw materials*. Brussels: European Commission.

Fisher, A. C. (1977). *On measures of natural resource scarcity* (International Institute for Applied Systems Analysis research report RR-77–19). Retrieved from http://pure.iiasa.ac.at/696/1/RR-77-019.pdf.

Generalic, E. (n.d.). *Abundance of elements*. Retrieved from www.periodni.com/rare_earth_elements.html.

Graedel, T. E., Barr, R., Chandler, C., Chase, T., Choi, J., Christoffersen, L., . . . Zhu, C. (2012). Methodology of metal criticality determination. *Environmental Science & Technology*, *46*(2), 1063–1070.

Hall, D. C., & Hall, J. V. (1984). Concepts and measures of natural resource scarcity with a summary of recent trends. *Journal of Environmental Economics and Management*, *11*(4), 363–379.

Halvorsen, R., & Smith, T. R. (1984). On measuring natural resource scarcity. *Journal of Political Economy*, *92*(5), 954–964.

Hanley, N., Shogren, J. F., & White, B. (2007). *Environmental economics in theory and practice* (2nd ed.). Basingstoke: Palgrave Macmillan.

Hilpert, H. G., & Kröger, A. E. (2011). Seltene Erden: Die Vitamine der Industrie [Rare earths: Industrial vitamins]. In S.-A. Mildner (Ed.), *Konfliktrisiko Rohstoffe?: Herausforderungen und Chancen im Umgang mit knappen Ressourcen* [Conflict risk: Raw materials? Challenges and opportunities in handling with scarce resources] (pp. 159–167). Berlin: German Institute for International and Security Affairs.

Knoeri, C., Waeger, P. A., Stamp, A., Althaus, H.-J., & Weil, M. (2013). Towards a dynamic assessment of raw materials criticality: Linking agent-based demand: With material flow supply modelling approaches. *Science of the Total Environment*, *461–462*, 808–812.

Krautkraemer, J. A. (2005). *Economics of natural resource scarcity: The state of the debate* (Resources for the Future Discussion Paper 05–14). Retrieved from http://core.ac.uk/download/pdf/9307837.pdf.

Long, K. R., Van Gosen, B. S., Foley, N. K., & Cordier, D. J. (2010). *The principal Rare Earth Elements deposits of the United States: A summary of domestic deposits and a global perspective* (U.S. Geological Survey Scientific Investigations Report 2010–5220). Retrieved from https://pubs.usgs.gov/sir/2010/5220/.

Malthus, T. (1798). *An essay on the principle of population* (Electronic Scholarly Publishing Project ed.). Retrieved from www.esp.org/books/malthus/population/malthus.pdf.

Merriam-Webster. (n.d.). *Dictionary*. Retrieved from www.merriam-webster.com/dictionary/dictionary.

Mulvaney, D. (2011). *Green energy: An A-to-Z guide*. Los Angeles: Sage Publications.

Nassar, N. T., Du, X., & Graedel, T. E. (2015). Criticality of the Rare Earth Elements. *Journal of Industrial Ecology*, *19*(6), 1044–1054.

National Research Council. (2008). *Minerals, critical minerals, and the U.S. economy*. Washingtonm, DC: The National Academies Press.

Neumayer, E. (2000). Scarce or abundant? The economics of natural resource availability. *Journal of Economic Surveys*, *14*(3), 307–335.

Neumayer, E. (2010). *Weak versus strong sustainability: Exploring the limits of two opposing paradigms* (3rd ed.). Cheltenham: Edward Elgar.

Norgaard, R. B. (1990). Economic indicators of resource scarcity: A critical essay. *Journal of Environmental Economics and Management*, *19*(1), 19–25.

Papp, J. F., Bray, E. L., Edelstein, D. L., Fenton, M. D., Guberman, D. E., Hedrick, J. B., . . . Tolcin, A. C. (2008). *Factors that influence the price of Al, Cd, Co, Cu, Fe, Ni, Pb, Rare Earth Elements, and Zn* (U.S. Geological Survey Open-File Report 2008–1356). Retrieved from https://pubs.er.usgs.gov/publication/ofr20081356.

Perman, R., Ma, Y., McGilvray, J., Common, M. S., & Maddison, D. (2011). *Natural resource and environmental economics* (4th ed.). Harlow: Pearson Education Limited.

Rademaker, J. H., Kleijn, R., & Yang, Y. (2013). Recycling as a strategy against Rare Earth Element criticality: A system evaluation of the potential yield of NdFeB magnet recycling. *Environmental Science & Technology*, *47*(18), 10129–10136.

Reynolds, D. B. (1999). The mineral economy: How prices and costs can falsely signal decreasing scarcity. *Ecological Economics*, *31*(1), 155–166.

Ricardo, D. (1817). *On the principles of political economy and taxation*. London: John Murray.

Seo, Y., & Morimoto, S. (2014). Comparison of dysprosium security strategies in Japan for 2010–2030. *Resources Policy*, *39*(1), 15–20.

Siebert, H. (1979). Indikatoren der Knappheit natürlicher Ressourcen [Indicators of natural resource scarcity]. *Wirtschaftsdienst*, *59*(8), 409–416.

Silberglitt, R., Bartis, J. T., Chow, B. G., An, D. L., & Brady, K. (2013). *Critical materials present danger to US manufacturing*. Santa Monica: RAND Corporation.

Stern, D. I. (1996). *The theory of natural resource scarcity indicators: Towards a synthesis*. (Boston University Center for Energy and Environmental Studies Working Paper Series No. 9604). Retrieved from https://openresearch-repository.anu.edu.au/bitstream/1885/40903/2/9604.pdf.

Tyrer, M., & Sykes, J. P. (2013). The statistics of the rare earths industry. *Significance*, *10*(2), 12–16.

United Nations Conference on Trade and Development. (2014). *Commodities at a glance: Special issue on rare earths*. Geneva: UNCTAD.

U.S. Department of Energy. (2011). *Critical materials strategy*. Washington, DC: US DOE.

U.S. Geological Survey. (1996–2016). *Mineral commodity summaries, vols. 1996–2016*. Retrieved from https://minerals.usgs.gov/minerals/pubs/commodity/rare_earths/index.html#myb.

U.S. Geological Survey. (2014). *Historical statistics for mineral and material commodities in the United States*. Retrieved from http://minerals.usgs.gov/minerals/pubs/historical-statistics/.

Valero Capilla, A., & Valero Delgado, A. (2015). *Thanatia: The destiny of the earth's mineral resources: A thermodynamic cradle-to-cradle assessment*. Singapore: World Scientific Publishing.

Wang, X., Lei, Y., Ge, J., & Wu, S. (2015). Production forecast of China's rare earths based on the Generalized Weng model and policy recommendations. *Resource Policy*, *43*, 11–18.

Weinstock, D. S. (1982). Using the Herfindahl index to measure concentration. *Antitrust Bulletin*, *27*, 285–301.

Weinstock, D. S. (1984). Some little-known properties of the Herfindahl-Hirschman index: Problems of translation and specification. *Antitrust Bulletin*, *29*, 705–717.

Weiszaecker, E. U., & Ayres, R. U. (2013). Boosting resource productivity: Creating ping-pong dynamics between resource productivity and resource prices. *Environmental Innovation and Societal Transitions*, *9*, 48–55.

Weng, Z., Jowitt, S. M., Mudd, G. M., & Haque, N. (2015). A detailed assessment of global Rare Earth Element resources: Opportunities and challenges. *Economic Geology*, *110*(8), 1925–1952.

Zhang, L., Guo, Q., Zhang, J., Huang, Y., & Xiong, T. (2015). Did China's rare earth export policies work? Empirical evidence from USA and Japan. *Resources Policy*, *43*, 82–90.

4 The optimal extraction path of Rare Earth Metals for China

As concluded in Chapter 3, REEs are scarce and therefore of economic interest. The fact that their prices do not indicate scarcity but have been stagnating since the 1990s has helped to shape the Chinese view that REEs were underpriced in the past. One quote attributed to the former Chinese Prime Minister Wen Jiabao states that REEs were sold at the price of salt in the 1980s but deserve to be sold at the price of gold (Ruhkamp, 2011). In order to further analyze this underpricing narrative, Chapter 4 will first introduce the Hotelling rule as a theoretical tool to model optimal paths of extraction and price development for exhaustible natural resources and explain the determinants for deviations from the optimal path. Then the Hotelling rule is utilized to compare the historical REEs' price path from 1965 to 2012 with a theoretical optimal price path in order to evaluate underpricing. Due to the fact that Chinese mines are expected to peak in 2024 at the current rate of production, the Hotelling rule is then used to model an optimal future REEs production path from China's point of view. Finally, the results are summarized and critically assessed in an intermediate conclusion.

The path of optimal extraction based on the Hotelling rule

The Hotelling rule for the determination of an optimal extraction path of a non-renewable resource was formulated by U.S. economist Harold Hotelling in his 1931 paper "The economics of exhaustible resources". The starting point of his rule was the contemporary emerging perception that exhaustible natural resources would be exploited and depleted too fast due to the low prices of resource assets. Future generations that would have to get along without natural resources were considered as disadvantaged parties of this development so that conservationists called for state regulation of natural resource mining in order to decelerate extraction and depletion. On the other hand, a deceleration of extraction could also lead to significant shortages of supply and sharply increasing prices that would hinder the economic development of the current generation (Hotelling, 1931, p. 137f.). Built upon this intertemporal dilemma, Hotelling derived a criterion for an optimal extraction path based on the intertemporal opportunity costs of resource owners in a market of perfect competition. According to Hotelling, resource owners should be indifferent in the decision to extract and sell one marginal resource unit in the current period or to extract and sell one marginal resource unit in the next period. If the resource owner extracted and sold one marginal unit in the current period, s/he could invest her/his revenue on the capital market. On the other hand, if s/he delayed the extraction and sale to the next period, s/he would expect higher revenues of mining due to increased resource prices. The Hotelling rule for temporal indifference is thus an intertemporal efficiency condition that is satisfied when the in situ shadow price of resources – or the real market price when marginal costs of extraction are constant or zero – increase at the discount rate. Resource owners with access to perfect future markets would be able to mine their deposits at an extraction rate that would lead to resource prices, which would increase at the discount rate (Hotelling, 1931, pp. 140–146).

Optimal extraction in perfectly competitive markets

In the standard case of perfectly competitive markets, and when extraction costs are neglected, the Hotelling rule is formulated as:[1]

$$p_t = (1+\delta)^t * p_0 \tag{4.1}$$

P_t = price of one resource unit in period t,
δ = discount rate,
p_0 = initial price of one resource unit in period 0.

An alternative way to highlight that the capital gain on an extractable unit of a specific resource must equal the rate of discount to fulfill the criterion of intertemporal indifference is then (Conrad, 2010, p. 157):

$$\frac{p_{t+1} - p_t}{p_t} = \delta \tag{4.2}$$

Then, two different situations are distinguished in the modeling of the optimal extraction path. The extraction is optimized either in finite time based on a linear inverse demand curve or in infinite time based on a constant-elasticity inverse demand curve. If a substitute or back-stop technology[2] for the resource exists, then a maximum or choke-off price for the demand of the resource is given by the price of the substitute or the technology. When the price for the extracted resource exceeds the price of the substitute or back-stop technology, the demand for this resource will drop to zero and the substitute or back-stop technology is demanded instead. On the optimal extraction path, the resource is therefore planned to be depleted at the date of exhaustion T, at which the corresponding price path will reach the choke-off price. The linear inverse demand curve is defined as (Conrad, 2010, pp. 157–160):

$$p_t = a - b * q_t \tag{4.3}$$

p_t = unit spot price for q_t in period t,
q_t = aggregate quantity supplied to the market in period t,
a = parameter, intercept of the demand curve on the price axis (when $a > 0$),
b = parameter, a/b is the intercept of the demand curve on the quantity axis (when $b > 0$).

The price on the optimal path of extraction will increase at the rate of the discount until the price in T is equal to a and the remaining reserves and extraction fall to zero. The price p_T at the known date of exhaustion T is thus defined as:

$$p_T = a = (1+\delta)^T * p_0 \tag{4.4}$$

This can be solved for the initial price p_0:

$$p_0 = a * (1+\delta)^{-T} \tag{4.5}$$

The price path p_t results then from substitution of equation 4.5 into equation 4.1:

$$p_t = a * (1+\delta)^{t-T} \tag{4.6}$$

When expressions 4.3 and 4.6 are equated, the extraction path can be derived by solving for q_t:

$$q_t = \left(\frac{a}{b}\right) * \left[1 - (1+\delta)^{t-T}\right] \tag{4.7}$$

The extraction path is optimal when the cumulative extractions from $t = 0$ to T-1 equal the initial reserves of R_0:

$$\sum_{t=0}^{T-1} q_t = \sum_{t=0}^{T-1} \left(\frac{a}{b}\right) * \left[1 - (1+\delta)^{t-T}\right] = R_0 \tag{4.8}$$

When there is no substitute or back-stop technology, there is also no choke-off price so that the net present value of the deposit is optimized in infinite time. The constant-elasticity inverse demand curve is given by:

$$p_t = a * q_t^{-b} \tag{4.9}$$

Without an exhaustion date of T, there is no finite terminal price so that 4.1 describes the price path without any modifications. Equating 4.1 to 4.9 yields the extraction path:

$$q_t = \left[\frac{a}{(1+\delta)^t * p_0}\right]^{\frac{1}{b}} \tag{4.10}$$

Due to the condition, that q_t is only zero as t and p_t approximate ∞, the cumulative extraction can be equated to initial reserves and the resulting expression can be solved for p_0 (Conrad, 2010, p. 161):

$$\sum_{t=0}^{\infty}\left[\frac{a}{(1+\delta)^t * p_0}\right]^{\frac{1}{b}} = \frac{\left[\frac{a*(1+\delta)}{p_0}\right]^{\frac{1}{b}}}{(1+\delta)^{\frac{1}{b}}-1} = R_0 \tag{4.11}$$

Solving for p_0 leads to the price path:

$$p_0 = \frac{a*(1+\delta)}{\left\{R_0 * \left[(1+\delta)^{\frac{1}{b}}-1\right]\right\}^b} \tag{4.12}$$

Figure 4.1 compares the optimal paths of extraction rates (upper chart) and prices (lower chart) of a linear inverse demand curve and constant-elasticity inverse demand curve when $a = 1$, $b = 0.1$, $\delta = 0.05$, and $R_0 = 75$.

The initial annual extraction rates are significantly higher in the scenario of constant-elastic demand than in the scenario with a choke-off price, but they abruptly and sharply decrease as R_0 is approximating zero quickly. The result is an optimal extraction path that is asymptotically approximating the x-axis. The resource is never exhausted but a tiny amount will remain in situ forever. The annual extraction rates in the case of the linear inverse demand curve are initially higher but decrease more steadily until the resource is exhausted in T. As a consequence, the later extraction rates of linear inverse demand are higher than in the case of constant-elastic demand.

The corresponding price path of the linear inverse demand curve steadily increases until it ends at the choke-off price of 1 in period 21, the date of exhaustion T resulting from the chosen parameters. The price path of the constant-elasticity demand curve does not end at any specific point but will increasingly rise sharper when the extraction rates approximate zero.

The path of optimal extraction in a monopolistic market

While the Hotelling rule has received little attention for almost four decades after its formulation, it suddenly received more attention due to the oil and energy crises of the 1970s (Norgaard, 1990, p. 20). On 17 October 1973, the Organization of Petroleum Exporting Countries, which was formed in 1960 as a collusion of oil-rich countries with the purposes to coordinate the extraction rates of crude oil in order to obtain higher prices from Western oil companies, announced that it would no longer export oil to countries which were supporting Israel in the Yom Kippur War. While this embargo only lasted until the end of March 1974, it was the first

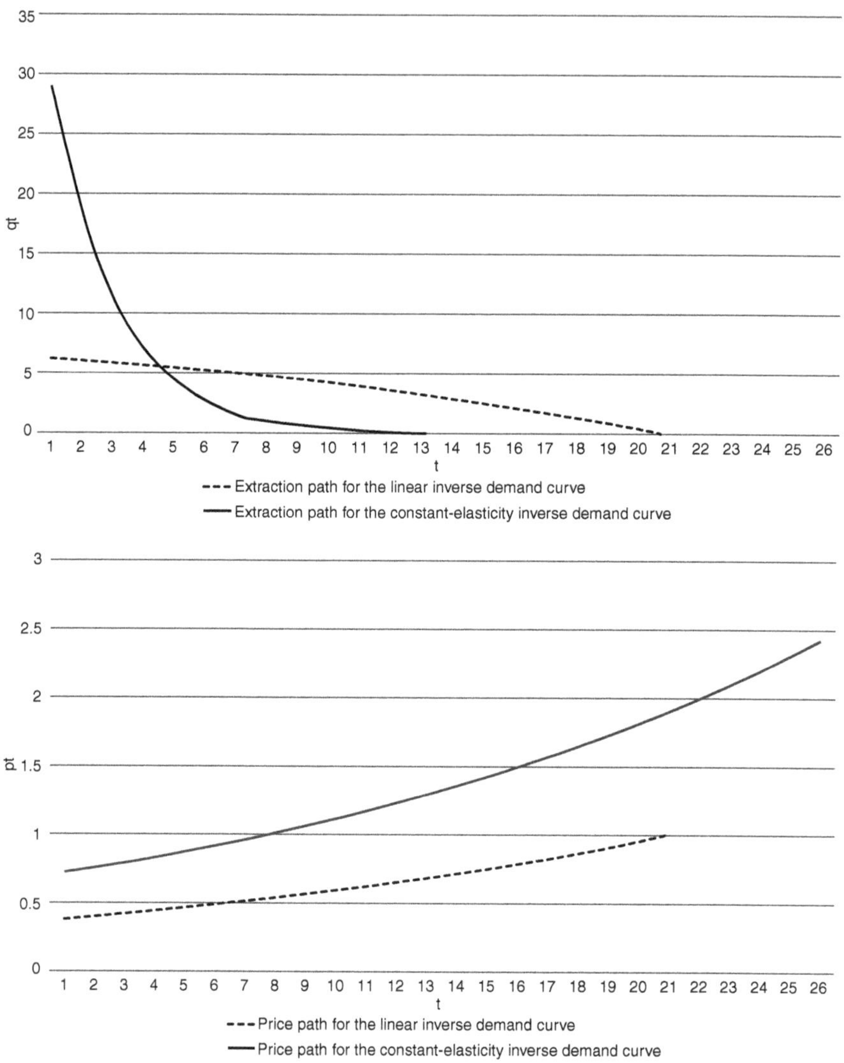

Figure 4.1 Comparison of optimal paths of extraction rates and prices in the cases of the linear and constant-elasticity inverse demand curves

in a series of events in the 1970s and 1980s that led to increasing real prices of crude oil. In January 1981, after the second oil shock due to the Iranian Revolution in 1979 and the beginning of the Iran-Iraq War in 1980, the real price of crude oil was more than seven times the real price in 1973 (Conrad, 2010, p. 162f.). Hotelling included deviations from the market structure of perfect competition and their impacts on the optimal paths of extraction and prices in the cases of monopoly and duopoly in his original paper, which was now used to analyze and explain the influence of OPEC on the development of crude oil prices.

In a monopoly market, the resource owner is assumed to maximize the net present value of revenues. In the case of a linear inverse demand curve, revenue in period t π_t is then given by (Conrad, 2010, pp. 164–167):

$$\pi_t = p_t * q_t = a * q_t - bq_t^2 \tag{4.13}$$

According to Hotelling, the monopolist would schedule the extraction to equate discounted marginal revenue. The marginal revenue of period t MR_t is defined as:

$$MR_t = a - 2b * q_t \tag{4.14}$$

Instead of shadow prices or real market prices, the marginal revenue has to increase at the discount rate:

$$MR_t = (1+\delta)^t * MR_0 \tag{4.15}$$

The marginal revenue will the equal price when the rate of extraction drops to zero so that $MR_T = a = p_T$. Analogous to equation 4.6, the marginal revenues can also be expressed as:

$$MR_t = a * (1+\delta)^{t-T} \tag{4.16}$$

Equating 4.16 to 4.14 yields the extraction path:

$$q_t = \left[\frac{a}{(2b)}\right] * \left[1 - (1+\delta)^{t-T}\right] \tag{4.17}$$

From the term $\frac{a}{(2b)}$ can be seen that the initial extraction rate of the monopolist will be approximately one-half of the extraction rate in a perfectly competitive market. Analogous to 4.11, the optimal extraction path in the monopoly is given by:

$$\sum_{t=0}^{T-1} q_t = \sum_{t=0}^{T-1} \left(\frac{a}{2b}\right) * \left[1 - (1+\delta)^{t-T}\right] = R_0 \tag{4.18}$$

Figure 4.2 compares the optimal extraction paths for the monopolistic and competitive mining industry facing a linear inverse demand curve when $a = 1$, $b = 0.1$, $\delta = 0.05$, and $R_0 = 75$. As indicated from expression 4.17, the initial extraction rates are lower in the monopolistic industry than in a mining industry in a perfectly competitive market. As a consequence, the date of exhaustion T in the monopoly is also further in the future and the extractions rate falls less steeply so that the extraction path of the monopolist intersects the extraction path of the perfectly competitive market from below. After the intersection, the rate of extraction is higher in the competitive path than in the monopolistic path. Through conservationist lenses, a monopolistic market for resources could be seen as preferable over a competitive

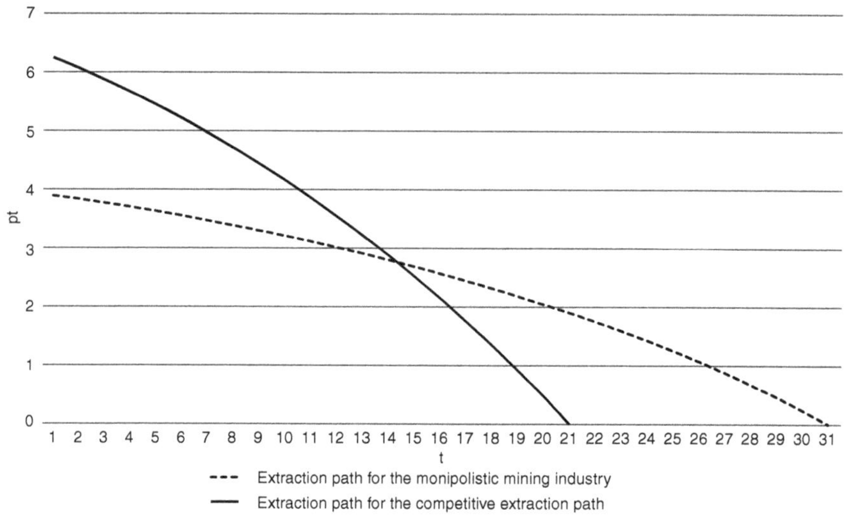

Figure 4.2 Comparison of extraction paths for the monopolistic and competitive mining industry

market because it reduces the concerns that non-renewable resources would be exploited too fast and future generations would have to get along without them.

In the case of the constant-elasticity inverse demand curve, the optimal paths of extraction and prices are identical for both market structures. All points on the constant-elasticity curve yield the same revenue so that the monopolist is unable to shift revenues to earlier periods in order to increase the net present value of revenues (Conrad, 2010, p. 166f.).

Empirical significance of the Hotelling rule

The empirical significance of the Hotelling rule has been tested in several papers since it has begun to get attention in the 1970s, but the findings are predominantly negative (Endres, 2011, p. 299). Slade (1982) tests the Hotelling rule based on the price development of 11 major metals and fuels with the exception of gold in the time from 1870 to 1978. She concludes that there are three basic long-term paths of falling, stable and rising prices. These curve courses can be explained by tradeoffs between a fall in prices influenced by improvements in technology and a rise in production costs induced by deposit grade deterioration. With regard to U-shaped price curves, extraction-cost reducing innovations can first overcompensate rising costs due to grade deterioration until the possibility for new technological developments has reached its natural limit. With constant technology and further ongoing grade deterioration, overall prices will begin to rise. Falling prices result from technological advances and the achievement of economies of scale in resource extraction and refining due to rapidly increasing consumption. Stable prices are found in the case of metals, whose demand has increased at a low rate and for which technological advances and grade declines are modest. The U-shaped price paths are further supported by the studies of Moazzami and Anderson (1994) and Pindyck (1999), while Berck and Roberts (1996) only find U-shaped price paths in their difference-stationary but not trend-stationary models.

Slade and Thille (1997) first state that the data of the last century show a decline in the relative prices of the majority of mineral commodities, which is contradictory to the Hotelling rule, before they formulate a modified Hotelling model unifying financial and product markets. It features risk-averse investors, resources that are risky in exploitation because of uncertainties in price development and extraction costs, and the possibility for risk diversification by investing in a portfolio on the capital market consisting of non-resource assets. The empirical test of their model, which is based on panel data of Canadian copper mining firms, shows some empirical support for the modified model, which can be used as an explanation for the poor empirical performance of the standard Hotelling model that does not include the possibility of risk diversification. However, the implied degree of required risk diversification is declared to be too high by Slade and Thille.

Ahrens and Sharma (1997) test whether the price development of resource commodities is either deterministic or stochastic in order to question the a priori assumption of trend stationarity for resource prices that is made by most studies. For their analysis, they select the same 11 fuels and metals that Slade (1982) analyzes in order to create comparability. They conclude that 6 of the 11 commodities are generated by trend-stationary processes, while the other 5 appear to be difference stationary. Cuddington and Nuelle (2013) analyzes the long run of trends of more than 100 real mineral commodity prices in a period of over more than 100 years. While their analysis shows that there are a few minerals with a monotonically increasing, a monotonically declining or a U-shaped price trend, there are also minerals with two or three switches in their price trend. Therefore, no single model would be able to explain the temporal behavior of all price series, but each exhaustible resource has to be individually analyzed.

Livernois et al. (2006) assume that the lack of strong empirical support for the Hotelling rule might stem from the initial estimation of scarcity rents. Because scarcity rents are not observable and have to be estimated, not only the Hotelling rule but also the models to generate scarcity rent data are empirically tested in most studies. In their paper, the authors try to avoid this by selecting old-growth timber as non-renewable resource for which scarcity rents are observable in the form of "stumpage prices bids made by logging firms competing to acquire the rights to harvest old-growth timber on federal land" (Livernois et al., 2006, p. 165) in the Pacific Northwest region of the USA from 1934 to 1998. In order to account for the rental value of the land itself, the authors use a modified optimal depletion model that includes the possibility to replant the land after it has been cleared of timber. Overall, they conclude that their results would be the strongest empirical support of the Hotelling rule up to the date of publication. The implicit discount rate estimated by using their basic Hotelling model without stock effects and historical stumpage return is 8.6%, which is referred as a reasonable estimate by the authors. However, while they do not generally reject the Hotelling rule, the tests of the basic model and its modified version do not provide strong fits.

Despite few empirical evidence for the basic model, Hotelling's contribution to the discipline of resource economics is undisputed. Devarajan and Fisher (1981) and Solow (1974b) express the view that the Hotelling model is a "canonical model for modern theorists to build on" (Devarajan & Fisher, 1981, p. 71) and that natural resource economics as an economic discipline can be traced to Hotelling's seminal article. Slade and Thille (2009) emphasize that deviation from the optimal Hotelling paths for production and prices could also come from violations of Hotelling's numerous and restrictive model assumptions. Especially deviations from the framework of perfect competition will lead to distortions of real price developments in relation to the theoretical planner's solution. Endres (2011) puts forward the thought that the Hotelling rule might be regarded as a self-destroying prophecy. Rising prices along the Hotelling path would be seen as a signal for emerging scarcity by economic agents, who would then engage in activities to slow down the scarcity process. These activities are not included in the basic model (Endres, 2011, p. 300).

Determinants for deviations from the optimal Hotelling paths

As mentioned before, the poor empirical significance of the Hotelling rule can be partially explained by the strict assumptions of the basic model, in which the extraction of a fixed stock of resources is optimized in a perfectly competitive market. While Hotelling has already included modifications of his model that include market concentration in the mining sector and state intervention through resource taxes, the possibility of the exploration of new deposits, substitution and other factors that lead to deviations from the optimal paths were not considered.

Variations in the relevant discount rate

The first major determinant for large variations in the indicated optimal paths for extraction and prices stems from the discussion of which interest rate should be utilized by resource owners to discount future scarcity rents or real market prices in order to maximize the net present value of their deposits. Hotelling addressed the choice of the relevant discount rate as a crucial factor for future availability of resources and intergenerational equity rather briefly.

> Hotelling mentions, but rather pooh-poohs, the notion that market rates of interest might exceed the rate at which society would wish to discount future utilities or consumer surpluses.
>
> (Solow, 1974b, p. 8)

The discount rate determines the tilt of the optimal extraction schedule and the date of exhaustion. When market rates of interest are used to discount the Hotelling rents and they are higher than the discount rate desired by society, then extraction rates will be too high and natural resources will be exhausted too early from a societal perspective. When market rates of interest are lower than the desired discount rate, then extraction rates and the level of natural resource availability for the current generation will be too low from a societal perspective. In the neoclassical framework of perfectly competitive markets, both interest rates are the same. When the assumptions of perfect competition are violated, market interest rates tend to be higher than the discount rate desired by society. One reason is the difference in risk assessment between individuals and the society as a group. The risk perception of individuals is higher than of groups so that higher market interests embody a high level of individual uncertainty. A second reason is based on the existence of taxes. While the society cares about the before-tax return, individuals pay more attention to the after-tax return on investment so that taxes on capital income are expected to be compensated by higher market interest rates (Solow, 1974b, p. 8).

Starting from Hotelling's mentioned societal concerns about the availability of exhaustible resources for future generations, the social discount rate should be used for optimization. The social discount rate "reflects a society's relative valuation on today's well-being versus well-being in the future" (Zhuang et al., 2007, p. 1). There are four different concepts to measure this relative valuation: the social rate of time preference, marginal social opportunity cost of capital, the weighted average approach and the shadow price of capital approach.

The social rate of time preference aims to measure the rate at which a society is poised to sacrifice current consumption in exchange for increased future consumption. One approach to empirically measure it was formulated by the British economist Frank P. Ramsey. In Ramsay's formula, the SRTP depends on the rate of pure time preference, the growth rate of consumption and the shrinkage rate of utility when consumption grows. The pure time preference embodies the impatience of individuals that tend to prefer current consumption to future consumption. In order to convince individuals to postpone consumption and to save, the discount rate has to be positive. High growth rates of consumption per capita lead to a low willingness to postpone current consumption in exchange of future consumption because people are already expecting increasing levels of future consumption without any sacrifices. The higher the shrinkage rate of utility is, the greater the impact on the growth rates of consumption (Markandya & Pearce, 1991, p. 137). Another approach for estimation is the approximation by the after-tax rate of return on low-risk, marketable securities, for example government bonds (Zhuang et al., 2007, p. 4).

The marginal social opportunity cost of capital is based on the idea that capital as a resource is scarce in any economy and that there is competition and crowding out between governmental and private investments. Each dollar invested in a public project could be invested in a project in the private sector instead. Thus, the benchmark interest rate for the society should be the return on private investments (Zhuang et al., 2007, p. 9). This embodies the concept of opportunity costs of capital investments. Especially in developing countries, where private lending rates are very high due to shortages of capital, the social discount rate has to be high (Markandya & Pearce, 1991, p. 143).

The weighted average approach aims to integrate the arguments of the SRTP and the SOC in one discount rate. Critics of the social opportunity cost of the capital approach emphasize that the concept neglects that not only private investment but also private consumption is displaced by public investment. However, the concept of SRTP neglects the impacts of public projects on private projects. Therefore, the discount rate of both concepts are weighted and aggregated into an average social discount rate. In the case of open economies with capital mobility, the international borrowing rate is also included in the average rate. On the one hand, the ability to borrow money abroad could lead to public investments that are displacing neither private investment projects nor private consumption. On the other hand, a high level of foreign debt could lead to lower credit ratings and to higher international borrowing rates, which would also lead to rising domestic borrowing rates. The main challenge of this concept is to estimate adequate weights (Zhuang et al., 2007, p. 10f.).

The shadow price of the capital approach takes the possibility to invest revenues and benefits of public projects in the private sector in order to generate future consumption into account. Therefore, revenues and benefits from public investment should be worth more than their immediate consumption. The total cost of a public project is then the sum of displaced current consumption and the foregone future consumption of displaced private projects. The total benefit is the sum of benefits immediately consumed and future consumption generated by reinvestment. In order to use the SPC approach for public project assessment, first the present value of streams of foregone consumption of displaced private investment or the present value of future consumption generated by the reinvesting of benefits in the private sector is estimated. This is then the SPC. Second, all displaced or generated costs and benefits are converted into consumption equivalents by multiplying them by the shadow price. Third, these costs and benefits are added to the direct costs of displaced current consumption and direct benefits of immediate consumption. Finally, total costs and benefits are discounted by the social rate of time preference to calculate the net present value of the public project. The main problem of this approach is the difficulty to apply it to actual projects. It requires information on the parameters of the SOC, SRTP, depreciation rate and marginal propensity to save in order to be empirically estimated and is very sensitive to changes and inadequate estimates of these parameters (Zhuang et al., 2007, p. 13f.).

When market interest rates and the social discount rate are not the same, the government could act as a social planner and implement regulatory measures which should enforce the use of the social discount rate in order to achieve social instead of private optimality (Solow, 1974b, p. 12f.). Nevertheless, even if these regulatory measures could be effectively implemented, the question of which social discount rate is appropriate remains. While the shadow price of capital approach is the least practicable to use due to its high information requirements, it is theoretically the most adequate because it embodies all costs and benefits of a project that are partially neglected in the other approaches. The second best choice is then the weighted approach, whose main source of error could be the estimation of weights that are not adequate for achieving social optimality. The concept of marginal social opportunity cost of capital neglects the aspects included in the concept of the SRTP, and vice versa, so that both concepts have major flaws and will not likely be equal to the rate at which society would wish to discount future utilities or consumer surpluses. Furthermore, John Rawls questioned the discount of future benefits from a moral point of view. Utility should be equal for all generations so that the current generation should not postpone consumption and save in order to benefit future generations but must not consume so much that future consumption would be reduced. Rawls then formulated a “just savings principle” that should achieve the intergenerational equity that was also the starting point of Hotelling’s considerations (Rawls, 1999, pp. 285–303). While Rawls’s approach was criticized for being too general, it fueled the development of new theories and models that more explicitly combine the optimal extraction of exhaustible resources and intergenerational equity in order to model constant-utility paths (for example, see Dasgupta, 1974; Dixit et al., 1980; Hartwick, 1977, 1978; Solow, 1974a). In the Hotelling rule, the implementation of Rawls’s criterion leads to discount rates of zero so that current and future Hotelling rents have the same value and the resource availability is divided evenly between all periods (Harris & Roach, 2013, p. 101).

Another deviation of the actual extraction path from the initial optimal path might come from a non-constant discount rate. In the basic Hotelling rule, a rise of the relevant discount rate will lead to faster extraction, while a decrease will lead to slower extraction (also called the conservation effect of a lower discount rate). However, Farzin (1984) shows that the allocative influence of discount rate changes is dependent on the capital intensity in the resource sector as well as in the sector that is producing the substitute for the extracted resource. The discount rate is not only a determinant for the price path but also for the capital cost per produced resource or substitute unit. When the resource stock is very large then the resource is treated like an ordinary good and priced close to the marginal costs of extraction. In this case, a decline in the discount rate leads to decreasing marginal costs and to increased extraction rates. In the opposing case of an extremely small resource stock, the resource is priced at a relatively high price that is set equal to the price of the substitute minus the marginal costs of extraction. In this case, a decline in the discount rate leads to a decline of the price of the substitute and consequently to a decline of the price of the resource. As a consequence, the resource will be extracted faster and exhausted earlier. Farzin calls the effect that a lower discount rate reduces the unit costs of the resource and the substitute and leads to higher rates of extraction “the disinvestment effect” (Farzin, 1984, p. 851).

In summary, the choice of the discount rate as well as changes of the discount rate could lead to paths of extraction that have been not initially predicted by the Hotelling rule and/or are not considered socially optimal. The implementation of Rawls’s criterion of intergenerational equity in the Hotelling rule would effectively reduce the concerns that future generations have to get along without resources. Nevertheless, it also contradicts Hotelling’s approach of net present value maximization from the perspective of individual resource owners.

Stock-dependent extraction costs and exploration of new deposits

One basic assumption of Hotelling is that extraction costs are constant. Conrad (2010) examines the impact of non-constant extraction costs on the paths of extraction and price development. He assumes that marginal costs of extraction increase as the level of remaining reserves decline. The consequence of this is a rise of Hotelling rents at less than the rate of discount so that the Hotelling rule itself is violated (Conrad, 2010, p. 168).

Another assumption is that the total stock of reserves is known prior to optimization. In practice, exploration is one of the major activities of economic subjects to reduce increasing scarcity of a natural resource and new reserves are found even in "some rather strange places" (Pindyck, 1978, p. 842). In general, additionally explored and developed reserves reduce scarcity rents and the present values of all deposits. With frequent new discoveries, the net price path could even show a declining instead of an increasing trend.

Pindyck (1978) examines the effects of exploratory activities as a means of accumulating or maintaining a specific level of reserves for the scenarios of constant and non-constant extraction costs. Under the assumption of mining costs that do not depend on the stock size of reserves, exploration will not affect the rate of change of the price path but only its level. The initial price is expected to be lower than in the basic model without exploration, and the date of exhaustion T is set further into the future. This scenario is illustrated in Figure 4.3.

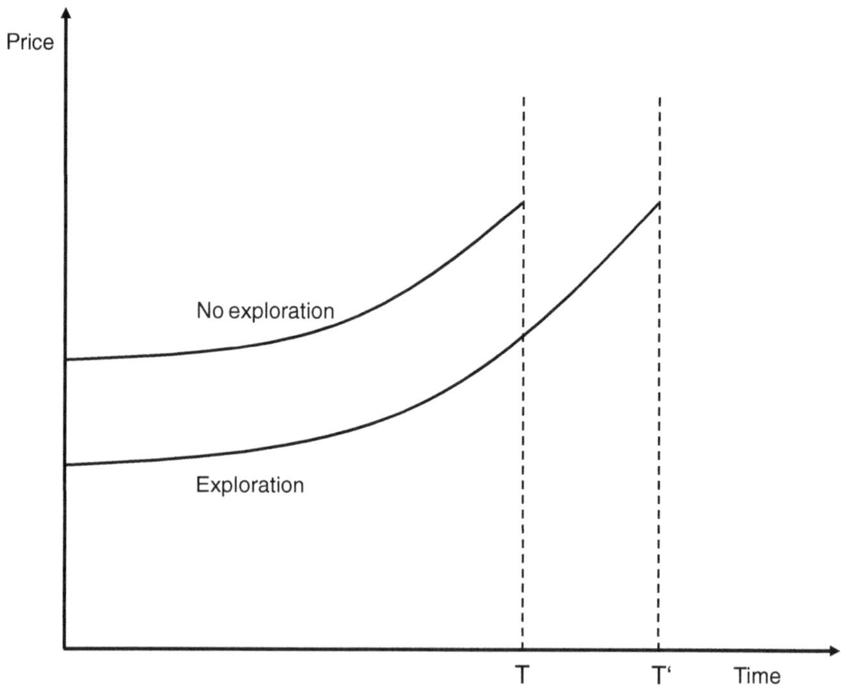

Figure 4.3 Price paths with and without exploration for zero extraction costs

Source: Reprinted with permission from Pindyck, R. (1978). The optimal exploration and production of a nonrenewable resource. *Journal of Political Economy*, *86*(5), 841–861. Copyright 1978 University of Chicago Press.

When stock-dependent extraction costs and exploration costs that increase as the known stock of reserves increase are assumed, then the level of exploration activities is determined by the initial value of the reserves. There is an intertemporal trade-off of gains from postponing exploration in order to discount its costs and the loss from higher extraction costs as the result of a shrinking reserve base (Pindyck, 1978). When the initial known reserve stock is large, then extraction costs will be low and exploration will be postponed. In this scenario, the price path will increase monotonously as in the basic model. When the initial known stock of reserves is small, then exploration will occur early in order to reduce extraction costs. The initial price will be high due to low reserves, will then decrease as a consequence of exploration and will finally increase again as all reserves have been explored and are declining again. In this scenario, the price path will form a U-shape (Pindyck, 1978).

In summary, a violation of the assumptions of constant extraction costs and/or of a known and fixed stock of resources leads to three main deviations from the competitive price path. When extraction costs are stock-dependent, and exploration is not possible, then the price path will violate the core principle of the Hotelling rule of prices and scarcity rents that increase at the rate of the discount rate. When extraction costs are constant and exploration is possible, then the price path will comply with the Hotelling rule at a lower level. When extraction costs are stock-dependent, exploration is possible and the initial known stock of resources is very small, then the price path will create a U-shape form.

In the case of a monopolistic mining market, the size of initial proved reserves is irrelevant because the monopolist chooses lower initial extraction rates in order to maximize the net present value of revenues. S/he will therefore be engaged less in exploration in the beginning but will undertake more exploratory activities later (Pindyck, 1978).

Changes in the extraction costs

In addition to the case of stock-dependent extraction costs, a change of the level of constant extraction costs could lead to deviations from the optimal path. For example, increasing wages could lead to an increased but constant level of costs for labor inputs required for mining. While the new net prices would be lower than the predicted optimal net prices in each period, they would still increase at the same discount rate. Due to net prices that are lower than optimal, the rates of extraction would be higher than on the optimal path in every period and the stock of extraction would be depleted before the choke-off price K is reached. Therefore, the new paths of extraction and prices are not optimal because demand does not fall to zero at the date of exhaustion (Pindyck, 1978).

Figure 4.4 illustrates the solution to this problem. In order to reach the choke-off price K in the date of exhaustion T, the initial price must be higher than the original price in period 0 ($p'_0 > p_0$). As a consequence, the initial rate of extraction will be lower than the original optimal extraction rate. The level of the price path for extraction at increased extraction costs will initially be higher than in the

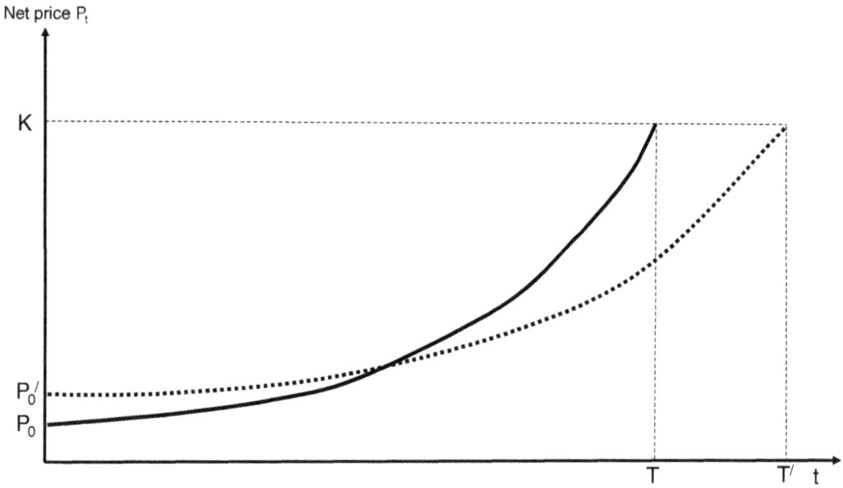

Figure 4.4 A rise in extraction costs

original path but will fall below the original price. The date of exhaustion will be postponed into the future (T' < T) so that the price is able to reach the choke-off price of K. However, when the increase of the level of extraction costs is very high, it could lead to an initial price that is higher than the choke-off price. The extraction of the natural resource would not be economically feasible (Perman et al., 2011, p. 527f.).

A decrease of the level of constant extraction costs leads to a diametrically opposing situation. The initial price will be lower, the initial extraction rate will be higher and the date of extraction will be earlier (Perman et al., 2011, p. 528).

Changes in demand patterns

There two main changes in the patterns of demand for a natural resource that could lead to a deviation from the predicted optimal path. The first change is an increase of the elasticity of demand. This could be the result of the discovery of good substitutes or a back-stop technology for the natural resource. Stiglitz (1976) investigates the effect of an elasticity that changes along the time path. He defines the elasticity of demand as $\left(\frac{1}{1-\alpha}\right)$ for $0 < \alpha < 1$ and derives a new condition for the price path as:

$$\frac{p_{t+1} - p_t}{p_t} = \delta - \frac{\alpha'}{\alpha} \tag{4.19}$$

The new optimal extraction paths in resulting from this modified Hotelling rule is illustrated in Figure 4.5 for both the competitive and monopolistic market.

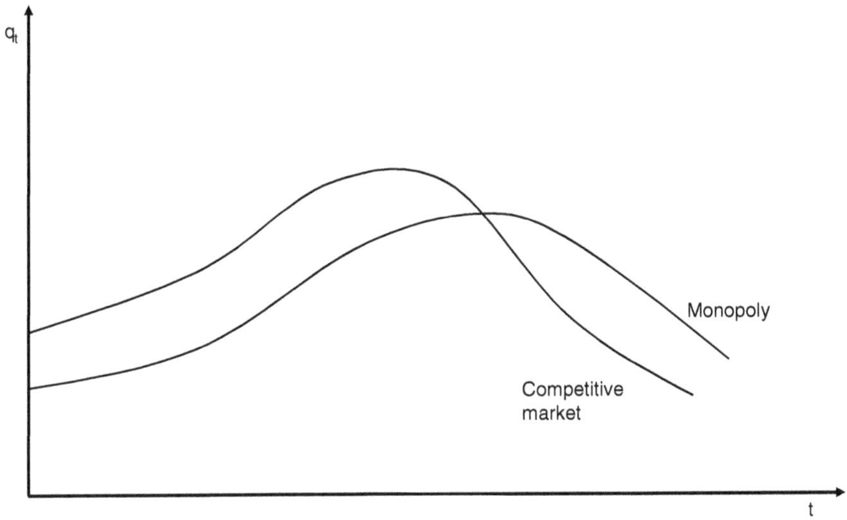

Figure 4.5 Increasing elasticities of demand

Source: Reprinted with permission from Stiglitz, J. E. (1976). Monopoly and the rate of extraction of exhaustible resources. *The American Economic Review*, *66*(4), 655–661. Copyright 1976 American Economic Association.

The rate of extraction will initially be lower and the rate of increase of the price will be slower in the monopolistic market than in the competitive market, which resembles the same pseudo-conservationist pattern as in the basic Hotelling rule. In both cases, extraction rates will be initially relatively low but increase as the elasticity increases over time in order to maintain the growth of the price path (Stiglitz, 1976, p. 657).

The second deviation is the increase of demand for the resource. This could happen due to newly found fields of applications for the natural resource, the growth of the population or rising real incomes, for example. As result of the increasing demand, the demand curve shifts outwards. On the original optimal price path, this would lead to higher rates of extraction so that the resource would be exhausted before the choke-off price is reached. Therefore, increased net prices are required to reduce the demand in every period in order to meet the optimality condition that the price is equal to the choke-off price at the date of exhaustion. The time until exhaustion is also shortened (Perman et al., 2011, p. 525). In the case of a sudden demand decrease for the resource, the solution would be analogous. The demand curve shifts inwards; net prices are required to decrease in order to increase the demand in every period. The time until exhaustion is lengthened.

Technological uncertainty and development of substitutes

According to Dasgupta and Heal (1974), technological uncertainties are the uncertainties with the greatest potential impact on the optimal extraction schedule. The existence of a substitute or back-stop technology with a known price leads to an optimization in finite time with prices that only increase up to the price of the substitute or back-stop technology. When a substitute or back-stop technology is not existing, then extraction will be optimized in infinite time and the increase of prices is without limits. However, the impetus for economic actors to engage in activities of research and development in order to find a substitute or back-stop technology is also steadily rising along the increasing price path so that it is uncertain whether the initially optimal extraction path will remain optimal. Technological change could even let an essential resource become inessential so that demand would suddenly fall to zero (Dasgupta & Heal, 1974, p. 26f.).

Dasgupta and Stiglitz (1981) compare the price paths under technological certainty and technological uncertainty. In the case of technology uncertainty and an unknown date of invention of a back-stop technology, the price path is divided into three phases: the pre-invention phase from period 0 to T_1, the post-invention and pre-innovation phase from T_1 to T_2 and the post-innovation phase from T_2 on. This is shown in Figure 4.6.

The path from A to C is the original optimal price path without a given choke-off price. The initial price p^u_0 is set higher than under technological certainty. In T_1, a back-stop technology with the fixed price of $\bar{p}$ is invented but does not immediately enter the market as innovation. As a consequence, the rate of extraction is adjusted in order to meet the fallback price $\hat{p}$. The new price path will then

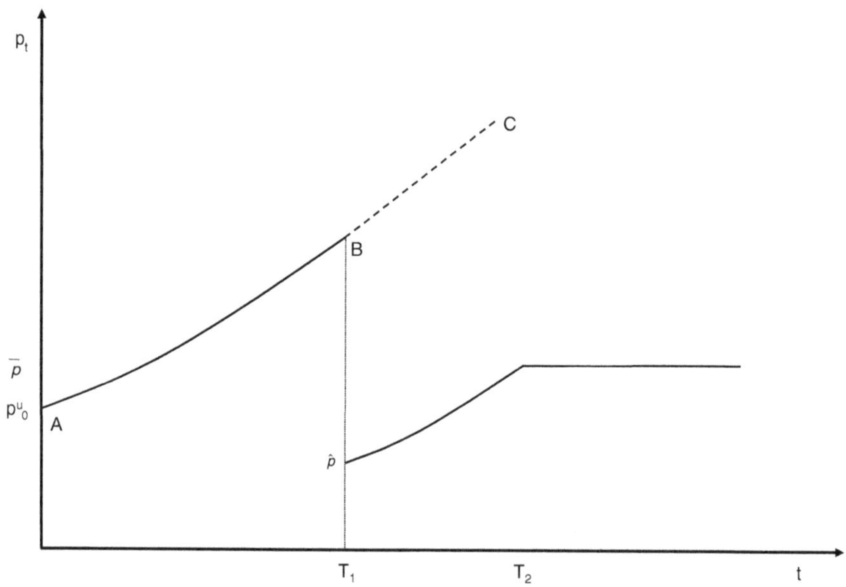

Figure 4.6 The optimal extraction path under technological uncertainty

Source: Reprinted with permission from Dasgupta, P., & Stiglitz, J. (1981). Resource depletion under technological uncertainty. *Econometrica*, *49*(1), 85–104. Published by Wiley-Blackwell on behalf of the Econometric Society. Copyright 1981 The Econometric Society.

increase until it reaches the choke-off price $\overline{p}$ in T_2. T_2 is the date of exhaustion of the natural resource as well as the date of innovation, on which the back-stop technology enters the market.

In summary, under technological uncertainty, the initial price of extraction is higher than the optimal price under technological certainty. When a back-stop technology is invented, extraction is adjusted in order to meet a fallback price that is below the choke-off and the price path transforms from the pattern of a constant-elasticity inverse demand curve to the pattern of a linear inverse demand curve. The paths of extraction and price are now optimized to meet the optimality criterion that the price is equal to the choke-off price at the date of exhaustion, which is also the date of market entry of the back-stop technology.

Common-pool externalities due to imperfect property rights

The basic Hotelling rule and the modeling of an optimal extraction is based on private resource owners as economic actors. When either private ownership of natural resources is absent due to the nonexistence of defined property rights or property rights are not well protected due to a defective legal system, then common-pool externalities that distort optimal extraction could arise. In the case of open-access to the extraction of an exhaustible natural resource, the condition of intertemporal indifference is overridden by the dilemma of competitive extraction. Each unit of the resource that is extracted and sold by one economic agent cannot be extracted and sold by another economic actor anymore. This leads to the so-called voracity effect of fast resource exhaustion. Each rival faction has the goal to extract as much as possible before the resource is depleted. The natural resource as a common asset is then transformed into private assets, for which excludability is given (Van der Ploeg, 2008, p. 1).

Van der Ploeg (2008) sets up a model of a closed economy with common-pool extraction of a natural resource. Each rivaling faction extracts the resource and invest it in private capital. His efficiency condition for optimal extraction is a modified version of the Hotelling rule:

$$\frac{p_{t+1}-p_t}{p_t}=\delta+\left(N-1\right)*\frac{\sigma}{K} \tag{4.20}$$

N = number of rivaling factions,

$\sigma=\sum_{i=1}^{N}\sigma_i$, σ_i = share of resource grabbed by faction i,

K = stock of private capital.

When the number of rivaling factions is only one (i.e. each deposit is privately owned and excludability is guaranteed), the solution of this variation, which is called the “political Hotelling rule” by the author (Van der Ploeg, 2008, p. 6), is equal to the solution of the basic Hotelling rule. For each number of factions above one, the modified Hotelling rule will lead to suboptimal solutions. As result, the rate of extraction and the rise of the resource price will be faster than optimal. Because extracted resource units are transformed into private capital, the substitution of natural resources by man-made resources occurs too rapidly and the country will save too much. The total output is too high but consumption too low. The more fractionalized the extraction is, the bigger are these effects (Van der Ploeg, 2008, p. 13). Due to the fast depletion of natural resources, the resource consumption of future generations is impaired. The level of consumption generated by investments in man-made capital is lower than in a homogenous county without fractionalization. Therefore, the whole society is worse off than in the basic Hotelling rule due to absence or deficiencies of a system of private property rights for natural resources (Van der Ploeg, 2008, p. 19).

Strategic extraction and exploration in the Cournot duopoly

The subject of strategic implications of a duopoly for extraction is raised in Hotelling's original paper but is only briefly discussed and not formalized. One formalization that deeply examines the case of the duopoly comes from Hartwick and Sadorsky (1990). In their model, two resource owners with a stock of known resources are rivals in extraction and exploration of new deposits in a two-period strategic game. The extracted quantity is the strategic variable that determines the price (Hartwick & Sadorsky, 1990, p. 277f.). The profit of each player (i = 1, 2) is defined as:

$$\pi^i = Q^i p\left(Q^1 + Q^2\right) - c^i\left(Q^i\right) - w^i\left(x^i\right) + \beta\Big\{\left(S^i + S^i\left(x^i\right) - Q^i\right) \\ * p\left(\sum_{i=1}^{2}\left(S^i + S^i\left(x^i\right) - Q^i\right)\right) - c^i\left(S^i + S^i\left(x^i\right) - Q^i\right)\Big\} \tag{4.21}$$

Q^i = firm i's output or exploration in period 1 ($Q^i \leq S^i$),
S^i = firm i's reserves of known stock in period i,
p (•) = the stationary demand schedule for output extracted by the two firms.
c^i (Q^i) = the total extraction cost for firm i,
x^i = physical resources devoted to exploration by firm i in period 1,
w^i (•) = the cost of exploration,
S^i (x^i) = the discovery of stock made in period 1 to be extracted in period 2,
β = the discount factor of 1/ (1-r),
r = discount rate.

The exploration of new deposits influences the market price. When the discovered deposits are large in relation to the remaining stock of resources, then resource owners will suffer a loss in value of unsold remaining quantities. However, resource owners are also able to increase their market share through successful exploration. Overall, competition promotes greater output and exploration but there is the tendency of the overexploration of duopolists in order to increase their own market share, while value loss is neglected (Hartwick & Sadorsky, 1990, p. 281).

Based on their model, Hartwick and Sadorsky test the strategic behavior in the three scenarios of a two-plant monopoly (i.e. a collusive duopoly with full cooperation in exploration and extraction), of a perfect duopoly and of the mixed case of cooperation of both players in exploration (the level of exploration is selected cooperatively) and Cournot competition in extraction. When there is cooperation in exploration, the same level of exploration is undertaken as in the case of a monopoly but extracted quantities differ. In the perfect duopoly, each player extracts more in period 1 and explores almost twice as much as in the monopoly and the mixed case. Overall, a rise in the discount rate will lead to a decline of extraction and exploration levels. When the initial stock reserves for firm 2 is assumed to be smaller than in the basic case, then the output of 2 in period 1 is reduced and the output of 1 increases. Both players engage more in exploratory activities than in the base case. When the extraction costs of 2 increase, then 2 will explore and extract less in the first period while player 1 will increase the levels of exploration and production in period 1. At the same time, the efforts of researching better exploration technology of 2 is reduced while the efforts of 1 increase. Finally, when the productivity of research efforts for firm 2 declines, then player 2 will explore and produce less in period 1, while player 1 will explore and produce more in period 1. In summary, the level of deviations is based on the patterns of strategic behavior of market players and the assumptions about cost structure and the distribution of the total initial stock. There is no clear pattern of long-term extraction, but there are strategic adjustments based on quantitative competition.

Optimal extraction of Rare Earth Metals in China

After an extended presentation of the Hotelling rule, it will consequently be applied to REEs in the following. First, the relevant demand curve will be estimated based on historical data of extraction quantities and real market prices, and a review of the substitutability of REEs. Second, different possibilities for the relevant discount rate will be discussed. In order to assess whether REEs have been undervalued in the past, the optimal paths of mining price development in the period of 1965 to 2012 will be modeled and compared to this period's historical price path. Due to the Chinese concern that REEs are depleted too fast, an optimal future extraction path will be modeled hereinafter. Finally, the results will be critically assessed in an intermediate conclusion.

Estimation of the relevant demand curve

In order to determine the relevant demand curve, a linear inverse demand function as well as a constant-elasticity inverse demand function will be estimated based on the USGS dataset for extraction rates and corresponding U.S. real market prices from 1922 to 2010 that has been used for the calculation of the growth rate of real REO prices in Chapter 3. Therefore, the same problem that there is no global

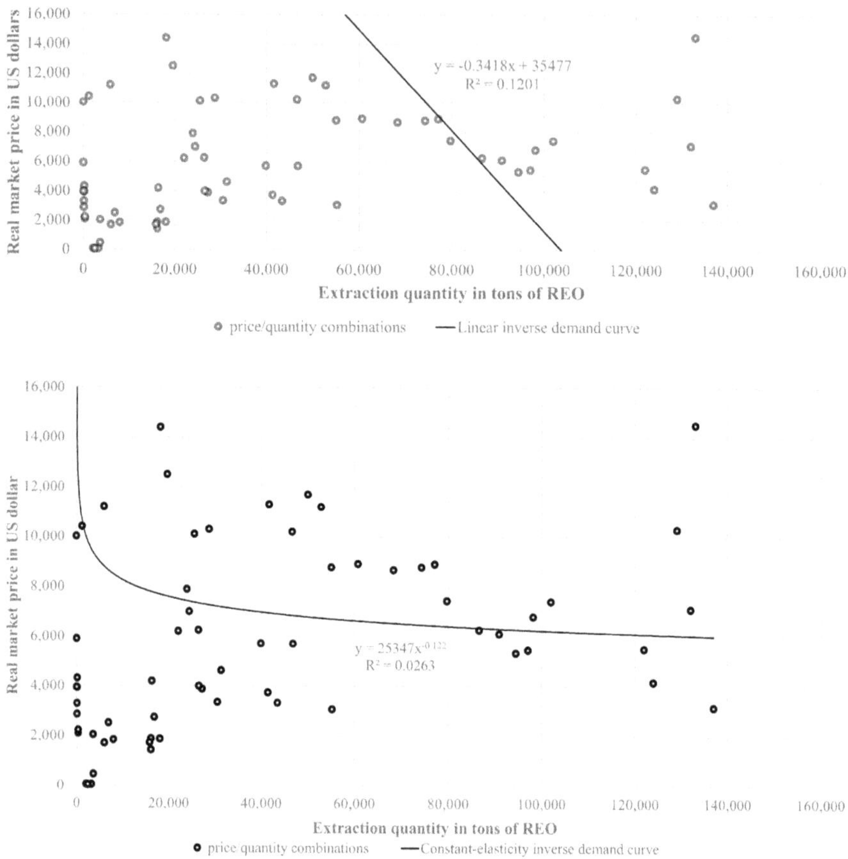

Figure 4.7 Estimations of the linear inverse and constant-elasticity demand curve
Source: Data retrieved from USGS, 2014.

market price for REO remains. Due to the lack of information about extraction costs, the functions are also estimated on price/quantity combinations instead of combinations of Hotelling rents and resulting extraction quantities. Figure 4.7 illustrates the estimation of the linear inverse demand curve (upper half) and of the constant-elasticity demand curve (lower half).

It is most noticeable that the coefficients of determination are very low in both cases. Thus, it seems that the extracted quantity of REO is not a good predictor for the real market price. This might be the result of shortcomings of the estimation. First and foremost, it is a very simplified approach that is purely built upon the basic microeconomic principle of price determination by the invisible hand of demand and supply. As it has been already highlighted in Chapter 3, it is not yet fully clear which factors influence the prices of natural resource in general and of REO in particular. Speculative activities and state regulations might have directly distorted prices, while several events such as wars, political crises and change, natural disasters and so on could indirectly affect them. Consequently, the low coefficients of determination reflect a high degree of abstraction of the price determination in the basic Hotelling rule. However, while the inclusion of additional factors might improve the empirical robustness of the demand curve, it also leads to a higher complexity of applying the Hotelling rule to the case of Rare Earths, for which the price determinants are even less evaluated than in the case of oil prices, for example. In the face of this dilemma, the simple versions will be used for further analysis despite their low values in R-squared.

As a second step, it must be decided whether the linear inverse demand curve or constant-elasticity demand curve will be used. This decision is related to the availability of adequate substitutes. It has been briefly mentioned in Chapter 3 that either no substitutes or less efficient substitutes exist for the major fields of REEs applications. One possibility of substitution is replacing one specific REM by a less critical REM. This is a feasible solution for some applications. Twenty-five percent of the neodymium content in NdFeB magnets could be substituted by praseodymium, which is less abundant but is also used in fewer applications. Dysprosium in permanent magnets could be partially replaced by terbium. However, terbium is also irreplaceable in green lamp phosphors but would be more available when fluorescent lamps will be replaced by light-emitting diodes. This would also decrease the criticality of europium, which is the only and irreplaceable REM that can be used in red lamp phosphors (Binnemans & Jones, 2015, p. 34). The substitution by other natural resources or technologies is also limited or economically undesirable. Cerium could be substituted by aluminum or iron oxide in the field of polishing materials. The light REEs used in nickel-metal hydride batteries are substitutable by a titanium-iron alloy. Because light REEs are cheap due to the oversupply resulting from the balancing problem, these two substitution possibilities are not seen as desirable (Binnemans & Jones, 2015, p. 35). Lithium-ion batteries could replace the NiMh batteries used in hybrid and electric mobility. In this field, the utilization share of Lithium-ion batteries was only 2% in 2009, which shows that this solution was not used before China's REEs embargo in 2010 (Schueler et al., 2011, p. 101). With regard to the performance-determining attributes of hybrid of electric motors, weight is the most important parameter because the energy consumption increases with additional weight. Induction motor technology is the most mature technology, which has been used in industrial applications for several decades and does not require special materials. Therefore, it is quite robust and cheap. It is also very efficient, so little energy is lost in the conversion from electric power into shaft power. On the downside, induction motors have a high weight and volume so that they are not optimal for the use in hybrid and electric vehicles. On the other side, permanent magnet synchronous motors require Rare Earths and cost about 20% more than alternative motor technologies but are also most efficient and do need a lot of maintenance. In combination with their low volume and weight, they have the highest power-to-weight and power-to-volume ratios and embody the first best solution for hybrid and electric mobility. Switched reluctance motors are based on ferromagnetic material, and are relatively cheap, efficient and very robust. They have a higher volume and weight than permanent magnet synchronous motors but are still seen as a second-best solution were it not for the loud noise emission coming from fluctuating variation of the motor torque that has impeded the wide use of this motor type (Bradshaw et al., 2013, p. 99f.). At the current level of technology, the renunciation of REEs-related technology in hybrid and electric mobility would lead to sub optimality. In offshore wind generation, turbines with gearboxes could substitute gearless turbines but would also create significant higher maintenance costs. As an alternative, an electromagnet based on copper could replace the NdFeB magnet in gearless turbines. This magnet type was used in the first generation of gearless turbines before the shift to NdFeB magnet turbines. Because they weigh more and are less efficient than REEs-based magnets, they have been substituted by NdFeB magnets (Bradshaw et al., 2013, p. 101). The trade-off between the price and the power-to-weight ratio is expected to be reassessed when the prices of REEs will rise due to increasing scarcity. At the current point in time, NdFeB magnet are not substitutable in gearless turbines without the loss of efficiency. The use of REEs for permanent magnets in hard disk drives is dependent on the expansion of the market share of solid state drives that do not require a voice-coil-motor containing a NdFeB magnet. Solid state drives are less susceptible to physical shock, are quieter and have lower access times to stored data but are also considerably more expensive than hard drive disks. Both technologies will therefore co-exist for an unpredictable time (Schueler et al., 2011, p. 99f.). In the field of catalysts, there is not even a less-efficient, known substitute now (Schueler et al., 2011, p. 103f.).

Overall, the general notion that no perfect substitutes or back-stop technology for REEs-based applications can be verified. This is even truer when REEs are analyzed from an aggregated view. As consequence, the constant-elasticity demand function will be used in the application of the Hotelling rule to Rare Earths:

$$p_t = 25347q_t^{-0.122} \tag{4.22}$$

The elasticity of –0.122 is lower than the estimated elasticity for copper (between –0.19 to –0.47), for aluminum (–0.25 in the short run and –0.3 in the long run) and for steel (between –0.2 to –0.3) but in the wide range of estimated elasticities for zinc, which vary between –0.005 and –0.78 (Pothen, 2013, p. 19f). Thus, this relatively high level of inelasticity of REEs demand reactions on price changes reflects the low level of substitution possibilities.

Determination of the relevant social discount rate

In order to determine whether the Chinese market interest rate is an adequate choice as a relevant discount rate, the Chinese financial system is briefly characterized. Since the beginning of economic reforms in 1978, the financial system has been transformed from a government-owned and internationally isolated mono bank system, which was only a policy tool of the central economic planning of the Chinese Central Government, into a diversified, partially internationally integrated system. This system includes a banking sector with a mixed private and/or public ownership structure as well as capital markets but is predominantly bank-based. However, despite almost four decades of ongoing reforms and steps of liberalization, the banking sector is still dominated by the State-controlled "Big Four" commercial banks "Agricultural Bank of China", "Bank of China", "China Construction Bank" and "Industrial and Commercial Bank of China", which supply almost 70% of the financing of the real economy (Fung & Liu, 2007, p. 119ff.; Yang, 2016). The Big Four are no longer officially listed as State-owned banks by the Chinese government because they have been equitized as joint-stock companies. Nevertheless, the amount of shares that are freely tradable represents only a fraction of the total equity, while the majority of shares is owned by the Chinese central bank "People's Bank of China", by the Ministry of Finance and other governmental agencies. As a consequence, the Chinese State still has highly influential possibilities concerning financing, credit allocation and commercial lending interest rates. This influence is completed the three wholly State-owned policy banks "Agricultural Development Bank of China", "China Development Bank" and "China Exim Bank" that are still directly controlled by the China's cabinet, the State Council (Martin, 2012, p. 2f.). The interest rates are not freely determined by the market mechanism but are regulated by the government. The PBOC sets maturity-specific benchmark rates for deposits and loans, and banks are allowed to offer interest rates within a band above and below them. Especially deposit rates have been kept artificially low so that savers are experiencing a situation of financial repression. The deposit rates are often so low that they are below the inflation rates. As a consequence, real deposit rates are occasionally negative (Lardy, 2008, p. 11f.). On the demand side for loans, the lending rates are more liberalized than deposit rates but are also assessed as being far too low. The consequence of this system is an investment-led growth path that is based on the underpricing of capital, low returns on deposits and excessive demand for capital (Lardy & Borst, 2013, p. 1ff.). However, the total supply with loans is limited because the PBOC allocates specific credit limits to Chinese bank (Martin, 2012, p. 9). Due to the banking system dominated by State-controlled institutes, the lion's share of funds is funneled into either State-owned enterprises or enterprises with strong ties with the government (Martin, 2012, p. 40f.). The commercial banks also benefit from this system because the difference between the benchmarks of deposit and lending interest rates guarantees stable net interest margins. Figure 4.8 illustrates Chinese inflation rates, the lending rates and deposit rates as listed by the World Bank. Due to data availability, the illustrated period is limited to the period from 1987 to 2014. It is observable that the difference between deposit and lending rate is almost steady from 1999 to 2014. The inflation rate was higher than in the deposit rate in the years 1987–1989, 1993–1996, 2004, 2007–2008 and 2010–2011 so that real deposit rates were negative in these years. When deposit rates would be chosen as discount rate for the optimization in the Hotelling rule, this would imply that real prices have to decrease in these periods. In order to achieve decreasing prices, the extraction rates would have to be excessive. This is not desirable not only from the view of resource owners but also from the view of the Chinese government that is

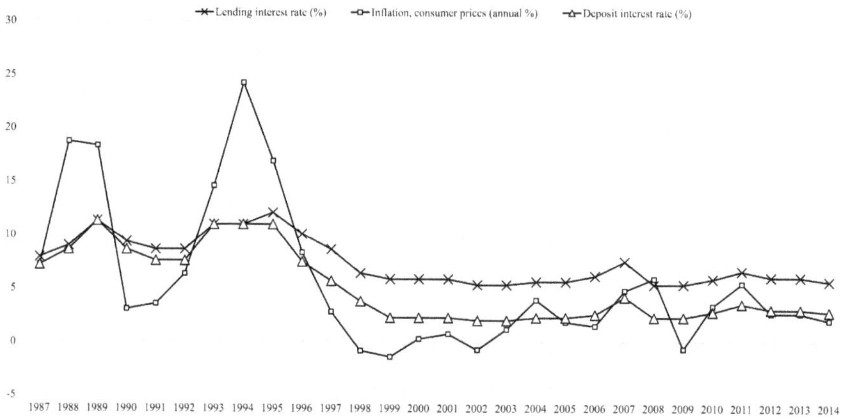

Figure 4.8 Inflation rates, lending interest rates and deposit interest rates in China, 1987–2014

Source: Data retrieved from The World Bank, 2016.

a warning of the excessive overexploitation of Rare Earths. Thus, deposit rates do not seem to be an adequate choice for the discount rate.

In order to achieve a market-compliant determination of deposit and lending rates, further financial reforms and interest rate liberalization have been a designated government goal since 2004. The actual progress has been slow and uneven because the government is concerned that liberalization could induce a rise in financing costs, which then imperil the highly indebted corporate sector. Furthermore, regulated and low interest rates decrease the cost of the PBOC to intervene in the foreign exchange market in order to regulate the value of the Chinese currency Renminbi and sterilize the money supply created because of intervention (Lardy & Borst, 2013, p. 2). In summary, the Chinese banking system remains highly controlled and does not even offer market interest rates that could be taken into consideration as an adequate discount rate at the moment.

He et al. (2014) analyze the impact of full interest rate liberalization on the determination of market interest rates. First, they estimate China's natural rate of interest, which is defined "as the equilibrium real interest rate consistent with stable low inflation and potential output, in the absence of transitory shocks to demand and supply" (He et al., 2014, p. 8), based on the approach of Laubach and Williams (2003) of applying Kalman filtering techniques to an equation system that describes the relations between the natural rate and observable values like inflation and output. Based on different assumptions for the intertemporal elasticity of substitution and the rate of time preference, the calculated natural rates of interest are in the range between 3.71% and 5.35%, which are the lower and upper boundaries of the estimation. A natural interest rate of 4% or slightly higher is finally identified as a reasonable baseline. A second approach to measure the natural interest rate adopted by the authors is the estimation of marginal returns of scale based on a standard macroeconomic production function with constant returns to scale. The natural interest rate is equal to the marginal product of the capital net of tax and depreciation. In the period of 1989 to 2012, the estimated natural interest rates are within a band between 3% and 6%. The average natural real interest rate is around 4.3%, which is consistent with the estimations of the calibration-based estimates (He et al., 2014, p. 9). The third approach adopted by He et al. (2014) is a linear regression model based on a cross-country panel data of 49 economies between 1973 and 2012. The model links the real interest rates to the real GDP growth rate, the aggregate saving rate and the degree of financial repression. The estimated natural rate of interest for 2012 is then estimated to be 4.31%. Summarizing the findings of all three approaches, the natural rate of interest of China is in an interval between 4% and 4.5% so that deposit rates would increase after liberalization while still being dependent on other market and institutional conditions. In general, the adequacy of the use of deposit rates as a discount rate would increase through liberalization.

In addition to market interest rates, estimations of the social discount for China will be considered as a relevant discount rate. According to Zhuang et al. (2007), the official social discount rate used in China is 8% for short- and medium-term projects and lower than 8% for long-term projects. These values come from the unpublished governmental document "The economic analysis of construction projects: methods and parameters" and is based on the weighted average approach (Zhuang et al., 2007, p. 17). The discount rate of 8% reflects China's level of development. Individuals in developing countries are assumed to have a high marginal propensity to consume and a low attention to intergenerational equity so that discount rates have to be high in order to achieve the people's willingness to postpone consumption. The social discount rates chosen in development countries are therefore between 8–15%. Multilateral development banks tend to apply a cut-off rate of 10–12% for projects in developing countries. If the calculated internal rate of return is below this cut-off grade, a project will not be implemented. At high levels of income in developed countries, the marginal propensity to consume is low and the willingness to save is high. More attention is paid to the aspect of intergenerational equity so that relatively low discount rates between 3–7% are used (Zhuang et al., 2007, p. 1f.). In general, the World Bank classifies all low- and medium-income countries as developing countries while emphasizing that this classification unites countries on different levels of development (The World Bank, n.d. b). Low-income countries are all countries with a gross national income per capita of 1,045 USD in 2014, middle-income countries are those with a GNI per capita of more than 1,045 USD but less than 12,736 USD and high-income countries are those with a GNI per capita above 12,736 USD. The middle-income country group is further subdivided into lower-middle-income economics ($1,046 to $4,125) and upper-middle-income economies ($4,126 to $12,735) (The World Bank, n.d. a). China reached a GNI per capita of 1,100 USD, and therefore the classification as middle-income country, in 2002. In 2015, the GNI per capita was 7,400 USD so that China is classified as an upper-middle-income country (The World Bank, 2016). Thus, a social discount rate of 8% intuitively seems to be adequate for a transition country that has rapidly developed from a low-income economy into an upper-middle-income.

Based on the social rate of time preference approach, the World Bank estimates a social discount rate of 8.26%. The pure rate of time preference was assumed to be 1.5% and the elasticity of consumption was set to one in the calculation in the Ramsey formula, while the annual growth of real per capita consumption has been 6.76% in the period from 1970 to 2008 (The World Bank, 2011, p. 116). While this discount rate is close to the official social discount rate of 8%, it could also be questioned because of the assumption of the pure rate of time preference. This is a standardized assumption and does not reflect a China-specific estimation. While the marginal propensity to consume should be relatively high, and the marginal propensity to save should be relatively low in China due to its level of development, it has been the other way around since 1978. Its gross national saving rate was in the range of 35% to 40% of the GDP in the period between 1980 and 1999 and then increased up to 53% of the GDP in 2010 while the aggregate consumption to GDP ratio declined from 62% in 1992 to 47% in 2010 (Ma & Yang, 2013, p. 1ff.). Especially the increase of the household saving rates, which increased from only 6–7% of the GDP at the end of the 1970s to about 22% in 2007, is positively correlated with increasing household incomes so that the marginal propensity to save was relatively high even in the period when China was a low-income country (Yang et al., 2011, pp. 15–18). In 2015, the households saved 30% of their disposable income while the consumption to GDP ratio further declined to 35% (Roberts, 2015). This development could be explained by the situation of low, and sometimes negative, real interest rates as well as the absence of a functioning social security and welfare system. Chinese households are savers that save in order to be able to pay educational fees for the household's children, purchase a private house or apartment, secure or increase pensions and pay the costs of medical treatment (Ma & Yang, 2013, p. 5ff.). Thus, it could be assumed that the individual rate of time preference should be relatively low in China and might even be close to zero when it is considered that saving rates are increasing despite of low net interest rates. In their estimation of the natural rate of interest, He et al. (2014) assume rates of time preference of only 0.3% or 0.45% in all scenarios. The resulting SRTP would be then only 7.06% or 7.21% respectively, which is very close to the upper boundary of social discount rates for developed countries. On the other hand, a study of Gong et al. (2014) shows that the individual rate of time preference is relatively high. This study is based on a web-based survey with 107 American participants, 86 Chinese participants from China and 110 Chinese participants that were currently living abroad. The survey included eight scenarios with choices between immediate and one-year delayed outcomes, for example the gain of 250 USD in a lottery win today versus the gain of a larger amount of lottery money a year from today (Gong et al., 2014, p. 113). Overall, the survey concludes that the Chinese participants discounted gains more than Americans did. Some Chinese even commented that they have considered the high inflation rate in China as a reason not to wait for larger gains in the future (Gong et al., 2014, p. 118). Therefore, the high marginal propensity to save might only reflect the imperfect financial system in China and the individual rate of time preference has to be higher than 1.5%.

The SOC of China can be calculated based on the following formula of Boardman et al. (2001):

$$SOC = \frac{\left(\left(\frac{Yield\ on\ AAA\ long-term\ corporate\ bonds}{1-corporate\ tax}\right) - expected\ inflation\right)}{1+expected\ inflation} \quad (4.23)$$

The yield on AAA long-term corporate bonds can be extracted from Cassola and Porter (2011), who measure the yields of long-term (120 months) AAA corporate bonds that are traded on the Chinese interbank market. The mean and median yields are 4.9%, while the minimum and maximum yields are 6.2% and 3.7% respectively (Cassola & Porter, 2011, p. 36). The average historical inflation rate as measured by the consumer price index can be used as proxy for the expected inflation. When the geometric mean of inflation rates in China is calculated for the period of 1987 to 2014, the average inflation rate is 5.38%. As an alternative, the geometric mean can also be calculated only for the period of 1996 to 2014. The legal status of the PBOC was first officially established by the "Law of the People's Republic of China on The People's Bank of China" in 1995. This law also defines the functions and responsibilities of the PBOC. Article 2 states that the PBOC "shall, under the leadership of the State Council, formulate and implement monetary policy, prevent and resolve financial risks, and maintain financial stability". Article 3 further defines that "the objective of monetary policy is to maintain the stability of the value of the currency" (PBOC, 2003, p. 2f.). Therefore, the control of inflation was not formulated before 1995 so that the average of the inflation rates from 1996 to 2014 might be a better proxy for expected future inflation rates. The geometric mean for this period is 2.25%. Information about the corporate tax rates in China is available from KPMG. The corporate tax has been 33% before 2008 and has been 25% since 2008. While this is the official tax rate, certain industries and businesses might enjoy lower corporate income tax rates such as 15% (KPMG, 2016). Based on this information, the SOC can be calculated. When the minimum yield for corporate bonds, the average inflation from 1987–2014 and the tax rate of 25% is taken as parameters, the SOC is -0.42. This would be the lower boundary. The upper boundary (maximum yields on corporate bonds, inflation from 1996 to 2014 and corporate tax of 25%) would then be 5.64%. The baseline SOC for mean yields is 1.09% for the higher expected future inflation rates and 4.19% for lower expected future inflation rates. The latter value is assumed to be the more adequate solution in this thesis due to the trend that the Chinese inflation rate was decreasing after monetary stability became an explicit goal of the PBOC in 1995. Furthermore, this value is in the range of the estimation of "4% or slightly above" by He et al. (2014).

Table 4.1 summarizes all finding of adequate discount rates for China that could be used in the modeling of the Hotelling rule.

Table 4.1 Summary of the estimations of relevant discount rates

Methodological approach	*Indicated social discount rate*
Natural real rate of interest (calibration-based estimates)	3.71%–5.35%; baseline: 4% or slightly higher
Natural real rate of interest (marginal returns to scale)	3%–6%; average: 4.3%
Natural real rate of interest (cross-country regression)	4.31% for 2012
Social rate of time preference (World bank estimation on basis of the Ramsey formula)	8.26%
Social rate of time preference (modified World Bank estimation)	7.06% or 7.21%
Marginal social opportunity cost of capital (real pretax rate of return on top-rated corporate bonds)	–0.42%–5.64%; baseline: 4.19%
Weighted average approach (official social discount rate)	8% for short- and medium-term projects; lower than 8% for long-term projects

There seems to be two generalizable levels for the social discount rate. It could be either in the range of 7.06% to 8.26% or around 4% or slightly higher. The former range reflects China's current development level, while the latter solution embodies future aspects affecting the discount rate. These aspects are the full liberalization of market interest rates or the expectation that inflation rates will not be so high as in the period of the 1980s to mid-1990s but will be relatively low as in the last two decades. Therefore, the official social discount rate will be used for the modeling of the historical optimal paths of extraction and prices, while the lower discount rates will be used for the modeling of future optimal paths.

Modeling of the optimal paths of mining and price development in the period of 1965–2012

In order to analyze whether REE prices have been undervalued in the past, the optimal paths of extraction and prices are modeled for the period of 1965 to 2012. The year 1965 is used as starting year for the analysis because it is the beginning of the USA-dominated, bastnaesite-based Mountain Pass Era. While the major techniques of extraction and processing had already been established since the mid-1950s due to the scientific contributions of the Ames Laboratory, the rates of extraction only increased in the mid-1960s due to the increasing demand for europium. The year 2012 is chosen as the ending year for the analysis because it is the year in which the EU, the USA and Japan jointly filed a WTO complaint against China's trade regime regarding Rare Earths that had been adjusted to be more restrictive in 2010.

As the first step before the Hotelling rule can be applied, the historical size of the reserve stock of the year 1965 has to be calculated. The USGS reported a global stock of 110 million tons of REO for the beginning of the year 2013. From that, 55 million tons were located in China and 55 million tons were located in the RoW. When the total global extraction rates in the period of 1965 to 2012 are added to the stock of 2013, the resulting global stock of reserves is 112,812,860 tons for 1965 (U.S. Geological Survey, 2014). The China-specific extraction rates are available from the USGS for the years 1994–2012 (U.S. Geological Survey, 1994–2012). The extraction rates for the years before 1994 are available in the 1986–1995 volumes of the BGS publication "World Mineral Statistics" (British Geological Survey, 1986–1995). Due to the adaptation of the USGS classification for reserves and resources in the mid-1980s, the compatibility of data is given. The aggregated extraction in China is 1,840,450 tons for 1984–2012 so that the stock of reserves was 56,840,450 tons in 1984. Because there are no reported data on extraction before 1984, this is also assumed to be the Chinese reserve stock for 1965. Thus, the resulting remaining stock of the RoW was 55,972,410 tons in 1965.

One additional assumption for the modeling is that only the stock of reserves of the RoW is available for extraction in the years 1965–1983. Due the isolation of China from Western countries until the Open Door policy and the beginning of economic reforms in 1978, foreign mining companies are assumed to have no access to Chinese deposits. Furthermore, the capital controls that impeded capital inflows in the 1970s and 1980s are assumed to have prevented the development of Chinese deposits by foreign companies for the period of 1978–1983 (Prasad & Wei, 2005, p. 4). Because the USA had the largest production share in this period, the U.S. discount rate will be used in the Hotelling rule. Hereby, the social discount of the U.S. EPA of 2% will be used, which is based on the SRTP approach (Zhuang et al., 2007, p. 18). In the period from 1984 to 2001, China is assumed to adapt to world market prices so that the discount rate of 2% is also adapted. Because China was a planned economy and has still the status of a non-market economy, it could be assumed that also the Chinese REEs prices were determined by the Chinese government or its agencies. However, the strategic parameter of state policies was rather the promotion of the expansion production than price setting. The government first voiced concerns over low REEs in 1996 when an official report stated that the "fierce competition causes the price decline of rare earth products" (Wuebbeke, 2013, p. 391). This implies that the price determination was not solely based on economic planning but also on the forces of demand and supply. Therefore, the assumption that the Chinese producers adapt to world market prices is justifiable due to the lack of the Chinese government to control REEs prices effectively. Furthermore, this assumption reflects another simplification that is required for the Hotelling rule, which does not include the case of a non-market economy. With the shutdown of the Mountain Pass Mine in 2002 and the emergence of the Chinese virtual monopoly, China is assumed to have switched to its official discount rate of 8%. The stock of reserves in the RoW are deemed to be inaccessible for Chinese mining companies due to capital controls and the prevention of Chinese investments in the REEs mining sector in foreign countries by their governments. For example, Chinese

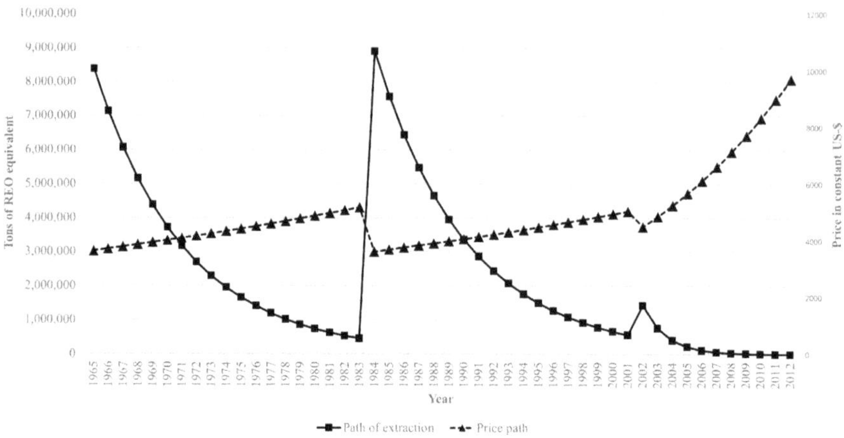

Figure 4.9 The optimal paths of extraction and prices, 1965–2012

SOEs intended to purchase a majority stake of the Australian Lynas Corp during the Global Financial Crisis but the Australian government blocked this (Ruettinger & Feil, 2011, p. 15). Figure 4.9 displays the resulting optimal paths of extraction and price development for the period of 1965–2012.

From 1965 to 1983, 53,410,269.19 tons of REO were extracted. The Chinese stock of reserves of 56,840,450 tons is then added to the total global stock in 1984. This has the same impact as the discovery of a significant large deposit like previously described. The price path falls to a lower level as extraction rates sharply increase. The total extraction in the period of 1984–2001 amounts to 56,204,229.04 tons so that the remaining total global stock equals 3,198,772 tons in 2002. Under the assumption that REO were proportionally mined, China would have a remaining stock of 3,060,512.38 tons in 2002 as it had a share of 95.69% of the global stocks in 1984 after the stock of the RoW had been mined for 19 years. As a consequence of the shift towards a higher social discount rate, the price path becomes steeper from 2002 on, and the path of extraction is rapidly approximating the asymptotic section. Figure 4.10 compares the modeled optimal price path with the historical price path for the years 1965–2012.

The historical prices were lower than the prices in the Hotelling path in the years 1965–1969, 1980–1983, 1985, 1988, 2005–2008 and 2009 but were still higher in most of the years. At the end of the 1980s, historical prices increased and finally spiked in 1992. There seems to be the general trend of declining real prices after 1992. While this might have helped to generate the impression of the Chinese government that REEs were undervalued in the 1990s and early 2000s, the thesis of an undervaluation cannot be confirmed by the comparison of the price paths because the historical prices were still higher than optimal. Finally, the sharp increase of prices in the years 2010–2012 presumably are the result of the Chinese embargo and restrictions in the trade of REEs.

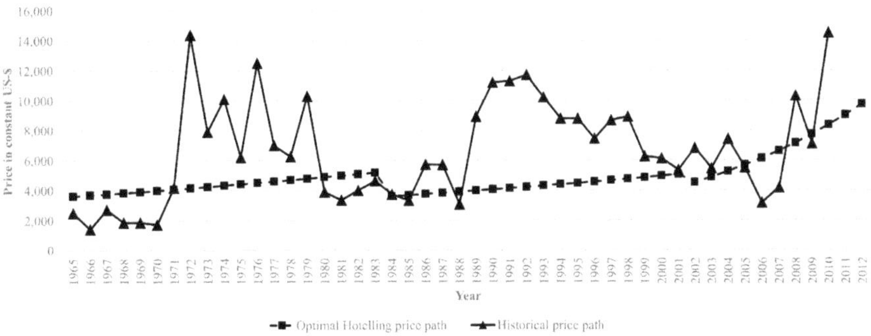

Figure 4.10 Comparison of the optimal price path with the historical price path, 1965–2012

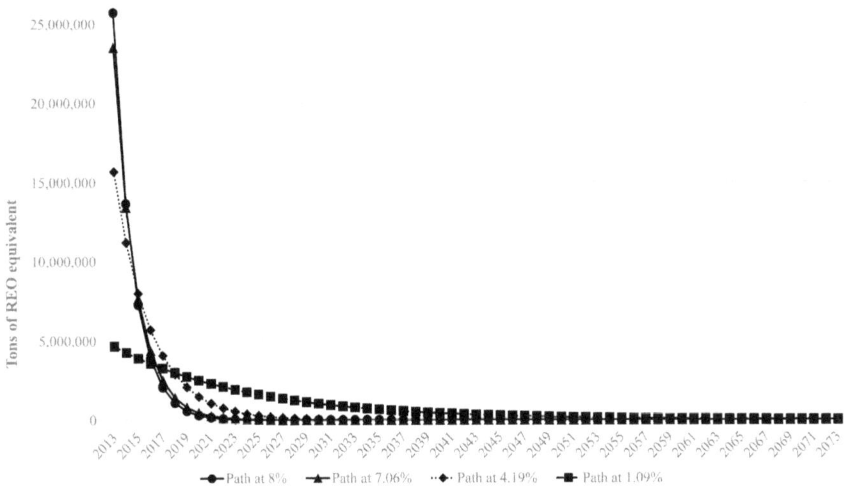

Figure 4.11 Variations of optimal future paths of extraction

Modeling of the future optimal extraction path

Four different scenarios of possible future extraction paths that are optimal for China in line with the Hotelling rule will be modeled. In this respect, the changing parameter is the choice of the relevant discount rates so that paths at 8% (the official social discount rate), at 7.06% (modification of the World Bank estimations) as well as at 4.19% (baseline SOC for low expected inflation rates) and at 1.09% (baseline SOC for high expected inflation rates) are calculated and plotted. The Chinese reserve stock of 55 million tons of REO will be used as relevant stock. Again, it is assumed that Chinese mining companies do not have access to offshore deposits so that only Chinese domestic reserves are considered. Figure 4.11 displays these four path variations.

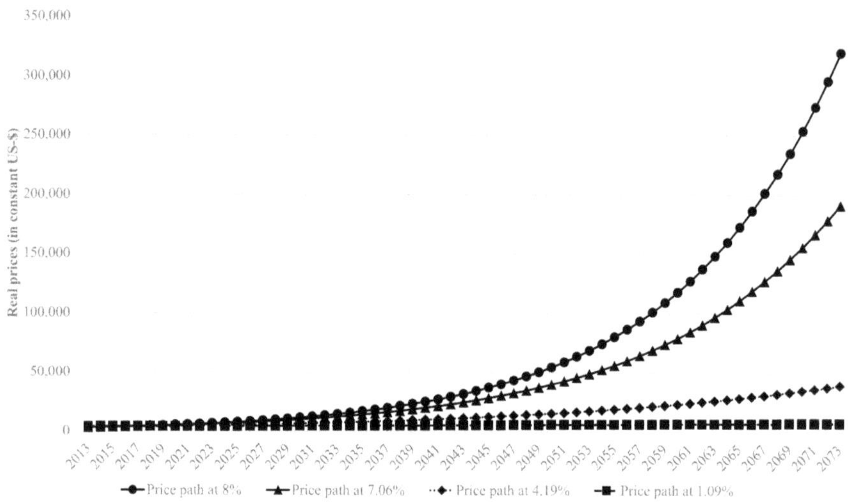

Figure 4.12 Variations of optimal future paths of price development

Because the discount rate is the determinant for the extraction rates and the slope of the extraction path, it is not at all surprising that the large differences in chosen discount rates lead to large differences in the optimal rates in the four scenarios. When 8% are chosen, 99.36% of the reserve stock has been exploited after eight years of ongoing mining at the end of 2020, while it is 98.86% at a discount rate of 7.06%, 93.22% at a discount rate of 4.19% but only 50.88% at 1.09%. While there is no total depletion of the Chinese stock due to the typical asymptotic pattern of the constant-elasticity inverse function, it is doubtful whether REEs are still of economic importance when only infinitesimally small quantities are extracted after 2020 in the former three paths. Furthermore, especially the choice of 8% or 7.06% leads to quickly increasing prices. This is illustrated in Figure 4.12, which shows the corresponding price paths for the four scenarios.

At a discount rate of 1.09%, the price path increases so slowly that it seems not to increase at all when it is compared with the other three scenarios. After a period of 61 years of ongoing extraction, the prices at a discount rate of 1.09% have increased from 3,892.21 USD per ton of REO to 7,459.13 USD per ton while the price at a rate of 8% has increased from 3,161.18 USD to 320,091.94 USD per ton. It can be derived that the higher the chosen discount rate is, the faster the economic pressure to find substitutes or to develop a back-stop technology rises. When the Chinese government is predominantly concerned that REEs are extracted too fast, and it wants to maintain an adequate high rate of extraction so that prices do not increase drastically and REEs are not threatened to rapidly lose their economic importance, the choice of the relatively low discount rate of 1.09% should be preferred. When intergenerational equity would be higher valued than the optimality of the Hotelling rule, then a discount rate of zero is the adequate choice according to Rawls's criterion. Because extraction rates equal zero when an infinite time horizon is considered in Rawls's approach, the Chinese government would have to determine a finite time horizon for REEs depletion. The paths of extraction and price development would be a constant straight in this case but the ever-increasing economic pressure to find substitutes is minimized.

Overall, it can be concluded that there are different paths of extraction and price development that are optimal and in line with the Hotelling rule. While the four utilized discount rates largely differ, they are calculated correctly and reflect different approaches to determine social discount rates. The path of extraction that is optimal from the perspective of Chinese resource owners and the Chinese government is mainly dependent on the difference goals of these actors. When the Chinese government is assumed to be a social planner that is predominantly concerned about resource conservation and intergenerational equity, as the government has claimed to be, then the chosen discount rate should be as low as possible. When extraction is optimized from the perspective of resource owners as independent economic agents, then a discount rate of around 4%, which embodies both the marginal social opportunity cost of capital and a market-compliant deposit rate after full interest rate liberalization, would be a more adequate choice.

Critical assessment and intermediate conclusion

Three main findings of this chapter can be summarized. The first finding is that, due to the lack of substitutes and the resulting use of a constant-elasticity inverse demand curve, China is unable to utilize its high market share of the virtual monopoly to influence the trajectories of optimal extraction and price development. The optimal solution is equivalent to the solution of competitive market. Second, the comparison of the historical price path with the calculated Hotelling price path for the years 1965–2012 has shown that the narrative of undervalued REEs prices cannot be supported. There is no structural undervaluation of prices because historical prices were higher than the calculated prices in most years. While there has been a decline in real prices in the 1990s and early 2000s, this is only a manifestation of the aggressive promotion of REEs extraction and export by the Chinese government. The rebate of the ad valorem tax of 16% and the non-consideration of the social marginal costs of extraction, which are the result of unregulated emissions from mining, have decreased the net costs of mining for Chinese resource owners so that they were able to expand their REEs production. Because the Chinese domestic demand for REEs was weak until 2004, the global total supply increased faster than demand in this period, which induced a decline in prices. This has led to the perception of the Chinese government that the market prices do not reflect the intrinsic value of REEs, or, in other words, that the exchange value of REEs is significantly lower than their use value. The other factor that contributes to fast extraction is the relatively high, official social discount rate of 8%, which reflects a preference of current consumption and a low attention to intergenerational equity. The third main finding is that the optimal future path of extraction is dependent on the preferences and expectations of Chinese economic actors. When the government is considered a social planner that is concerned about fast depletion and intergenerational equity, it should try to enforce a low discount rate in order to keep extraction rates low. When the Chinese government is not a social planner or is not able to effectively implement regulatory measures that enforce the use of a low discount rate, then the resource owners would freely choose a relevant discount rate. This would be most likely a discount rate of around 4%, which is both the natural real interest rate as estimated by He et al. (2014) and the baseline estimation for the real pretax rate of return on top-rated corporate bonds as calculated in this thesis. The optimal rates of extraction are then significantly higher than the optimal rates at 1.09% until 2018 but are lower in the period after 2018.

One major shortcoming of the application of the Hotelling rule to the case of REEs is the low empirical significance of the demand functions. This mainly comes from the relative simplicity of the basic Hotelling model in contrast of the complexity of natural resource price determination. Another shortcoming might result from the abstraction of the demand side. While the demand side is included in the form of the inverse demand function, it could be questioned if real demand would be able to fully assimilate the supply with REEs. The extraction pattern that is optimally in line with the Hotelling rule has extremely high rates of extraction at the beginning and subsequently diminishing low rates in later periods. In the theoretical world, it is assumed that all quantities are consumed in the same period they were extracted so that there are no stockpiles. In the current REEs' market outside of the theoretical world, demand is expected to increase but is still significantly lower than the optimal extraction rates. It is doubtful whether the REEs processing sectors could be able to adapt their capacities to assimilate the supplied quantities. Therefore, all findings are the result of a high level of abstraction, which stems from the restrictive assumption of Hotelling, and should be treated with some caution.

Appendix

Calculated rates of extraction and price development in the optimal Hotelling paths, 1965–2012

Year	*Rate of extraction (tons REO)*	*Price (USD)*	*Year*	*Rate of extraction (tons REO)*	*Price (USD)*
1965	8,386,235.205	3,624.527391	**1990**	3,360,772.787	4,052.29439
1966	7,129,742.213	3,697.017939	**1991**	2,857,234.864	4,133.340277
1967	6,061,507.074	3,770.958298	**1992**	2,429,141.03	4,216.007083
1968	5,153,323.488	3,846.377464	**1993**	2,065,187.646	4,300.327225
1969	4,381,211.249	3,923.305013	**1994**	1,755,764.676	4,386.333769
1970	3,724,783.055	4,001.771113	**1995**	1,492,701.936	4,474.060444
1971	3,166,706.195	4,081.806535	**1996**	1,269,053.365	4,563.541653
1972	2,692,244.885	4,163.442666	**1997**	1,078,913.616	4,654.812486
1973	2,288,871.172	4,246.711519	**1998**	917,262.1279	4,747.908736
1974	1,945,934.143	4331.64575	**1999**	779,830.5621	4,842.866911
1975	1,654,378.689	4418.278665	**2000**	662,990.0952	4,939.724249
1976	1,406,506.41	4,506.644238	**2001**	563,655.6039	5,038.518734
1977	1,195,772.344	4,596.777123	**2002**	1,431,858	4,496.83312
1978	1,016,612.145	4,688.712665	**2003**	761,964.5058	4,856.579769
1980	734,799.5323	4,878.136657	**2004**	405,480.0883	5,245.106151
1981	624,705.9754	4,975.69939	**2005**	215,776.589	5,664.714643
1982	531,107.5178	5,075.213378	**2006**	114,825.7034	6,117.891814
1983	451,532.7315	5,176.717645	**2007**	61,104.60002	6,607.323159
1984	890,0172.394	3,598.32145	**2008**	32,516.86715	7,135.909012
1985	7,566,677.212	3,670.287879	**2009**	17,303.87973	7,706.781733
1986	6,432,976.969	3,743.693637	**2010**	9,208.27496	8,323.324272
1987	5,469,136.786	3,818.567509	**2011**	4,900.191696	8,989.190213
1988	4,649,706.866	3,894.93886	**2012**	2,607.641362	9,708.32543
1989	3,953,050.506	3,972.837637			

Calculated rates of extraction in the future Hotelling paths at different discount rate

Year	*Path at 8%*	*Path at 7.06%*	*Path at 4.19%*	*Path at 1.09%*
2013	25,731,701.17	23,557,543.57	15,713,112.46	4,676,491.209
2014	13,693,147.62	13,467,400.68	11,223,986.95	4,278,862.663
2015	7,286,820.665	7,699,057.437	8,017,372.963	3,915,043.324
2016	3,877,688.087	4,401,405.055	5,726,865.999	3,582,158.494
2017	2,063,515.158	2,516,199.758	4,090,740.736	3,277,577.899
2018	1,098,101.424	1,438,463.659	2,922,044.932	2,998,894.913
2019	584,355.6475	822,342.3806	2,087,237.284	2,743,907.537
2020	310,965.3767	470,117.5359	1,490,928.299	2,510,601.001
2021	165,480.5013	268,757.2752	1,064,980.589	2,297,131.846
2022	88,060.59569	153,643.4349	760,723.1389	2,101,813.357
2023	46,861.52418	87,835.03648	543,389.8983	1,923,102.236
2024	24,937.4017	50,213.62378	388,147.2332	1,759,586.405
2025	13,270.46046	28,706.17596	277,256.3036	1,609,973.853
2026	7,061.887314	16,410.77613	198,046.1313	1,473,082.424
2027	3,757.989604	9,381.729333	141,465.747	1,347,830.479
2028	1,999.817505	5,363.356651	101,049.9799	1,233,228.344
2029	1,064.204661	3,066.129233	7,2180.71266	1,128,370.499
2030	566.317455	1,752.847906	51,559.19165	1,032,428.413
2031	301.3663365	1,002.069889	36,829.09389	944,644.0058
2032	160.3723636	572.8643424	26,307.28127	864,323.6533
2033	85.34229565	327.495675	18,791.47638	790,832.7084
2034	45.41497841	187.2230635	13,422.88398	723,590.4865
2035	24.16762108	107.031873	9,588.06061	662,065.6765
2036	12.86082102	61.188091	6,848.819253	605,772.1435
2037	6.843897322	34.98007064	4,892.15985	554,265.087
2038	3.641986037	19.99744268	3,494.504252	507,137.5269
2039	1.938086103	11.43215855	2,496.14901	464,017.0872
2040	1.03135424	6.535548127	1,783.016826	424,563.0539
2041	0.548836075	3.736248859	1,273.621482	388,463.6832
2042	0.292063604	2.135942581	909.756799	355,433.7377
2043	0.155421906	1.221077846	649.8456918	325,212.2332
2044	0.082707906	0.698067036	464.1893566	297,560.3759
2045	0.044013085	0.399071679	331.5737282	272,259.6763
2046	0.023421602	0.228141707	236.8454504	249,110.222
2047	0.012463827	0.130424285	169.180374	227,929.0991
2048	0.006632636	0.074561089	120.8467333	208,548.9458
2049	0.003529563	0.04262516	86.32167307	190,816.6311
2050	0.00187826	0.024367995	61.66017931	174,592.0438
2051	0.000999518	0.01393072	44.04430055	159,746.9864
2052	0.000531894	0.007963929	31.46115423	146,164.1614
2053	0.000283048	0.004552827	22.47292415	133,736.2447
2054	0.000150624	0.002602765	16.05256807	122,365.0379
2055	8.01548E-05	0.001487951	11.46646248	111,960.692
2056	4.26545E-05	0.000850633	8.190574943	102,440.9976

Year	Path at 8%	Path at 7.06%	Path at 4.19%	Path at 1.09%
2057	2.26986E-05	0.000486291	5.850585394	93,730.73537
2058	1.20791E-05	0.000278003	4.179114371	85,761.08155
2059	6.4279E-06	0.000158929	2.985170842	78,469.06439
2060	3.42061E-06	9.08568E-05	2.132328566	71,797.06639
2061	1.82028E-06	5.19411E-05	1.52313732	65,692.36912
2062	9.68664E-07	2.96938E-05	1.08798772	60,106.73664
2063	5.15476E-07	1.69754E-05	0.777157294	54,996.03436
2064	2.74311E-07	9.70449E-06	0.555128931	50,319.88034
2065	1.45975E-07	5.54787E-06	0.396532507	46,041.32619
2066	7.76806E-08	3.17161E-06	0.283245964	42,126.56515
2067	4.13378E-08	1.81315E-06	0.202324588	38,544.66494
2068	2.19979E-08	1.03654E-06	0.144521879	35,267.32336
2069	1.17062E-08	5.92573E-07	0.103232996	32,268.64468
2070	6.22948E-09	3.38763E-07	0.073740057	29,524.93498
2071	3.31502E-09	1.93664E-07	0.052673042	27,014.515
2072	1.76409E-09	1.10714E-07	0.037624725	24,717.54879
2073	9.38763E-10	6.32931E-08	0.026875606	2,2615.88698

Rates of extraction in the future Hotelling paths at different discount rate

Year	Price path at 8%	Price path at 7.06%	Price path at 4.19%	Price path at 1.09%
2013	3,161.18133	3,195.41084	3,357.24143	3,892.21041
2014	3,414.07583	3,421.00685	3,497.90985	3,934.6355
2015	3,687.2019	3,662.52993	3,644.47227	3,977.52303
2016	3,982.17805	3,921.10454	3,797.17566	4,020.87803
2017	4,300.7523	4,197.93453	3,956.27732	4,064.7056
2018	4,644.81248	4,494.3087	4,122.04534	4,109.01089
2019	5,016.39748	4,811.6069	4,294.75904	4,153.79911
2020	5,417.70928	5,151.30634	4,474.70944	4,199.07552
2021	5,851.12602	5,514.98857	4,662.19977	4,244.84545
2022	6,319.2161	5,904.34677	4,857.54594	4,291.11426
2023	6,824.75339	6,321.19365	5,061.07711	4,337.88741
2024	7,370.73366	6,767.46992	5,273.13624	4,385.17038
2025	7,960.39235	7,245.25329	5,494.08065	4,432.96874
2026	8,597.22374	7,756.76818	5,724.28263	4,481.2881
2027	9,285.00164	8,304.39601	5,964.13007	4,530.13414
2028	10,027.8018	8,890.68637	6,214.02712	4,579.5126
2029	10,830.0259	9,518.36883	6,474.39486	4,629.42929
2030	11,696.428	10,190.3657	6,745.672	4,679.89006
2031	12,632.1422	10,909.8055	7,028.31566	4,730.90087
2032	13,642.7136	11,680.0377	7,322.80209	4,782.46769
2033	14,734.1307	12,504.6484	7,629.6275	4,834.59658

(*Continued*)

(Continued)

Year	*Price path at 8%*	*Price path at 7.06%*	*Price path at 4.19%*	*Price path at 1.09%*
2034	15,912.8611	13,387.4766	7,949.30889	4,887.29369
2035	17,185.89	14,332.6324	8,282.38493	4,940.56519
2036	18,560.7612	15,344.5163	8,629.41686	4,994.41735
2037	20,045.6221	16,427.8391	8,990.98943	5,048.8565
2038	21,649.2719	17,587.6446	9,367.71188	5,103.88903
2039	23,381.2137	18,829.3323	9,760.21901	5,159.52142
2040	25,251.7108	20,158.6831	10,169.1722	5,215.76021
2041	27,271.8476	21,581.8862	10,595.2605	5,272.61199
2042	29,453.5954	23,105.5673	11,039.2019	5,330.08346
2043	31,809.8831	24,736.8204	11,501.7445	5,388.18137
2044	34,354.6737	26,483.2399	11,983.6676	5,446.91255
2045	37,103.0476	28,352.9567	12,485.7832	5,506.2839
2046	40,071.2914	30,354.6754	13,008.9376	5,566.30239
2047	43,276.9947	32,497.7155	13,554.012	5,626.97509
2048	46,739.1543	34,792.0542	14,121.9251	5,688.30912
2049	50,478.2866	37,248.3732	14,713.6338	5,750.31169
2050	54,516.5496	39,878.1084	15,330.1351	5,812.99008
2051	58,877.8735	42,693.5028	15,972.4677	5,876.35167
2052	63,588.1034	45,707.6641	16,641.7141	5,940.40391
2053	68,675.1517	48,934.6252	17,339.0019	6,005.15431
2054	74,169.1638	52,389.4097	18,065.5061	6,070.61049
2055	80,102.6969	56,088.1021	18,822.4508	6,136.78015
2056	86,510.9127	60,047.9221	19,611.1115	6,203.67105
2057	9,3431.7857	64,287.3054	20,432.8171	6,271.29107
2058	100,906.329	68,825.9891	21,288.9521	6,339.64814
2059	108,978.835	73,685.104	22,180.9592	6,408.7503
2060	117,697.142	78,887.2723	23,110.3414	6,478.60568
2061	127,112.913	84,456.7137	24,078.6647	6,549.22248
2062	137,281.946	90,419.3577	2,5087.5608	6,620.60901
2063	148,264.502	96,802.9644	26,138.7296	6,692.77365
2064	160,125.662	103,637.254	27,233.9423	6,765.72488
2065	172,935.715	110,954.044	2,8375.0445	6,839.47128
2066	186,770.572	118,787.399	29,563.9589	6,914.02152
2067	201,712.218	127,173.79	30,802.6888	6,989.38435
2068	217,849.195	136,152.259	32,093.3214	7,065.56864
2069	235,277.131	145,764.609	33,438.0316	7,142.58334
2070	254,099.301	156,055.59	34,839.0851	7,220.4375
2071	274,427.245	167,073.115	36,298.8428	7,299.14027
2072	296,381.425	178,868.477	37,819.7643	7,378.7009
2073	320,091.939	191,496.591	39,404.4124	7,459.12873

Notes

1 In the course of this study, the adaption and modification of Conrad (2010) will be used for illustrating the Hotelling rule and its application to Rare Earths.
2 "Back-stop technology: A technology that is able to supply an input (such as energy), but is currently uneconomic to employ" (Grafton et al., 2004, p. 471).

Bibliography

Ahrens, W. A., & Sharma, V. R. (1997). Trends in natural resource commodity prices: Deterministic or stochastic? *Journal of Environmental Economics and Management, 33*, 59–74.

Berck, P., & Roberts, M. (1996). Natural resource prices: Will they ever turn up? *Journal of Environmental Economics and Management, 31*(1), 65–78.

Binnemans, K., & Jones, P. T. (2015). Rare earths and the balance problem. *Journal of Sustainable Metallurgy, 1*(1), 29–38.

Boardman, A., Greenberg, D., Vining, A., & Weimer, D. (2001). *Cost-benefit analysis: Concepts and practice* (2nd ed.). Upper Saddle River: Prentice-Hall.

Bradshaw, A. M., Reuter, B., & Hamacher, T. (2013). The potential scarcity of rare elements for the Energiewende. *Green, 3*(2), 93–111.

British Geological Survey. (1986–1995). *World mineral statistics, vols. 1986–1995*. Retrieved from www.bgs.ac.uk/mineralsuk/statistics/worldArchive.html.

Cassola, N., & Porter, N. (2011). *Understanding Chinese bond yields and their role in monetary policy* (IMF Working Paper WP/11/225). Retrieved from www.imf.org/en/Publications/WP/Issues/2016/12/31/Understanding-Chinese-Bond-Yields-and-their-Role-in-Monetary-Policy-25265.

Conrad, J. M. (2010). *Resource economics* (2nd ed.). Cambridge et al.: Cambridge University Press.

Cuddington, J. T., & Nuelle, G. (2013). *Variable long-term trends in natural prices: The ongoing tug-of-war between exploration, depletion, and technological change* (Colorado School of Mines, Division of Economics and Business Working Paper No. 2013–02). Retrieved from http://econbus.mines.edu/working-papers/wp201302.pdf.

Dasgupta, P. (1974). On some problems arising from Professor Rawls' conception of distributive justice. *Theory and Decision, 4*, 325–344.

Dasgupta, P., & Heal, G. (1974). The optimal depletion of exhaustible resources. *The Review of Economic Studies, 41*(5), 3–28.

Dasgupta, P., & Stiglitz, J. (1981). Resource depletion under technological uncertainty. *Econometrica, 49*(1), 85–104.

Devarajan, S., & Fisher, A. C. (1981). Hotelling's 'economics of exhaustible resources': Fifty years later. *Journal of Economic Literature, 19*(1), 65–73.

Dixit, A., Hammond, P., & Hoel, M. (1980). On Hartwick's rule for regular maximin paths of capital accumulation and resources depletion. *The Review of Economic Studies, 47*(3), 551–556.

Endres, A. (2011). *Environmental economics: Theory and policy* (Revised and extended English version). Cambridge et al.: Cambridge University Press.

Farzin, Y. H. (1984). The effect of the discount rate on depletion of exhaustible resources. *Journal of Political Economy, 92*(5), 841–851.

Fung, H., & Liu, Q. W. (2007). The banking system: Development and current issues. In K. C. Chan, H. Fung, & Q. W. Liu (Eds.), *China's capital markets: Challenges from WTO membership* (pp. 119–138). Northampton: Edward Elgar.

Gong, M., Krantz, D. H., & Weber, E. U. (2014). Why Chinese discount future financial and environmental gains but not losses more than Americans. *Journal of Risk and Uncertainty*, *49*(2), 103–124.

Grafton, R. Q., Adamowicz, W., Dupont, D., Nelson, H., Hill, R. J., & Renzetti, Steven (2004). *The economics of the environment and natural resources*. Malden: Blackwell Publishing.

Harris, J. M., & Roach, B. (2013). *Environmental and natural resource economics: A contemporary approach* (3rd ed.). Armonk: M.E. Sharpe.

Hartwick, J. M. (1977). Intergenerational equity and investing of rents from exhaustible resources. *The American Economic Review*, *67*(5), 972–974.

Hartwick, J. M. (1978). Substitution among exhaustible resources and intergenerational equity. *The Review of Economic Studies*, *45*(2), 347–354.

Hartwick, J. M., & Sadorsky, P. A. (1990). Duopoly in exhaustible resource exploration and extraction. *The Canadian Journal of Economics*, *23*(2), 276–293.

He, D., Wang, H., & Yu, X. (2014). *Interest rate determination in China: Past, present, and future* (Hong Kong Institute for Monetary Research Working Paper No. 04/2014). Retrieved from www.hkimr.org/uploads/publication/375/wp-no-04_2014-final-.pdf.

Hotelling, H. (1931). The economics of exhaustible resources. *Journal of Political Economy*, *39*(2), 137–175.

KPMG. (2016). *Corporate tax rates table*. Retrieved from https://home.kpmg.com/xx/en/home/services/tax/tax-tools-and-resources/tax-rates-online/corporate-tax-rates-table.html.

Lardy, N. (2008). *Financial repression in China* (Peterson Institute for International Economics Policy Brief No. PB08–08). Retrieved from https://piie.com/publications/pb/pb08-8.pdf.

Lardy, N., & Borst, N. (2013). *A blueprint for rebalancing the Chinese economy* (Peterson Institute for International Economics Policy Brief No. PB13–02). Retrieved from https://piie.com/publications/policy-briefs/blueprint-rebalancing-chinese-economy.

Laubach, T., & Williams, J. C. (2003). Measuring the natural rate of interest. *Review of Economics and Statistics*, *85*(4), 1063–1070.

Livernois, J., Thille, H., & Zhang, X. (2006). A test of the Hotelling rule using old-growth timber data. *Canadian Journal of Economics*, *39*(1), 163–186.

Ma, G., & Yang, D. T. (2013). *China's high saving puzzle* (IZA Discussion Paper No. 7223). Retrieved from https://papers.ssrn.com/sol3/papers.cfm?abstract_id=2223150.

Markandya, A., & Pearce, D. W. (1991). Development, the environment, and the social rate of discount. *The World Bank Observer*, *6*(2), 137–152.

Martin, M. F. (2012). *China's banking system: Issues for Congress* (CRS Report for Congress 42380). Retrieved from https://fas.org/sgp/crs/row/R42380.pdf.

Moazzami, B., & Anderson, F. J. (1994). Modelling natural resource scarcity using the 'error-correction' approach. *The Canadian Journal of Economics*, *27*(4), 801–812.

Norgaard, R. B. (1990). Economic indicators of resource scarcity: A critical essay. *Journal of Environmental Economics and Management*, *19*(1), 19–25.

PBOC. (2003). *Law of the People's Republic of China on the people's bank of China*. Retrieved from www.pbc.gov.cn/english/130733/2941519/2015082610501049304.pdf.

Perman, R., Ma, Y., McGilvray, J., Common, M. S., & Maddison, D. (2011). *Natural resource and environmental economics* (4th ed.). Harlow: Pearson Education Limited.

Pindyck, R. (1978). The optimal exploration and production of a nonrenewable resource. *Journal of Political Economy*, *86*(5), 841–861.

Pindyck, R. (1999). The long-run evolution of energy prices. *The Energy Journal*, *20*(2), 1–27.

Pothen, F. (2013). *The metal resources (METRO) model: A dynamic partial equilibrium model for metal markets applied to Rare Earth Elements* (ZEW Discussion Paper No. 13–112). Retrieved from http://ftp.zew.de/pub/zew-docs/dp/dp13112.pdf. 22.11.2014.

Prasad, E., & Wei, S.-J. (2005). *The Chinese approach to capital inflows: Patterns and possible explanations* (IMF Working Paper WP/05/79). Retrieved from www.imf.org/external/pubs/ft/wp/2005/wp0579.pdf.

Rawls, J. (1999). *A theory of justice* (Revised ed.). Cambridge: The Belknap Press of Harvard University Press.

Roberts, D. (2015, May 1). The Chinese can't kick their savings habit. *Bloomberg Businessweek*. Retrieved from www.bloomberg.com/news/articles/2015-05-01/chinese-consumers-cling-to-saving-suppressing-spending.

Ruettinger, L., & Feil, M. (2011). *Sustainable prevention of resource conflicts: New risks raw materials for the future? Case study and scenarios for China and rare earths* (Report 3.4). Berlin: Adelphi.

Ruhkamp, C. (2011, October 7). Seltene Erden: Aus Salz wurde Gold [Rare earths: Salt became gold]. *Frankfurter Allgemeine Zeitung*.

Schueler, D., Liu, R., Buchert, M., Dittrich, S., & Merz, C. (2011). *Study on rare earths and their recycling* (Oeko-Institute. V. final report for the Greens/EFA group in the European Parliament). Retrieved from www.oeko.de/oekodoc/1112/2011-003-en.pdf.

Slade, M. E. (1982). Trends in natural-resource commodity prices: An analysis of the time domain. *Journal of Environmental Economics and Management*, *9*, 122–137.

Slade, M. E., & Thille, H. (1997). Hotelling confronts CAPM: A test of theory of exhaustible resources. *The Canadian Journal of Economics*, *30*(3), 685–708.

Slade, M. E., & Thille, H. (2009). Whither Hotelling: Tests of the theory of exhaustible resources. *Annual Review of Resource Economics*, *1*(1), 239–260.

Solow, R. M. (1974a). Intergenerational equity and exhaustible resources. *The Review of Economics Studies*, *41*, 29–45.

Solow, R. M. (1974b). The economics of resources or the resources of economics. *The American Economic Review*, *64*(2), 1–14.

Stiglitz, J. E. (1976). Monopoly and the rate of extraction of exhaustible resources. *The American Economic Review*, *66*(4), 655–661.

U.S. Geological Survey. (1994–2012). *Minerals yearbook, vols. 1994–2012*. Retrieved from https://minerals.usgs.gov/minerals/pubs/commodity/rare_earths/index.html#myb.

U.S. Geological Survey. (1996–2016). *Mineral commodity summaries, vols. 1996–2016*. Retrieved from https://minerals.usgs.gov/minerals/pubs/commodity/rare_earths/index.html#myb.

U.S. Geological Survey. (2014). *Historical statistics for mineral and material commodities in the United States*. Retrieved from http://minerals.usgs.gov/minerals/pubs/historical-statistics/.

Van der Ploeg, F. (2008). *Voracious transformation of a common natural resource into productive capital* (Oxford Centre for the Analysis of Resource Rich Economies Research Paper No. 2008–02). Retrieved from www.oxcarre.ox.ac.uk/images/stories/papers/ResearchPapers/oxcarrerp200802.pdf.

The World Bank. (n.d. a). *Country and lending groups*. Retrieved from http://data.worldbank.org/about/country-and-lending-groups.

The World Bank. (n.d. b). *How does the World Bank classify countries?* Retrieved from https://datahelpdesk.worldbank.org/knowledgebase/articles/378834-how-does-the-world-bank-classify-countries.

The World Bank. (2011). *The changing wealth of nations: Measuring sustainable development in the new millennium*. Washington, DC: The World Bank.

The World Bank. (2016). *World Bank data: Indicators*. Retrieved from http://data.worldbank.org/indicator.

Wuebbeke, J. (2013). Rare Earth Elements in China: Policies and narratives of reinventing an industry. *Resources Policy*, *38*(3), 384–394.

Yang, D. T., Zhang, J., & Zhou, S. (2011). *Why are savings rate so high in China?* (NBER Working Paper No. 16771). Retrieved from www.nber.org/papers/w16771.

Yang, Y. (2016, March 30). Profit growth flattens at China's biggest banks. *Financial Times*. Retrieved from www.ft.com/intl/cms/s/0/31772348-f668-11e5-803c-d27c7117d132.html#axzz49y9E4epY.

Zhuang, J., Liang, Z., Lin, T., & De Guzman, F. (2007). *Theory and practice in the choice of social discount rate for cost-benefit analysis: A survey* (Asian Development Bank ERD Working Paper Series No. 94). Retrieved from www.econstor.eu/handle/10419/109296.

5 Adjustments in the regulatory framework of the Chinese Rare Earths sector

Chapter 5 deals with the adjustments in the regulatory framework of the Chinese Rare Earths sector. First, the regulatory measures in the period before the Global Financial Crisis will be reviewed. Second, it will be discussed why the GFC has given the impetus for new adjustments in the regulatory framework. Then, the implemented measures concerning the structure of the domestic REEs sectors, the trade regime for REEs and environmental standards and their impact on market power, price-setting power and global welfare, and consequently on the resource policy of the main consumer countries in the rest of the world will be analyzed. Finally, the implications of implemented regulatory measures of China and implemented countermeasure of the rest of the world for the optimal Hotelling extraction path will be highlighted.

Characteristics of the regulatory framework before the Global Financial Crisis

The period before the Global Financial Crisis can be divided into two phases of distinct approaches to the regulation of the Chinese REEs sector: the phase of industry liberalization from the late 1970s to the early 2000s and the phase of mild reregulation of the REEs industry from the early 2000s to 2009. Reregulation is hereby defined as a state involvement in market evolution with the goal to control the market and industry through reformulating old rules and creating new ones in order to achieve state goals (He, 2014, p. 239). Reregulation is mostly used in China concerning industries and sectors that have been extensively liberalized in the course of the economic and structural reforms since 1978 but whose current direction of development and evolution are supposed to be in conflict with the current national goals, which have been formulated in the different Five-Year-Plans, for example.

The first phase is marked by the initiated transition from a planned economy towards a market-based economic system. The formulated main goal of the Five-Year-Plans in the phase was the doubling of the gross national product of 1986 by 2000, and the subsequent doubling of the gross national product of 2000 by 2010. The start of industrial liberalization was accompanied by the decentralization of power. The most important reform in this first stage of reforms was the implementation of the "contract-responsibility system" in the early 1980s that adjusted the official relationships between central and local governments, which should transition from resource-receiving and finance-subsidizing agents of the central State to financially independent entities, and between the State and enterprises, which became independent self-financing units and were no longer "state puppets" (Zhao & Zhang, 1999, p. 256f.). The central government decided to give up a part of its authoritarian power in favor of local cadres that gained the rights to formulate and implement their own economic policies, to supervise firms and to plan local expenditures. By the mid-1980s, these local cadres were primary promoted, rewarded or punished based on the economic performance of their assigned administrative areas so that local cadres had the impetus to prefer the promotion of fast economic growth to all other issues such as environmental protection. This was further reinforced by the strong link between local revenues and local budgets. The result was the promotion of REEs mining, especially in regions in which other economic structures were underdeveloped. As explained in Chapter 2, the production and exportation of Rare Earths were promoted by the central government in order to acquire foreign currencies and to establish links with Western countries. On the local level, cadres promoted REEs mining in order to foster the development of the local economy and to increase tax revenues. They used their rights to sell land and to license mining and processing projects, which led to an easy access to mining permits and to a sharp and sudden increase of the number of licensed REEs mining companies (He, 2014, p. 240ff.; Ruettinger & Feil, 2011, p. 19f.). This has induced a voracity effect described by van der Ploeg (2008) especially in the regions of ion adsorption deposits in southern China. As explained before, these deposits are mined under the use of decentralized and mobile small-scale plants that do not require high initial capital investments or a high level of technology. Due to the high number of licensed companies, the Rare Earths from these deposits could be seen as a common-pool resource so that all licensed companies compete with each other for mining as many of these deposits before they are exhausted. This is one of the contributing factors for the excessive extraction that the Chinese government has been addressing more vigorously since 2010. However, the first attempts of reregulation were made at the end of this first phase. In 1997, the State Planning Commission[1] made an announcement to put new REEs projects on hold. In 1999, an export quota was introduced and a list of companies with the allowance to export was published. The export of unprocessed, primary REO was banned and the government announced the stop of the issuance of new mining permits and introduced limits of foreign investment in the REEs processing sector. In 2000, production plans for REEs mining were finally established. Nevertheless, all of these measures could not stop the further expansion of mining and did not curb the production (He, 2014, p. 242).

In the second phase from the early 2000s to 2009, measures of mild reregulation were implemented. With ongoing market reforms, and the accumulation of domestic industrial production capacities and foreign currency reserve through increasing trade volumes, REEs were no longer necessary for the acquisition of foreign currency but were domestically consumed more and more because of the growing demand for industrial products as a consequence of the rising disposable incomes of the Chinese people. Instead of solely focusing on GDP-based economic growth, President Hu Jintao announced the pursuit of a qualitative economic development that should include socio-economic issues such as social welfare, environmental protection and social equality. The regulatory structure of REEs was reformed so that the Ministry of Commerce gained the responsibility for issuing export licenses and quotas, the Ministry of Land Resources was responsible for issuing mining licenses and production quotas and the Chinese MEP gained the responsibility for environmental and occupational safety standards and inspections. The Ministry of Industry and Information Technology should set production quotas for Rare Earth Oxides and other refined products in this new structure. The NDRC was instated to coordinate the activities of all regulating agencies and to plan the longer-term development of the domestic industry. In 2004, the MLR announced the shutdown of all unlicensed mines, and mining and processing facilities that would violate environmental, industry and safety policies and standards. The export tax rebates for refined and processed REEs product was abolished by the MOFCOM in 2005 (He, 2014, p. 242ff.). It also reduced the number of companies that are licensed to export Rare Earths. In 2006, 47 Chinese domestic and 12 joint venture companies in the REEs sector were allowed to export. This was reduced to 23 domestic and 11 joint venture companies in 2009 (Morrison & Tang, 2012, p. 16). In 2007, export duties at a rate of 10% were implemented. In 2008, these rates were individually raised for specific REEs commodities so that they were now in the range between 10–25%. In 2009, the minimum rate was raised to 15%. In the same year, the MIIT started to issue production quotas. This has been the responsibility of the MLR since the early 1990s. Overlapping competencies of two or more administrative bodies on the same hierarchical level are not rare in the Chinese regulatory structure and are known to lead to regulatory inaccuracies or contradictions (Ferris Jr. & Zhang, 2005, p. 88f.). Due to the conflict of competences and a lack of communication between the two ministries, the production quota of the MIIT was significantly higher in the years of 2008 (MLR quota: 90,180 tons of REO equivalent; MIIT quota: 119,500 tons of REO equivalent) and 2009 (MLR quota: 87,620 tons of REO equivalent; MIIT quota: 110,700 tons of REO equivalent) (Tse, 2011, pp. 4–8). This illustrates that there were still clear inefficiencies in the regulation of the domestic industry by the agencies of the central government that impeded the planned consolidation and restructuring. Furthermore, there were inconsistencies between the formulation and enforcement of waste disposal fees. The Chinese government issued the "Waste Disposal Fee Regulation" in 2003, which sets specific fees and fines that should compensate for the cleaning up of environmental damage. After vigorous protest from REEs mining and processing companies that claimed that their business would suffer from rising costs, most REEs companies only had to pay half of the amount necessary to restore the local environment (He, 2014, p. 245).

In addition to deficiencies on the national level, the behavior of local cadres further prevented an effective regulation. Due to the importance of mining for the local economy and tax revenues, local cadres were hesitant to abide by the goals of the central government or even actively resisted the enforcement of new regulations. Because the control of the local REEs production is directly connected to economic benefits of the cadres, local cadres are not willing to abandon their possibilities to control companies that are located in their administrative area directly. The central government intended to merge several local REEs mining and processing companies together into one company that should be under the direct control of the central government. The major share of taxes would then be paid to the central government and not to the local government anymore. While the local governments would be financially compensated by transfer payments, total local tax revenues would still decrease (Liu et al., 2013, p. 33). As stakeholders of local companies, local governments also tend to block or delay the implementation of new environmental standards and regulations that might hamper investments and economic growth or prevent their effective enforcement. The local environmental protection bureaus that are responsible for the enforcement of environmental standards and the penalization of non-compliant companies are financially dependent on local governments, which determine the salaries of EPBs' officials, their office space and staff cars. Therefore, local governments are able to pressure EPBs into giving up effective enforcement of new environmental standards or at least into raising only minor fines in the case of environmental violations (Economy, 2005, p. 108; Gang, 2009, p. 39ff.). Due to this dependence structure, local REEs mining companies were not affected much by stricter new environmental standards. Furthermore, companies that are mining without licenses are sometimes protected by local cadres out of personal self-interest. Dong and Torgler (2010) analyze the causes of corruption in China and find out that both the abundance of natural resources and the decentralization of administration are significantly correlated with higher levels of corruption in China. While local bureaus of the MLR tried to chase down unlicensed mining operations, local cadres sometimes formed a "cooperative umbrella" consisting of the cover-up of illegal operations, the purchase of company shares and the suppression of complaints of stakeholders that were negatively impacted by these operations. Especially in southern China, the MLR was able to temporarily stop illegal mining activities but not to arrest illegal miners, who managed to flee the mining area in order to begin the production in new illegal mines before the MLR has even obtained all evidence. Meanwhile, the most successful series of consolidation was achieved by the Ganzhou Rare Earth Mineral Industry Co Limited. This company was established in 2004 by the city government of Ganzhou, which is also called the "Rare Earth capital" of the Jiangxi province. This local-government-owned company managed to expand and gain control of all 88 mining licenses in Ganzhou (He, 2014, p. 243ff.).

In summary, the mild attempts of reregulation were not effective. The output of all unprocessed REEs and processed REMs materials was higher than the production quotas of the MIIT during the whole phase (Tse, 2011, p. 5). Even companies that complied with quotas were able to use regulatory loopholes. Because production and export quotas were only based on tonnage and did not differentiate between the monetary value of individual REMs, mines focused on the extraction, processing and exportation of higher-valued REMs in order to maximize their profit while lower-valued REMs were disposed as waste. This also led to very low recovery rates of REEs. Although the market entry of new processing plants should have been limited, the full capacity of processing plants reached 200,000 tons in 2009. This overcapacity led to the illegal trading of export quotas between REEs processing companies (He, 2014, p. 245). Although the measures of mild reregulation were intended to slow down the expansion of the domestic REEs sector and eliminate the disruptions that were created by State promotion in the first of industry liberalization from the late 1970s to the early 2000s, they did not succeed but only created new structural imbalances and disruptions.

Reregulation in the wake of the Global Financial Crisis

The Global Financial Crisis has given a new impetus for a new wave of intensified efforts of reregulation or an "industry reregulation storm", as it is called by He (2014, p. 245). This can be only partly explained by the failure of the mild attempts in the phase from the early 2000s to 2009 and the necessity to further improve the regulatory framework in order to regain State control over the REEs market and industry. An additional explanatory approach, which is elaborated on in this study, is based on the implications of the GFC for the Chinese economic growth path and the importance of Rare Earths as a strategic natural resources for economic rebalancing.

Implications of the GFC for the Chinese economic growth path

Prior to the GFC, especially in the period since the accession to the WTO in 2001 (OECD, 2013, p. 19), the Chinese economic growth path was predominantly based on the systematic underpricing on the factor markets for capital, labor, land, energy and environment. Although the prices of 95% of the products have been liberalized, these markets remained under the control of the government (Fabre, 2013, p. 6). As explained in Chapter 4, the cost of capital is kept low especially for SOEs and large firms with close connections to the government and the State-controlled "Big Four" banks through the financial repression of the saving households. Because the households are target and precautionary savers, their marginal propensity to save increase and their marginal propensity to consume decreases when real interests decrease. Therefore, the financial repression also induced a repression of private consumption in China. While low interest rates enabled companies to invest in production capacities extensively so that investment in fixed capital almost reached 50% of the GDP in 2011, household consumption decreased from 46% of the GDP in 1996 to 35% of the GDP in 2011 (Lardy & Borst, 2013, pp. 2–6). The factor labor was underpriced due to the exploitation of rural migrant workers in labor-intensive manufacturing industries. Due to the Chinese household registration system of "hukou", urban employers are not required to pay social welfare contributions to migrant workers that have left their registered rural area in order to work in factories in urban areas. As informal workers, rural migrants tend to work 50% more than formal employees while receiving only 60% of their salaries

(Fabre, 2013, p. 6). As consequence of the underpricing of labor, the wage share of GDP has decreased from 55% to 49% in 2009, which is even low for an emerging economy (Lardy & Borst, 2013, p. 8). The land in China is owned by the State or local authorities in rural areas while firms and individuals are able to obtain land use rights. In the countryside, the rural population holds inheritable long-term use rights but the State has the power to withdraw these rights for development purposes. In order to attract investments of domestic and especially foreign-invested companies in their administrative area, local governments made use of their right to withdraw land use rights and offered it for industrial use below cost. While the rural population is compensated for withdrawn land, the sale price for developed land with connection to infrastructure could be sold for a price 30 to 50 times the requisition price (Fabre, 2013, p. 7). The prices of electricity, gasoline and all other liquid fuels are controlled by the NDRC. When the price of one barrel of crude oil increases above 80 USD, the full pass through from price increases to refined petroleum products is abandoned. When it increases above 130 USD, the cost pass through is completely abandoned. While the rates paid to electricity generators is generally raised by the NDRC when the price of coal increases by more than 5% over six months, the NDRC failed to raise electricity prices to offset price increases of coal in 2007, 2008, 2010 and 2011 so that increasing costs were not effectively passed through to electricity consumers. As consequence, energy- and electricity-intensive industrial firms, especially in the manufacturing sector, benefited from these indirect subsidies of energy underpricing (Lardy & Borst, 2013, p. 5ff.). The underpricing of fuels and electricity also raised the level of waste, emissions and environmental pollution. Although local cadres are responsible for the environmental conditions in their region since 1989, and environmental factors are also included in the valuation of cadre promotion system, economic growth was still seen as the most important goal before the GFC (Economy, 2005, p. 106). Due to the lack of political elections, the Chinese Communist Party does not have a democratic legitimacy to rule while the ideological legitimacy to rule has eroded since the beginning of the economic reforms in 1978. The ability to promote economic growth as a means to foster the modernization of China and to create new employment opportunities has become the major legitimacy of the government (Schueller, 2006, p. 27). As a consequence of the negligence of environmental aspects, the pollution of air, water and land has reached such a severe level that the health of the population and even productivity is threatened (Fabre, 2013, p. 7). In addition to these factors, the systematic undervaluation of the Chinese currency Renminbi through foreign exchange market interventions by the PBOC increased the profitability of export-oriented manufacturing industries so that China had a persistent, large, current account surplus until 2008 (Lardy & Borst, 2013, p. 3ff.). However, a major share of Chinese exports stem from the labor-intensive assemblage of intermediate goods from third countries so that the value-added of Chinese exports is low, especially for high-tech goods. For example, the value-added for an Apple IPhone was estimated to be 178.96 USD in 2009. While China exported IPhones worth 2.02 billion USD in that year, the Chinese share of value-added was only 3.6%, while the share of value-added of Japan was 34%, of Germany was 17%

and of South Korea was 13% (Batson, 2010). In summary, the Chinese economic growth path can be characterized as investment-driven, export-oriented growth that worsened social and environmental issues. The abandonment of a solely GDP-based economic policy that was announced in 2003 has failed.

In the fall of 2008, the GFC showed that this growth model cannot be sustained in the long-term. While China was hardly affected via the financial channel of mortgage-backed assets or collateralized debt obligations due to the restriction of oversea investment opportunities through capital outflow controls, its real sector was severely impacted via the export channel due to the slump in demand induced by the emerging global recession. Especially the recession of the G3 economies of the EU, Japan and the USA as main import economies had an impact of the economic growth in China. Based on a near vector autoregression model and data on the changes of output and prices in the G3 and China, Liu (2009) shows that a 1% decline in economic growth in the G3 leads to a 0.73% decline in growth in China (Liu, 2009, p. 22f.). While net exports contributed one-third of China's GDP growth in 2007, exports and imports in February were down 25.7% and 24.1%, respectively, on a year-on-year basis (Morrison, 2009, pp. 1–4). FDI inflows have also decreased so that the number of newly approved foreign-invested enterprises were 21% lower from January to September 2009 compared to the same period of the previous year (De Beule & Van den Bulcke, 2010, p. 13). Especially export-oriented companies in Coastal China were affected by this slump of demand for export goods so that local companies had to close down and lay off workers. While there are no official, reliable numbers, it is assumed that at least 20 million workers lost their jobs in the period from the third quarter of 2008 to the first quarter of 2009 (Overholt, 2010, p. 28). While the GDP growth forecast was only 6.6% at the beginning of 2009 (Morrison, 2009, p. 4), China managed to maintain a growth rate of 9.2% (The World Bank, 2016) through an economic stimulus package of circa 4 trillion RMB. While this package made a short-term economic recovery possible, it has been criticized for focusing too much on the construction sector and the creation of redundant infrastructure. Therefore, it would not promote long-term economic development (Schueller, 2009, pp. 4–7). The growth rates after the GFC might reflect this. While the growth rate was 10.6% in 2010, it subsequently fell to 9.5% in 2011, 7.8% in 2012, 7.7% in 2013, 7.3% in 2014 and finally 6.9% in 2015 (The World Bank, 2016). This might indicate that the current economic growth model has reached its limits while the problems of environmental degradation and social inequalities still remained unsolved and might be an increasingly prominent threat to the eroding legitimacy of the CCP. As consequence, the Twelfth Five-Year-Plan for the period of 2011–2015 stressed the necessity to rebalance the economic growth and to decouple the Chinese business cycle from foreign business cycles (Holbig & Gilley, 2010, p. 399ff.). Instead of the investment-driven, export-oriented growth path, a growth pattern led by domestic consumption should be achieved. Specific goals are maintaining a stable growth rate of 7%, the removal of social and regional disparities in income and development, the improvement the environmental framework and the promotion of seven key sectors: three sectors aligned with sustainable growth (energy savings and environmental protection, new energy and clean energy vehicles) and four sectors that should help China to move up the value chain (biotechnology, new materials, new IT and high-end manufacturing). These industries should contribute 8% of the GDP instead of the 2% they contributed in 2010 (British Chamber of Commerce, 2011). In order to be able to achieve these, the adjustment of the regulatory framework of Rare Earths seemed to be essential, as will be explained in the next section.

The role of Rare Earths in rebalancing the economic growth path and main goals of the new regulatory framework

Rare Earths are directly mentioned on two occasions in the Twelfth Five-Year-Plan. First, Section 4 of Chapter 9, which covers the overall goals of improvements and promotion of manufacturing, names the REEs industry as one of the industries which should be restructured by mergers and reorganization of enterprises. Advantaged enterprises of the sector should carry out alliances, cross-regional mergers and reorganization in order to increase the concentration of the REEs industry and to develop large enterprises with core competencies. This increase of concentration should be primarily based on market-based operations and not on governmental orders, for example. Second, Section 2 of Chapter 10, which covers the fostering and development of strategic emerging sectors, lists the promotion of R&D and industrialization of high-performance Rare Earth Materials in the category of new materials (British Chamber of Commerce, 2011). Thus, Rare Earths are included as one of the four key sectors that should help to move up the value chain and to increase the value-added of Chinese exports.

Apart from explicitly formulated goals, the rebalancing of the growth path had further implications for the REEs sector. As explained in the course of study, Rare Earths are almost indispensable in the three key sectors aligned with sustainable development except for a few cases in which substitutes or alternative technologies exist. They are also directly included in the key sector of new materials and are needed in many products of the IT sector and high-end manufacturing. Therefore, the promotion of these key sectors indicates that the domestic demand for REEs could be expected to steadily increase. While 70% of REMs were exported until 2004, the domestic demand increased with an annual average rate of 11% in the period of 2005 to 2011 while the demand in the RoW only grew with annual rates of 4% (Massari & Ruberti, 2013, p. 40). With a consumption of 60% of the global supply in 2013, the PRC has become the largest REEs demanding country in the world (Ting & Seaman, 2013, p. 238). Thus, China needs an increasingly growing share of its domestic REEs production for itself in order to secure the supply to domestic companies. The concerns of the Chinese government are that China would become a net importing country of REEs if the rate of REEs extraction and the quantity of exported REEs could not be reduced. Especially heavy REEs, which are needed for application in the three environmental sectors, will be scarce after the peak of the Chinese deposits of southern China. While the revenues of Chinese REEs exports were low due in the past to the factor of the China discount explained in Chapter 3, an increase of Chinese REEs import would lead to rising prices according to the factors that influence the price determination of REEs by Papp et al. (2008). Therefore, one major goal of the regulatory adjustments of the regulatory framework was the reduction of excessive production and exportation of REEs in order to secure the domestic supply for a longer term and to delay the dependency on expensive REEs imports. The restructuring of the sector by merging firms into a few large companies would hereby ease the supervision and control of the sector. This would also reduce the voracity problem that has been created through the policy of easy access to mining permits. The licenses to extract and export would only have to be allocated to a few actors, which could be controlled more easily whether they comply with their quotas and with other industrial standards.

The second main goal of regulatory adjustment is directly connected to the first goal. The movement up the value chain should also be achieved in industries that require REEs as input materials. While the global REO production sector is relatively small and is only worth 1.3 billion USD, the REEs-reliant industries are worth 4.8 trillion USD (Seaman, 2010, p. 22). Thus, the promotion of downstream industries is beneficial for China as derived from the dependency theory of Prebisch (1950) and Singer (1950). Prebisch and Singer state that the relative prices of primary commodities would decrease over time so that the terms of trade of countries that export primary commodities and import manufactured goods would consequently deteriorate and their underdevelopment would be cemented. The solution to this is the restriction of commodity exports and the development of downstream, commodity-processing sectors. China has already moved up in the chain value in upstream REEs goods by banning the exportation of unprocessed minerals for processing abroad due to the impression that REEs' price would be too low. This impression seemed to be confirmed in 2009. Due to the global recession, the demand for REEs was especially weak so that their prices further plunged. As a consequence, Inner Mongolia Baotou Steel Rare Earth Hi-Tech Co Ltd realized losses of 60 Million Renminbi (RMB) while having a global market share of 50% (Zhang, 2013, p. 22). China has also already upgraded the production of intermediate and some downstream goods so that China produces over 70% of the world total production of permanent magnets as well as luminescent, hydrogen storage and polishing materials (Information Office of the State Council, 2012, p. 6). The next step is the development of high-value downstream industries, in which China has been only used as a location for assembly so far. This would not only increase the value-added of Chinese exports but would also be a major step towards the rebalancing to a consumption-driven growth model. China will need to create 300 million extra jobs by 2020 in order to prevent the unemployment of future Chinese graduates. The creation of high-valued, high-quality goods–producing industries offers the opportunity to create new job positions that are also better paid than the current jobs in assembly facilities (Seaman, 2010, p. 21f.). The necessity to undervalue the RMB in order to enhance the cost advantage of Chinese labor-intensive, low value-added economic activities also disappears.

The third main goal of regulatory adjustment is based on the narrative of environmental concerns as explained by Wuebbeke (2013). The environmental regulation and the monitoring of the compliance with new standards that should diminish the environmental impact of REEs mining and processing should become easier with increasing concentration of the industry. Furthermore, REEs are strategic materials required for the pursuit of a sustainable development path so that the environmental and human health and social development are not jeopardized by an absolute focus on economic growth any longer. While the regulation of wastes and emissions of REEs mining and processing is required to protect the local environmental and human health in the surroundings of mines and processing plants, the utilization of Rare Earths for the expansion of domestic capacities in the fields of energy savings and environmental protection, new energy and clean energy vehicles enhances the possibilities to protect the environment and human health on the national level. This is also needed to sustain the legitimacy of the CCP after the level of economic growth rates declined. In the years 1996 to 2011, the number of environmental pollution–related protests increased by an annual average of 29% (Ruettinger et al., 2015, p. 10). The former popular governmental belief that China should first focus on "getting rich" and would later have sufficient financial resources to clean up the environment seems to no longer be shared by the Chinese population (Wen, 2006, p. 50). When the environmental is irreversibly damaged and economic growth is impeded by the poor environmental and human health, then it will be "stay-dirty-and-get-poor" instead of "get rich-cleaning up later" (Zhang et al., 2007, p. 8).

In summary, the adjustments in the regulatory framework in 2010 can be explained by three interlocked main goals that are both connected to the narratives established by Wuebbeke (2013) and to the special role of Rare Earths for the rebalancing of the Chinese development path towards a consumption-led, sustainable growth model.

Implemented measures of reregulation

The implemented measure of reregulation can be divided into three categories: reregulation of the domestic production sector that should precipitate consolidation and reorganization, restrictions in REEs trade and the implementation of stricter environmental standards and regulations.

Consolidation of the domestic Rare Earths sector

The main goal of consolidation has been already announced in the "National Plan for Mineral Resources Plan (2008–2015) that was issued in 2008. In this plan, the objectives of tighter regulation and control of the industry, the restriction of exploitation, the restriction of new market entries and the comprehensive utilization of REEs and other protected minerals were formulated. In 2009, the responsibility for registering, examining and approving of the exploration, development and mining of Rare Earths was taken back from the local authorities by the central government (Information Office of the State Council, 2012, p. 17f.). In the same year, the "2009–2015 Plans for Developing the Rare Earth industry" was issued by the MIIT. This mid- to long-term plan states that the provinces and regions, in which REEs are mined will be grouped into three large districts of south, north and west China with 11 sub-districts overall, which are shown in Map 5.1. This should simplify the control and regulation over REEs resources.

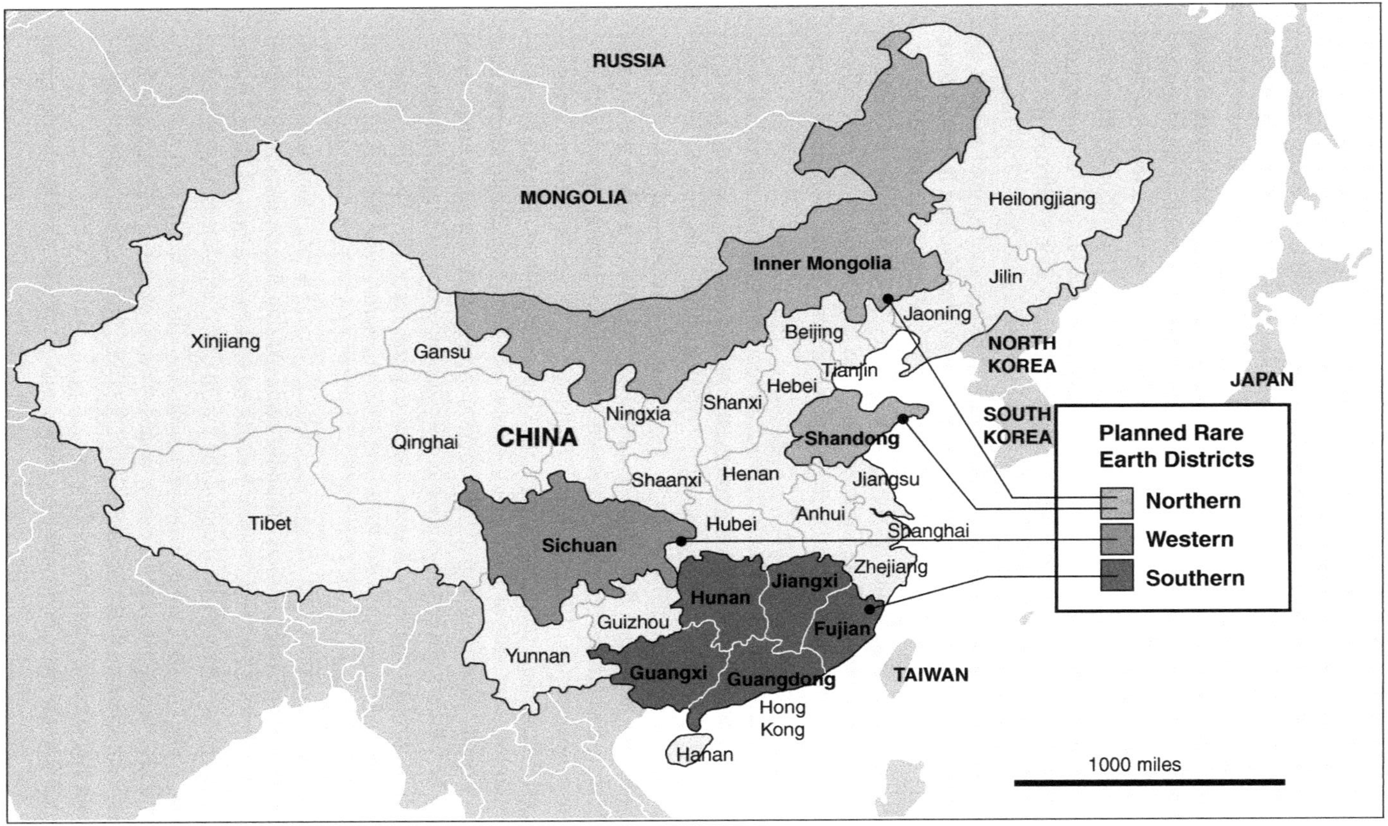

Map 5.1 Rare Earths production districts in China

Source: Morrison & Tang, 2012, p. 14.

Furthermore, the planned production of REEs should be between 13,000 and 15,000 tons of refined REMs annually, while the production capacity of separating and smelting enterprises should be between 12,000 and 15,000 tons (Schueler et al., 2011, p. 31). This roughly equals 130,000 to 140,000 tons of REO (Biedermann, 2014, p. 280). These production limits should be achieved by tightening mining permits and production quotas. Thus, the MIIT announced that, from 2009 to 2015, no new mining permits would be issued but that existing companies should improve their level of technical equipment, environmental protection and management capabilities. Small and/or illegal REEs mines as well as inefficient separating and smelting enterprises were designated to be shut down. This should reduce the number of enterprises from 100 to 20 (Schueler et al., 2011, p. 31). Separating companies are required to meet minimum output capacities of 8,000 tons per year of REO of mixed REEs, 5,000 tons per year of bastnaesite and 3,000 tons per year of ion adsorption REEs. Metal smelting producers are required to have an annual output capacity of at least 1,500 tons. It was also decided that new Rare Earths separation and smelting projects would be denied approval until 2015 (Tse, 2011, p. 9). The responsibility to oversee the industry by creating an examination and inspection system for Rare Earths mining was transferred to the MIIT. This should guarantee that the national directive plans are effectively implemented and executed (Schueler et al., 2011, p. 31).

In May 2010, the MLR started a five-month long, nation-wide inspection with the goal to identify and close down mines and processing firms that do not have legit operation licenses or do not comply with industrial standards or allocated production quotas (He, 2014, p. 247). The Chinese government also used this inspection tour to explain the complete halt of exports in 2010 when the accusations of neomercantilism emerged as consequence of the embargo. According to a Chinese mining expert, 100 owners and managers of illegal mines were arrested in the mining area in the hills of northern Guangdong alone (Bradsher, 2010). Inspection tours are seen as the sole solution to crackdown on illegal mining that has been on the rise since official production quotas were cut at end the of the 1990s. The Chinese government tried to estimate the extent of illegal mining and production through the recording of illegal exports the RoW. The discrepancy between the REEs exports to the RoW and REEs imports of the RoW from China in official custom statistic were 20,000 tons in 2008. An official from the mining city of Baotou estimated that smuggling of REEs from his city alone was 40,000 tons in 2010. The State Council officially reported that the imports of REEs of the RoW from China were 1.2 times the official Chinese exports in 2011. These estimated numbers only partly indicate the extent of the problem of illegal mining and smuggling, but the factual numbers might easily be higher. It is assumed that REEs are also smuggled over the hardly guarded green border to Vietnam and then shipped from Vietnam to REEs consuming countries. Second, the Chinese estimation does not consider that REEs that are smuggled out of China might also be smuggled into the main consuming countries without registration by the customs office. The smuggled quantities could therefore be higher than recorded (Kilby, 2014, p. 545f.; Zhang, 2013, p. 23f.). In addition, illegally mined REEs could also be used for the domestic market so that they are also not covered by the official estimation approach.

Also in 2010, the MIIT issued the "Entry Criterions for Rare Earth Industry" document, which sets minimum standards for the production capacity, capital ratio for fixed assets, utilized production techniques and machinery and resource recovery rates for existing companies and new market entrants (He, 2014, p. 247). For example, these new criterions determine that the mining of pure monazite minerals is banned because they contain thorium. This will induce a shrink of Chinese REEs reserves while reducing the potential environmental impact of mining. The usage of separation through electrolyzing metals by their chlorides was not explicitly banned but marked as a technique that should not be used. The recovery rate of mixed REEs and bastnasite should be not less than 72% while the loss rate through mining should not be more than 10%. The recovery rate for ion adsorption should not be less than 70%. Refined REMs should have a purity of at least 92% (Schueler et al., 2011, p. 52f.). Especially the companies located in south China failed to meet these new criteria so that 80% of all processing companies were expected to be closed down (He, 2014, p. 248). Overall, one-third of the 23 mining companies and almost half of the 99 smelting enterprises failed to meet the new standards and were expected to be shut down (Biedermann, 2014, p. 284). This is a major step forward towards the ultimate goal of the central government as formulated in the "Guidelines for Merger & Acquisitions and Reconsolidation of Companies", which were issued by the State Council in 2011 and list key industries in which internationally competitive, large enterprise groups should be developed in order to upgrade the industry. Through mergers and acquisitions, six State-owned conglomerates should arise as national champions under the direct control of the central government. As large, vertically integrated companies, these national champions should amass 80% of China's national capacity in mining and processing (He, 2014, p. 246f.). The designated six chosen firms are Inner Mongolia Baotou Steel Rare Earth Hi-Tech Co Ltd, Minmetals Mining Corp. Ltd., Aluminium Corp. of China Ltd. (Chinalco), Ganzhou Keli Rare Earth New Material Co. Ltd., Guangdong Rising Nonferrous Metals Group Co. Ltd. and Xiamen Tungsten Co. These companies will receive easier approvals in M&As, more quotas for mining, separation and exportation and additional governmental support such as government purchase and fiscal subsidies (Jacobsen, 2014). Due to its high annual production and share of total Chinese REEs reserves, Inner Mongolia is seen as the most important region. Here, the Inner Mongolia Baotou Steel Rare Earth Hi-Tech Co Ltd has been designated to become the monopoly in the industry. According to the Chinese government–owned newspaper *China Daily*, 22 of the original 35 licensed REEs companies have been shut down and received financial compensations, whereas the other 12 were integrated into the Baotou Steel Rare Earth Group. The companies and their shareholders have "handed over" 51% of their shares and will be provided production and export quotas by their new mother company ("Baotou Steel integrates", 2012). It is unclear if this "handing over" included compensation payments. According to Biedermann (2014), at least 9 companies of the 34 received no retaliation at all. In Sichuan, the licenses were reduced from 18 to 7.

The central government also fostered cross-region collaboration to raise the effectiveness of regulation and prevent the lowering of standards and regulations as a means of regional competition. Under the leadership of the MLR, 15 city governments in southern China formed a joint regulatory regime in 2010. This joint regime should coordinate the production of heavy REEs and issue new, locally specific regulations that are in line with national goals. In 2011, three cities in light REEs mining areas formed a similar joint regulatory regime. In 2012, the "Association of China Rare Earth Industry" was established as a national level industry association in order to serve as a mediator in industry consolidation and international communications. It is designated to assist the coordination of supply and demand between firms to negotiate prices and other supply conditions with foreign governments and firms (He, 2014, p. 246ff.). Furthermore, unitary pricing systems were established in southern China that unify the provinces of Jiangxi, Fujian, Guangdong and Hunan in order to set a common price for REO and prevent dumping and cut-throat competition. Such a unitary pricing system had been already established in Inner Mongolia prior to the start of M&A activities (Seaman, 2010, p. 19). In 2012, the China Rare Earth Exchange was finally founded in Baotou. This national exchange has the responsibility to regulate the domestic market flows and price fluctuations (He, 2014, p. 247). In addition, a guideline issued in 2011 enabled the strategic State and corporate stockpiling of REEs at different processing stages, whereas previous regulations included only the stockpiling of REEs concentrates. The creation of stockpiles is another measure to balance the temporary differences between REEs demand and supply in order to stabilize market prices. Since the first half of 2012, the State has been reportedly purchasing REEs (United Nations Conference on Trade and Development, 2014, p. 28ff.).

Nevertheless, there is still local resistance against the consolidation due to the aspects related to the cadre promotion on the one hand and to corruptive behavior on the other hand. One illustrating example is the case of the Jiangxi province where the Ganzhou Rare Earth Mineral Industry Co Limited has already monopolized the industry in the surroundings of the city of Ganzhou. When designated enterprises of the central government entered Jiangxi in order to push national consolidation forward, both the municipal government and its company heavily resisted the transfer of mining rights, and smelting and separation operations so that the consolidation and reorganization ended in a deadlock (Liu et al., 2013, p. 33). Although the central government subsidized M&A activities, M&As were planned to be primary based on market operations and not on administrative measures and directives. Thus, the resistance against the consolidation of local REEs industries by State-controlled firms is successful at the moment. The Vice Secretary of Jiangxi Rare Earth Association stated that "in the face of state polices, we will walk our own path" (He, 2014, p. 249). This quote illustrates that the national plans of consolidation and reorganization might be facing unanticipated obstacles.

In summary, the implemented measures that mainly target the domestic mining and production sector should lead to a consolidation of the REEs sector and the development of six large, vertically integrated companies that each have a local monopoly. The first advantage of the promotion of these conglomerates is that the regulation and supervision would be simplified. This would guarantee the compliance with the production quotas are set lower than the previous growth of extraction rates in order to prevent excessive mining and delay the date of exhaustion. The voracity effect that was established through the easy access policy in the 1980s could therefore be eliminated by consolidation and reorganization of the REEs industry in China. According to the latest available data, over 90% of production quotas are now allocated to these six large firms since the end of 2015 (Mancheri, 2015, p. 268). The second advantage of these conglomerates is based on their increased market share and pure size that should increase their negotiation power on the international market. In the case of close coordination through State agencies such as the "Association of China Rare Earth Industry", these conglomerates could really act as a cartel as long as the global market share of China remains unchanged in the field of REEs. This would transform China's virtual monopoly situation into an actual monopoly situation, in which Chinese producers benefit from monopolistic prices while REEs are conserved for a longer time. However, local governments are still resisting the complete reorganization of the industry so that the main goals of the central government have not been achieved yet. Illegal mining is expected to remain a critical issue even after a successful and complete consolidation. Due to the mining technique of in-situ leaching in remote areas of the Nanling mountain areas, illegal mining can only be discovered through extensive inspection tours or by informants, whom are rewarded with up to 3,000 Yuan for information on illegal mining operations (Hayes-Labruto et al., 2013, p. 59). Nevertheless, illegal mining in southern China can only be limited for a certain time but not wholly prevented permanently.

Trade restrictions

With regard to restrictive regulatory adjustments of the trade regime for REEs, three main measures are used in China: export licenses, export duties and export quotas. While it was used in 2010, the export ban as a restriction to trade has been used only in this incident.

According to an OECD survey authored by Fliess and Mard (2012), which covers the restrictive trade measures of 100 countries that have been implemented since 2009, export licensing requirements are the second most often used type of measures (Fliess & Mard, 2012, p. 15). These requirements are divided into two categories: non-automatic export licensing and automatic export licensing. In the case of automatic export licensing, the approval for export is granted in almost all cases upon a standardized application. This measure is only intended to simplify the statistical recording of exports. In the case of non-automatic export licensing, exporters have to acquire an export permit in order to be allowed to export. The application for export authorization can be rejected or existing permits can be withdrawn for economic reasons and non-economic reasons. Economic reasons include the promotion and protection of further processing or value-adding activities in the home country or the control of illegal exports. Non-economic reasons include concerns about the national security, the protection of health, safety and the environment, and the compliance with international obligations. Export licenses can further specify the permitted export conditions so that the exportation of specific variations or processing stages of one good is restricted or that exports are restricted by destination (Fliess & Mard, 2012, pp. 16–23). China implicitly used automatic export licensing in the Rare Earths sector until 1999. There were no specific restrictions in this period of REEs export promotion. In 1999, the State first published a list of companies that were eligible with export licenses and also banned the export of primary REO for processing purposes. Instead of primary REO, the export of processed REEs should be promoted (He, 2014, p. 242). This was the shift from automatic to non-automatic export licensing. Since 2006, the responsible MOFCOM has gradually reduced the number of export permits. While 47 domestic REEs producer and traders and 12 Sino-foreign joint venture REEs companies were allowed to export in 2006, this number was subsequently first reduced to 23 domestic and 11 joint venture companies in 2009, then to 22 domestic and 10 joint venture firms in 2010 and finally to only 22 domestic and 9 joint venture REEs companies and traders in 2011 (Tse, 2011, p. 6). The reduction of permits does not only simplify the control over the quantity and the level of value-added of REEs exports but is also a tool for both industry consolidation and ensuring the security of supply on the domestic market. As the consolidation of the industry advances, the number of export permits for domestic firms will be supposedly reduced to six, which are then allocated to the six conglomerates. While foreign companies cannot be fully exempted from the right to export in accordance to paragraphs 5.1 and 5.2 of China's WTO Accession Protocol (Kilby, 2014, p. 545), their export would be only minimal when the State-owned conglomerates amass 80–90% of China's total production. This could make the Chinese system of export quotas for REEs redundant.

According to Fliess and Mard (2012), only China has been using the measure of export quotas during the investigation period. Export quotas are defined as "restrictions or ceilings imposed by an exporting country on the total volume of certain products" (Fliess & Mard, 2012, p. 13). The rationales of export quotas are similar to the rationales of export licenses. A quantitative limitation of exports will lead to a higher domestic supply with goods subject to a quota while the supply on the world market will be reduced. As a consequence, the scarcity and therefore the price on the global market rise while the scarcity and therefore the price on the domestic market decline. When the export of specific goods negatively affects the national security, the protection of health, safety and the environment, and the compliance with international obligations, then export quotas might be used in order to reduce these impacts (Kim, 2010, p. 7f.). While China has been utilizing export quotas for REEs since the early 1990s, these quotas did not seem to have effectively restricted the physical availability of REEs on the global market and affected their prices until the embargo of 2010. Figure 5.1 illustrates the export quotas in tons of REO equivalent content for the years 2000–2014, for which data was available.

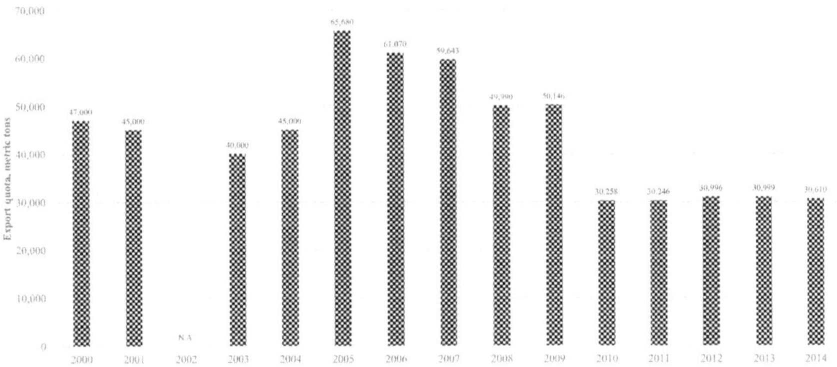

Figure 5.1 Chinese REO export quotas, 2000–2014

Source: Data retrieved from Tse, 2011, Statista, 2015.

After quotas were raised in 2005, quotas were annually reduced between 2005 and 2008. In the year 2009, Chinese exporters did not fully made use of the quota due to a sharp decline in the global demand of REEs in the GFC (Korinek & Kim, 2010, p. 21). The adjustment of the quota from 2009 to 2010 was a hard cut as the 2010 quota was 40% lower than the 2009 quota. Since then, the total quota has been relatively stable around 30,000 tons per year. This is clearly lower than the maximum export quantity of 35,000 tons, which was formulated in the MIIT's 2009–2015 development plan (Mancheri, 2015, p. 266). Because exporters began to focus on high-valued REEs exports in order to optimize their revenues, the MOFCOM has started to set separate export quotas for light and heavy REEs in 2012 (Pothen & Fink, 2015, p. 8). Over 87% of the annual total quotas is for the exportation of light REEs (Morrison & Tang, 2012, p. 18). This especially increases the domestic availability of heavy REEs, which are relatively scarcer and more critical than the more abundant light REEs. The announcement system of exports quotas was also changed. Until 2012, the MOFCOM announced a provisional quota at the beginning of the year, which was then readjusted in a second announcement. The first announcement only represented two-thirds of the total quota in 2010 and only about half of the total quota in 2011. In 2012, the ministry switched to three announcements per year (Mueller et al., 2014, p. 11f.). The introduction of a third announcement had the advantage of greater flexibility. The quota can be set relatively low in the first announcement in order be able to better adapt to the demand developments on the domestic and international market. When it becomes apparent that the domestic demand is extraordinarily high or the international demand is extraordinarily low in a specific year, then the second and third announcements could incorporate this. This could have helped to prevent the sharp price decline in 2009 as consequence of the REEs demand slump in the wake of the GFC.

Export duties are the most frequent utilized measure in the country sample of the OECD survey. Export duty is defined as "a tax collected on goods or commodities at the time they leave a customs territory" (Fliess & Mard, 2012, p. 23). Export duties are levied on either a per unit basis (specific tax per unit of volume) or an ad valorem basis (a tax that equals up to 30% of the value of the exported good). The measure can also implicitly include the trade measure of minimum export prices when the government prescribes a minimum monetary amount that the exporter has to pay per volume unit of exported goods (Fliess & Mard, 2012, p. 15). In general, export duties are used to stabilize commodity prices on the global market, to influence resource allocation in order to increase the supply on the domestic market, to alter domestic and global income distribution outcomes and to increase the fiscal revenues. Furthermore, export duties could also prevent the deterioration of the terms-of-trade of commodity-exporting countries when the relative prices of primary goods are declining as in the Prebisch-Singer hypothesis. When the exporting country has a large of the global market in the exported economy, then an export duty would increase the world price for the exported commodity and to an increase of the relative price of total exports to imports (Piermartini, 2004, p. 7). China first imposed export duties in the year 2006 after it had abolished the rebates of the export tax of 16%[2] in 2005. The initial tax was set as an ad valorem tax of 10% but was not applied to every REEs product (Tse, 2011, p. 8). The export tax mainly covered Rare Earth Oxides. At the same time, 41 kinds of REO, metal alloys containing REMs and REEs salts, were prohibited from trade for processing purposes. In 2007, the export tax was adjusted to the range of 10–15%. In 2008, ferroalloys with REMs content were included in the duty scheme at a tax of 15% (He, 2014, p. 244). Since 2008, the export duties have also been increased to 15–25% and are applied to an increasing number of REEs products. Since the last adjustments of the export tax scheme in 2011, the duty for ferroalloys that contain more than 10% of REEs are subject to a 25% export duty (Tse, 2011, p. 8). An extended overview of the export duty rate for various specific REEs products is given in the Appendix.

Because export duties and export quotas are used in tandem in China, the main goal of export duties is assumed not to be the increase of fiscal revenues but the restriction of exports (Mancheri, 2015, p. 267). This reflects the important role of REEs for rebalancing the Chinese growth path the necessity to retain a larger part of domestic production for domestic supply. In addition, the tightening of Chinese supply is also intended as a means to attract FDI from foreign high technology companies. While foreign companies are prohibited to invest in mining operations in China and are not permitted in smelting and separation activities without a Chinese partner, they are encouraged to invest in downstream processing, and the production and development of REEs-dependent goods. They are guaranteed a stable supply or relatively cheap REEs in exchange for the transfer of technology. This is called the "technology for resources" strategy, which should assist the industrial upgrading in China (Morrison & Tang, 2012, p. 18f.). If this strategy turns out to be successful, the expectations of Fifarek et al. (2008) that high technology downstream sectors, which utilize Rare Earths as inputs, will relocate to Asia would likely be fulfilled.

Adjustments of environmental regulation

The adjustments in the framework of environmental regulation of the REEs industry mainly consist of the implementation of new, stricter environmental standards and of a raise of the resource tax for mining.

According to Siebert (1990) and Morgenstern et al. (2001), the implementation of new and stricter environmental laws regarding emission level standards and production might induce and indirect price decrease. When companies invest in abatement technology in order to be able to comply with a new, permitted level of emission standards, these investments have to be seen as an additional cost driver that raises the average cost of extraction for all resource deposits within the legal domain of the new law. In addition, the investments in environmental protection capacities reduce the net investment level of productive capacities. This leads to a decreased level of production.

The first catalog of new environmental standards for the Chinese REEs industry were included in the MIIT's new entry criterions. In addition to the new requirements explained previously, the document also determines that facilities for the processing of bastnaesite and mixed minerals are obliged to have a complete treatment system for wastewater, waste gas and solid waste. The techniques of ponding and heap leaching are banned, while the in-situ method is declared the first best practice for the mining of ion adsorption deposits. In the process stage of refining, the saponification with ammonia is banned. Facilities for the electrolysis under the use of molten salt fluoride are required to install a treatment system that is capable of dealing with fluorine-containing wastewater and waste gas. Fluor-containing solid waste has to be disposed separately and must not be mixed with other wastes. Companies are also required to use energy-efficient production techniques and comply with indicated maximum values for the energy demand per ton of Rare Earths produced. At least 85% of the water that is used in ore dressing in the cases of bastnaesite and mixed minerals should be recycled. In the case of ion adsorption deposits, the required minimum water recycling rate is 90%. In the case of ion adsorption mining, at least 90% of plants and vegetation has to be rehabilitated in the affected area when a deposit is exhausted (Schueler et al., 2011, p. 51f.). The Chinese MEP then issued the second catalog of new standards in 2011. The "Pollutant Discharge Standards for the Rare Earth Industry" further tightened the emissions standards for pollutants in water and air, and for the total discharge of wastewater, waste air, thorium, and uranium. It was expected that 80% of REEs firms would fail to meet the new standards, which raise the production costs by an estimated 70%. As a concession to the industry, only new market entrants are required to immediately comply with these standards, while existing companies were given some time to upgrade their environmental technology and treatment facilities in order to ensure their compliance (Wuebbeke, 2013, p. 388f.). Since 1 January 2015, the new standards are obliging for all REEs companies (Mancheri, 2015, p. 268). These two new catalogs are obviously designed to reduce the severe environmental impact of REEs mining and processing on the environment and human health, which has been described in Chapter 2. However, they are also used in conjunction with industry consolidation and restriction of trade. REEs companies that do not comply with the environmental standards will be deprived of their production quotas, which would then be reallocated to complying companies. The allocation of export licenses and export quotas is also predicated upon the compliance with the environmental standards since 2012. In this year, only 9 companies received licenses and quotas in the first round of allocation while another 17 firms had to undergo an audit in order to investigate if they would comply with the environmental standards (Morrison & Tang, 2012, p. 16). Therefore, the new standards seem to be also a tool to reduce the number of producing and exporting companies deliberately. The companies that will most likely meet the new standards are the six designated national champions, which receive extensive financial support from the central government.

The second environment-related regulatory adjustment is the raise of the resource tax. This tax is based on the concept of the Pigouvian tax as an economic policy instrument for the internalization of externalities. Pigou (1932) established the idea of externalities as a divergence of marginal private interests from marginal social interests. Profit-maximizing firms rather focus on the marginal private net product of their investments and business activities than the marginal social net product. The activities of firms might be harmful to third parties and induce indirect social costs. In the case of negative technological externalities, emissions and environmental pollution are an example for indirect costs that are not borne by firms and are not included in the market price for goods, whose production are causing emissions and pollution. The market price of one unit only reflects the marginal or average production costs but not the marginal costs of damaging the environment or human health that the production of one unit causes. Because the market price does not reflect all direct or indirect costs, technical externalities lead to market failure, which justifies state intervention. Pigou (1932) had the idea of a tax that should compensate for the full extra costs. Thus, the tax on the production of one marginal unit of a product should be equal to the marginal social costs that the marginal unit causes. Baumol (1972) further developed Pigou's concept and put forward the idea of an acceptable externality level that is defined by the government. The advantage of this approach is that it does not require specific information on the marginal social cost of production, which is not measurable. Instead, the Pigouvian tax should be set so high that an output quantity is reached that bears the acceptable externality level. In order to find the optimal tax that leads to the acceptable externality level, Baumol considered a rather simple trial-and-error process.

Until 2011, the resource tax for the mining of Rare Earths was relatively low. It was between 0.4 RMB (for xenotime and ion ad absorption deposits) to 2 RMB (for bastnaesite and monazite) per extracted ton of REEs-bearing mineral. In 2011, the tax was raised to 60 RMB per ton of minerals that mainly contain light REEs and to 30 RMB per ton of minerals that mainly contain heavy REEs (Information Office of the State Council, 2012, p. 18). According to the concept of the Pigouvian tax, this resource tax should increase the Rare Earths market prices and decrease the overall output of Chinese REEs mines. The adjustment of the tax is especially significant in the case of heavy REEs, whose tax was raised by a factor of 750, that are found in minerals with lower concentrations than light REEs.

In summary, new environmental standards and the raise of the resource tax should prevent further severe environmental pollution. This also provides the adequate time to clean up the existing environmental damages in the main mining area. The resource tax has also a secondary effect of resource conservation. Due to the decrease of output, the exhaustion is delayed further in time. In addition, the tax increases REEs markets prices and indirectly helps to eliminate the impression that REEs are sold below their intrinsic value at least partially. In addition to the pure goals of environmental protection, the new standards are also used to enforce and accelerate the consolidation of the domestic industry.

Impact and implications of reregulation

After the implemented measures were introduced, their impact will be investigated. First, the impact especially of the regulatory adjustment of the trade regime for REEs on the price formation for and the global distribution of welfare will be discussed. Because the consolidation of the Chinese industry is not yet complete, and the new environmental regulations have been only enforced since 2015, there are no quantitative studies to measure the effects of reregulation in these fields. Second, the impact on the resource policy of major REEs consuming countries in the rest of the world will be assessed. Finally, the implications of reregulation for the optimal future path of extraction will be analyzed.

Impacts on the global price formation and the distribution of global welfare

The impacts of the restriction of exportation on the global price formation and the distribution of global welfare have been widely researched and are described in the standard literature on international trade theory. For example, according to Devarajan et al. (1996); Piermartini (2004) and WTO (2010), the theoretical effects of the restriction of trade are the direct influence on prices and the distribution of global welfare. Large economies with significant market power are able to benefit from imposing export duties on goods they are producing and exporting as the main suppliers. The optimal export tax that will maximize the domestic welfare is hereby given by the inverse demand elasticity. The price on the world market for the resource will rise due to the export duty. Because the demand for goods that are now subject to an export tax declines on the global market due to their increased prices, previously exporting companies offer a larger share of their production on the domestic market. Due to increased supply, this would lead to decreased domestic prices. This benefits domestic consumers and disadvantages foreign consumers. Producers will face exactly opposing effects. Domestic producers experience an overall decrease of product prices, which induces a reduction of their welfare, of their production and of their employment, while foreign producers will experience an increase of prices for their products, of their output and of their employment.

The export tax–imposing government will receive additional tax revenues coming from foreign consumers. Overall, the aggregate welfare effects are positive for the producing large country and negative for importing countries so that the imposition of an optimal export tax is a redistribution of global and domestic income and a welfare shift from foreign countries to the large economy. While domestic producers are faced with a producer loss, the welfare increases of the consumers, who benefit from decreased domestic prices, and of the government, which benefits from increased tax revenues, will more than make up for the producer loss. Export quotas, which should increase the physical resource availability on the domestic market, are a key element for upgrading the domestic industrial structure in the dependency theory but also have an implicit tax effect. Due to the reduction of physical availability on the global market, the international prices will also increase while prices on the domestic market will decrease due to the increased availability. Thus, export quotas have also the same welfare effects, like export taxes in the case of large economies.

Sanyal et al. (2013) estimate the effects of natural distances, traditional demand factors (e.g. changes in the GDP per capita) and trade costs on Rare Earths exports in the period from 2001–2009 (the period of mild reregulation) on the basis of a stochastic frontier estimation in a gravity trade modeling framework. The trade costs are divided into "behind the border costs", which are improvements of the trade and transport infrastructure, custom and port procedure reforms and investment in storage infrastructure of the exporting country, "explicit beyond the border costs", which include export taxes and real exchange rate, and "implicit beyond the border costs", which are the removal of regulations to trade with China by the importing countries. Their results show significant export losses due to the increase of losses in the "behind the border" trade costs. At the same time, revenues in some foreign markets such as Italy, Germany and Japan increased due to the reduction in "implicit beyond the border" trade costs while they increased in other markets due to an increase of these costs. The authors attribute this to the efforts of some countries to diversify their importing sources, to develop domestic REEs mines or to substitute REEs with other materials. They conclude that the export restrictions might not have been beneficial for China in this period.

In the current period of the "industry reregulation storm", the immediate impact on the formation of short-term prices for specific individual REEs came from the export ban. Table 5.1 displays the price development of selected REMs for the years 2007–2013. Due to the demand slump in 2009 as consequence of the GFC, prices predominantly decreased in this year. In 2010, they skyrocketed as a consequence of China's embargo, which induced scarcity on the global market but also fueled speculation with REEs. Speculation is seen as the major driver for sharp declining prices, while it is not clear how the other specific protective measures, for example the quota cuts of 2010 or the further increases of export duties in 2010 and 2011, directly and individually attributed to the price increases.

In 2011, REEs prices further skyrocketed and climaxed. The price for lanthanum oxide increased from 4.9 USD/kg in 2009 to 22.4 USD/kg in 2010 and finally to 104.1 USD/kg in 2011. This 21-fold increase represents the largest price

Table 5.1 Prices of individual Rare Earth Oxides in USD/kg, 2007–2013

Element	*2007*	*2008*	*2009*	*2010*	*2011*	*2012*	*2013*
Lanthanum oxide	3.4	8.7	4.9	22.4	104.1	25.2	8.0
Cerum oxide	3.0	4.6	3.9	21.6	102.0	24.7	8.3
Praesodymium oxide	29.1	29.5	18.0	48.0	197.3	121.0	92.3
Neodymium oxide	30.2	31.9	19.1	49.5	234.4	132.2	70.7
Samarium oxide	3.6	5.2	3.4	14.4	103.4	64.3	15.6
Europium oxide	323.9	481.9	492.9	559.8	2843.9	2484.8	1161.4
Terbium oxide	590.4	720.8	361.7	557.8	2334.2	2030.8	974.0
Dysprosium oxide	89.1	118.5	115.7	231.6	1449.8	1035.6	550.4

Source: Data retrieved from Golev et al., 2014, p. 55.

increase of all REMs. Beginning in 2012, prices started to decrease while being still higher than in the period before the embargo. Meanwhile, the terms-of-trade effects are negligible. According to the Prebisch-Singer hypothesis, commodity export restrictions lead to an improvement of the terms-of-trade. However, Rare Earths have only a small share in total exports. The shares were between around 0.06% in 2002 and circa 0.03% in 2009. At the climax of REEs prices in 2011, the share increased to 0.14%, which is still too low to positively affect the terms-of-trade significantly (Pothen & Fink, 2015, p. 11). An effect that was realized was the establishment of a dual pricing system for REEs, in which Chinese domestic prices and global prices differed between 68.5% and 557.2% for some REO at the climax of prices in 2011 (Morrison & Tang, 2012, p. 27). This dual pricing was perceived as pressure to invest more in China by foreign companies in order to secure the supply with REEs. According to Biedermann (2014), 50 foreign companies have been already operating in the Baotou Rare Earth Hi-Tech Industrial Development Zone in Inner Mongolia, which is the designated investment location for the "technology for resources" strategy, in 2014. For example, the German car manufacturer Daimler formed a joint venture with the Chinese firm "Build your Dreams" in order to build electric cars. The Korean Development Bank signed a cooperation agreement with the Baotou High-Tech Zone in order to encourage FDI of Korean electronics firms or car manufacturers in processing plants. In return, Korean firms are offered low local taxes and discounts on Rare Earths materials (Biedermann, 2014, p. 284).

Zhang et al. (2015) conduct a market power analysis and a price sensitive analysis for REEs prices in Japan and the USA for the years 2001 to 2010 in order to estimate the effects of China's trade restriction on the price formation. The market power is measured by the Lerner index, which represents the difference between the market price and marginal costs of REEs. A value of zero equals low market power while a value of one equals high market power. They conclude that the Chinese market power have increased by 140.18% on the U.S. and by 244.22% on the Japanese markets after the tightening of export restrictions. However, the market power is still 1.14 times higher on the U.S. market than on the Japanese market. In their price sensitivity analysis, the authors estimate the sensitivity of Chinese REEs when the export volume decreases by 5%, 10%, 15% and 20%. While the price sensitivity is in general higher on the U.S. market than on the Japanese market, which shows a higher competitiveness of Chinese REEs on the U.S. market, the price gaps between both markets decline as the Chinese exports decline. Therefore, the pricing power has increased with a tightening of export restrictions. These results illustrate that the strict reregulation has helped China to obtain price-setting power. Through reregulation, China is able to utilize their virtual monopoly effectively in order to adjust prices so that the perceived situation that REEs are sold below their intrinsic value could be eliminated.

Pothen (2013b) estimates the impact of the Chinese REEs export restrictions on its market power and on the distribution of global welfare based on the dynamic equilibrium model "Metal Resource (METRO) model" of Pothen (2013a). In his business-as-usual scenario, he assumes that export quotas and tariffs remain unchanged at the level of 2013 until 2020. The production is assumed to increase to 150,000 tons in 2018 and the global demand should increase up to 285,000 tons per year by 2020. While secondary mining from recycling activities is assumed to be prevented by high prohibitive costs in this scenario, the market entry of new mining projects is included. The mining capacities of the RoW are set to increase from 32,000 tons in 2014 to 137,000 tons in 2020. The business-as-usual simulation shows that China would be able to utilize its market power to affect prices until 2019. Until 2015, prices in China and the RoW diverge significantly. In 2014 and 2015, the prices of light REO are about 30% and the prices of heavy REO are about 170% higher in the RoW. However, RoW prices are expected to decrease and approximate the lower prices on the Chinese market due to increasing supply on the global market by new mines. Pothen estimates the welfare changes due to the export restrictions in comparison of his business-as-usual-scenario with a free trade situation. The simulated welfare gains of China until 2020 are 1.4 billion USD. The gains of other countries, in which new mines can be developed, are 0.66 billion USD. The losses of the USA, Europe and Asia, except China, are -0.58, -0.57 and -1.46 billion USD, respectively. This represents a global welfare shift from countries that only consume REEs and do not have domestic mines to REEs-producing countries. The total global welfare loss equals -0.55 billion USD.

Mueller et al. (2014) estimate the wealth effects of export quota announcements for listed companies in the REEs industry in China and the USA in the period of 1 January 2008 to 31 August 2014. Wealth effects are hereby measured in the form of abnormal returns, which are calculated as the residuals of regressing the individual companies' stock returns on the market portfolio. They come to the conclusion that extreme REEs price increases benefited Chinese companies in the front of the REE supply chain but were unfavorable for REE users in the U.S. manufacturing sector. Thus, China was able to utilize its virtual monopoly situation to transfer wealth from the end-use industries in other countries to its domestic industry. However, this result is only applicable to the period with two annual announcements. With the shift to three annual announcements at the beginning of the WTO trial, U.S.

end-use companies showed more positive reactions than Chinese supplier firms did. In addition, Mueller et al. find out that the reaction of companies is in accordance to their position along the REEs supply chain. Chinese and global REEs suppler would benefit from extreme price increase while U.S. end-users would react negatively.

In summary, the restrictive adjustments in the trade regime in the wake of the GFC benefitted China's ability to actively utilize its virtual monopoly. As predicted in the theoretical considerations of the effects of trade restrictions, export duties and export quotas induced increasing REEs prices in the RoW and decreasing prices in China. As a consequence of diverging prices, a dual pricing system was established, and global welfare was redistributed to Chinese REEs downstream users and mining firms in the RoW at the expense of Chinese mines and end-users in the RoW. In addition, China was able to increase its market power on the U.S. and Japanese REEs markets. As a consequence of the significant increases of the price sensitivity on both markets, further reductions of the export quotas would lead to higher price spikes than in previous periods. However, the analysis of Pothen (2013b) also shows that China's increase in market power is only temporary. As briefly mentioned in Chapter 4, increasing natural resource prices will most likely trigger new economic activities such as recycling or the exploration and development of new mines in order to decrease prices again. The next section will take a close look at the efforts of the governments and companies of main consuming countries.

Countermeasures of main consuming countries in the rest of the world

Similar to the First Rare Earth Crisis in the 1940s, the governments of main consuming countries and private companies in the rest of the world began to actively seek solutions in order to reduce the dependency on Rare Earths imports from China through the diversification of supply sources, the exploration and development of new mines and efforts in R&D for recycling techniques or materials that could substitute REEs. In addition, they were also able to make an official WTO complaint against China's trade restriction in order to initiate an investigation if China's REEs trade regime would violate the WTO rules. This opportunity was unavailable for the USA in 1947 due to the nonexistence of a dispute settlement in the international trading system before the foundation of the GATT/WTO.

Paradigm shifts in the resource policy

Prior to 2010, Rare Earths were not in the focus of the resource policy of the main consuming countries outside of China. The securing of supply with REEs was only an issue for the resource management of the private sector. Although China used export quotas, these quotas were effectively non-binding and did not lead to an undersupply and increasing scarcity on the global market so that prices were low and state interventions seemed to be unnecessary. Neither governments, companies nor the broad public paid much attention to the Chinese virtual monopoly in spite of the 2008 report of the U.S. NRC "Minerals, critical minerals, and the U.S. economy", which analyzed the criticality of Rare Earths for the U.S. economy. The lack of attention to REEs reflects the general lack of attention for nonfuel minerals. While the USGS still has the largest international database on minerals, the quantity and quality of data and its analysis were declining prior to 2010 due to reductions in budget, staff and data coverage (National Research Council, 2008, p. 8). After the quota was cut by 72% for the second half of 2010 and, of course, after the full export ban in the fall of 2010, the attention for REEs suddenly and sharply increased.

Inside the EU, Reinhard Buetikofer, a member of the European parliament from the German Green Party, was among the first of those who called for a paradigm shift in the resource policy on the European and international levels. On the international level, he suggested a Trans-Atlantic cooperation between the EU and USA in order to collect reliable data on global deposits and potential production capacities and to coordinate all efforts in R&D for substitutes, recycling possibilities and resource-augmenting technologies (Buetikofer, 2010). He also suggested a technological cooperation in the field of REEs with China similar to the cooperation in energy resources in the framework of the "EU-China Clean Energy Centre" (Buetikofer, 2014, p. 5). On the EU level, he launched the study of Schueler et al. (2011) and influenced the new European raw materials strategy by his "Report on an effective raw materials strategy for Europe" (Buetikofer, 2014, p. 5ff; European Parliament, 2011). The original raw materials strategy "Tackling the challenges in commodity markets and on raw materials", which was published in February 2011 by the European Commission in order to update its "Raw Materials Strategy" of 2008, was based on three pillars (European Commission, 2011b). The first and most important pillar should be trade and resource diplomacy, the second pillar consisted of domestic mining and the third and least important pillar was the promotion of resource efficiency and recycling (Buetikofer, 2014, p. 6). The new report by Buetikofer reversed these pillars so that promotion of resource efficiency and recycling is the main goal of the final strategy "A resource-efficient Europe-Flagship initiative under the Europe 2020 strategy" (European Commission, 2011a). Furthermore, the "European Rare Earths Competency Network" was founded in 2013 based on the initial idea of Buetikofer and Matthias Buchert of the Oeko Institute (ERECON, 2015, p. 11). The task of this network is to examine challenges and find solutions for REEs mining in the EU, for recycling and substitution possibilities and for fostering resilient, sustainable and competitive REEs supply chains in the EU (ERECON, 2015, p. 17).

In February 2011, the cooperation in the field of REEs with Japan was initiated after a hearing of the deputy director of the "Manufacturing Industries Bureau" of the Japanese Ministry of Economy, Trade and Industry on the Japanese resource strategy. Japan was especially vulnerable to the export ban of 2010 because it is the largest REEs consuming country outside of China. Furthermore, the threat that China might use REEs as an economic weapon in geopolitical disputes again led to a high urgency to reduce the dependency on Chinese REEs imports. The general Japanese strategy, which was formulated in the 2009 "Strategy for Ensuring Stable Supplies of Rare Metals", include the securing of overseas sources of critical materials in order to maintain a stable supply, the recycling of scrap metals, the development of substitutes and the stockpiling of some rare metals (U.S. Department of Energy, 2011, p. 62f.). The immediate policy that rapidly decreased the level of dependency on China and thus the urgency to find solutions based on recycling and R&D was the diversification of import sources. While 80% of Japanese REEs imports came from China in 2010, this share decreased to below 50% in 2012. The imports from the USA and France, which are both traditional intermediaries in the global REEs trade, and Vietnam, increased at the same time (Seaman, 2012, p. 3ff.). As part of the diversification strategy, the Japan Oil, Gas, and Metals Corporation, which is an independent agency but is reporting to the METI, was tasked to launch and financially support partnerships with foreign companies such as the Lynas Corporation, which is mining the Mt. Weld mine in Australia, Lavreco from Vietnam and Indian Rare Earths from India. Lynas was granted a 325 million USD loan by the Japanese trading house Sojitz Corporation. The Japanese government provided 50% of this loan. Sojitz also purchased 25 million USD in Lynas's shares. In return, Lynas should supply 8,500 tons of REMs, or 28% of Japan's annual consumption, annually for ten years. The cooperation with India was mainly channeled through the Toyota Tsusho Corporation, which founded a wholly foreign subsidiary in India named "Toyotsu Rare Earths India Private Limited". This subsidiary should produce REEs from monazite sands provided by Indian Rare Earths Limited. In addition, Japan and India also signed a trade agreement in Indian exports to Japan in November 2012 and considered the forming of joint venture activities in third countries. In Vietnam, Toyota Tsusho Corporation established a joint venture with Sojitz Corporation and the Vietnamese SOE mining company Lavreco, which should supply 20% of Japanese REEs demand. In addition to REEs project, Japan also invested in regional infrastructure projects in order to strengthen the general supply lines in South and Southeast Asia to enhance the government-to-government as well as business-to-business ties and to reduce trading costs. In Kazakhstan, the Sumitomo Corporation formed the joint venture "Summit Atom Rare Earth Company" with the national nuclear company Kazatomprom in March 2010. Kazatomprom also established a joint venture with Toshiba Corporation in September 2011. With the support of JOGMEC, Toshiba also began to research techniques for the effective recovery of REEs from uranium-pregnant solutions and uranium extraction in Kazakhstan. In October 2010, Japan also established a cooperation with Mongolia with the goal of drilling for REEs (Mazza et al., 2013, pp. 8–10). According to the minerals investors' guide of the Mongolian government, Mongolia has three untapped deposits of commercial interest (Elsner et al., 2011, p. 265). In November 2012, Japan and Mongolia began to negotiate an economic partnership agreement to establish a strategic partnership between both countries and strengthen existing political and economic ties (Mazza et al., 2013, p. 10). Due to its fast reaction to the Chinese export ban and implementation of immediate countermeasures, Japan was seen as an adequate cooperation partner for the EU and as a role model for the strategic direction of its own resource policy. As a third cooperation partner, the USA was finally called in for trilateral consultation talks.

Despite a 2002 USGS report that warned about the emerging Chinese virtual monopoly, which would threaten the U.S. leadership in REEs expertise and would make U.S. markets dependent on the continued stability in China's internal politics and economy as well as on China's relation to other countries (U.S. Geological Survey, 2002, p. 4), and the 2008 NRC report, the USA was not prepared for the export restrictions implemented in 2010. After the cut of export quotas, the first reaction was a congressional hearing, "Rare Earth Minerals and 21st Century Industry" on 16 March 2010. Among the experts that gave testimony was the 80-year-old senior metallurgist of Ames laboratory, Professor Karl A. Gschneidner, who stressed that the dissolvement of the domestic REEs industry also led to a decline in the intellectual infrastructure in REEs technologies that would hamper a rapid revitalization of the domestic industry (Goldman, 2014, p. 139). Therefore, the state funding and support of REEs-related research and education would be indispensable for ensuring the independency from Chinese imports. This view was supported by the testimony of a representative of the National Research Council, who advocated for the state funding of basic and policy research on minerals, materials and global supply, as wells for the establishment of new collaborations in education and applied research between academic organizations, the industry and the government. Mark A. Smith of Molycorp demanded governmental loan guarantees for capital-intensive REEs projects in the private sector, the training of personnel for REEs study, the reestablishment of the information networks between policy makers about the impact of strategic materials on natural security and the provision of grants for private and public REEs research. Steven Duclos, the Chief Scientist at General Electric, also called for federal support for public-private collaborations of resource and research sharing (Goldman, 2014, p. 157ff.). In short, the pursued paradigm shift in the U.S. resource policy for Rare Earths was suggested to be a return to the former supportive system centered on the Ames Laboratory and its Rare Earth Information Center. The U.S. Department of Energy then formulated the new "Critical Materials Strategy", which is similar to the EU concept. It is based on the three pillars of supply diversification, substitute developing and improvement of recycling. The role of R&D for these three pillars is also highlighted in this strategy. While R&D is not considered a primary mechanism for supply diversification in the U.S. DoE report, it is emphasized that it might boost the supply from new and existing sources throughout the world as a consequence of more efficient and environmentally friendly technologies for mining and processing. For the fields of developing substitute and finding recycling techniques, it is deemed the primary mechanism (U.S. Department of Energy, 2011, p. 6f.). As the new central institution of the emerging knowledge infrastructure, the "Critical Materials Institute" was founded in 2013 by the DoE, which made an announcement about providing up to 120 million USD for the years 2013–2017. The institute is led by a team of scientists from the Ames Laboratory and should bring together scientists from universities, public research institutes and the private sector. Its main goal is the coordination of research and development of the known and new reserves and improvements in the efficiency of mining, processing and manufacturing of Rare Earths (Goldman, 2014, p. 158). The new U.S. strategy also stresses the importance of international cooperation in order to achieve a secure global REEs supply jointly. Therefore, scientists, politicians and representatives from the private sector of the EU, Japan and the USA started the trilateral talks in order to exchange information on each other's resource strategy and on the issues in the fields of recycling, efficiency, substitution and mining (Buetikofer, 2014, p. 5). As a result of these talks, the EU, Japan and the USA decided to jointly request a formal WTO consultation with China over its limit on REEs exports, which will be subsequently discussed.

In summary, the EU, Japan and the USA initiated a paradigm shift in their resource policy in 2010. Prior to 2010, the securing of nonfuel minerals was predominantly seen as the task of the private sector. Although Chinese REEs exports were theoretically restricted, these restrictions were neglected or ignored due to low global REEs prices. As a consequence of the restrictive adjustments in the trade regime of 2010, the EU, Japan and the USA decided to adopt more active resource policies that are based on the diversification of REEs sources as well as the resource and development of technologies for the improvement of REEs efficiency and of recycling possibilities. Emerging international collaboration in these fields were soon recognized to be a key element for breaking the Chinese virtual monopoly.

Exploration and development of new deposits for primary mining

The restriction of Chinese REEs exports in 2010 and 2011 triggered many activities in primary mining projects in addition to the Japanese projects mentioned earlier even without the governmental direction and support. The increase of prices on the global market led to a new consideration of the commercial exploitability of known or indicated deposits that could be developed as new mines as well as mines that were mined since the decline of prices in the 1990s. There have been more than 400 projects related to exploration of deposits outside of China. Forty-five locations in China and in the rest of the world are now known to have an estimated ore grade at 2% or higher. This is the cut-off grade used by many companies that are engaged in large-scale mining operations (Terrascope project, n.d.). The locations outside of China are mainly located in the USA, Canada, Australia, Brazil, India, Russia and other members of the Commonwealth of Independent States and South Africa (U.S. Department of Energy, 2011, pp. 29–32).

The largest project in the USA was the reopening of the Mountain Pass mine, where extraction activities were discontinued in 2002, but separation from stockpiles has continued since 2007. Due to its size and high concentration, it is still the most adequate principal source for REEs for covering the U.S. demand. Because incidents of environmental contamination from wastewaters and tailings impoundments were one of the reasons why the active mining had to be discontinued in 2002, the new mining and processing facilities at Mountain Pass have been planned to utilize multiple new technologies and management strategies in order to minimize the environmental impact of the reopened mine. Instead of transporting wastewaters and tailings to evaporation ponds through pipelines, tailings will be dewatered and stored as a paste on an onsite location. Ninety percent of the wastewater will be treated through a reverse osmosis process and reused. This treatment of tailings eliminates the need of 120 acres of evaporation ponds. In addition, the rejection of the osmosis process can be treated in an onsite chlor-alkali facility in order to produce sodium hydroxide, hydrogen chloride and other valuable products that could be sold or reused (U.S. Environmental Protection Agency, 2012, pp. 4–8ff.). The projected extraction rates were planned to be 18,000 tons of REO in the planned starting year of 2012 and 40,000 tons of REO in the following years. In addition, the deposits of Bear Lodge in Wyoming, Pea Ridge in Missouri and Round Top Mountain in Texas were explored and drilled in order to estimate their potential. Because most mines outside of China only provide large amounts of light REEs, the Round Top Mountain Project is seen as especially promising due to its large inferred content of heavy REEs (U.S. Environmental Protection Agency, 2012, pp. 2–8f.). Due to the high regulatory barriers for new mine developments in the USA – the Mountain Pass mine had the advantage of being just a reopening – these projects do not have a projected starting date and could only begin to supply REEs in the medium-to-long term.

In Australia, the efforts to start mining at the Mt. Weld mine increased due to the high global prices. The construction of the mining and beneficiation facilities began in 2007 and was sped up as consequence of Chinese export restrictions (Haque et al., 2014, p. 621f.). The extraction started in 2012 but the extraction quantity stayed, as already mentioned, below the mine's projected potential in the first year. In addition, Arafura Resources further developed its mine at Nolans Bore in the Northern Territory. In 2008, a demonstration pilot project for processing ore was constructed. In 2010, the company announced that it would plan to produce REEs on a large scale by the fourth quarter of 2013 (British Geological Survey, 2011, p. 29). However, the projected production start has been delayed to 2019 (Volling, 2016).

In South Africa, the Great Western Minerals Group started to develop the Steenkampskraal deposit. This monazite mine was mined from 1950 to 1963 especially for its thorium content but was abandoned when uranium became the standard material for nuclear technology. Although the deposit is relatively small and would only annually provide 5,014 tons of REO, the advantages of this deposit were seen to be low investment costs of only 60 million USD that would be required to reopen the mine. The company also formed a joint venture with the Ganzhou Qiangdong Rare Earth Group of Jiangxi in order to build a separation facility near the mine. The hope of the mining company was to start production in early 2012 as the first new REEs mine outside of China and to be the first to benefit from high global REEs prices (Jepson, 2012, pp. 23–26). The project was delayed as the feasibility and environmental impact studies were only published in 2014 (Market Wired, 2014). In October 2015, the Steenkampskraal Thorium Limited Group announced that it has acquired the mine from the Great Western Minerals Group and is planning to begin production in October 2017

(Steenkampskraal Thorium Limited, 2015). The other large domestic deposit at Zandkopsdrift was purchased by Frontier Rare Earths. While this carbonite deposit is associated with higher costs than the Steenkampskraal deposit due to greater technical difficulties in extraction and separation, its annual extraction rate was projected to be 20,000 tons. It also contains more critical REEs like europium and less thorium than the Steenkampskraal deposit so it was estimated to be one of the most promising projects outside of China (Jepson, 2012, p. 26). The associated costs for Frontier Rare Earths are also reduced through a partnership with the Korean government–owned mining and natural resource investment company Korea Resources Corporation (Kores) that acquired a 10% stake of the mine and the right to purchase up to 50% of the mine production. As a return, it will provide funding on the best available market terms as well as technical and operating experience for the design, construction and operation of the facility. Frontier and Kores will also jointly investigate downstream business opportunities. The beginning of production was scheduled for 2015 (Frontier Rare Earths, 2012, p. 3ff.). However, the most recent company information shows that only the pre-feasibility study was finished in 2015 and that the production will not start before the end of 2018. The projection of annual extraction rates has also been adjusted. The mine should now annually provide 8,000 tons of REO for the first four years of production and then up to 16,000 tons for the total life of the mine: 45.5 years (Frontier Rare Earths, 2015, pp. 50, 60).

The Kvanefjeld project, which has been already discussed, is not the only project in Europe.[3] The Norra Kaerr deposit is located in south-central Sweden and contains large amounts of heavy REEs. Exploratory drilling began in 2009 and the current owner plans to start production in 2017. In addition, there are also the Kringlerne project and Sarfartoq project in Greenland, the Olserum project in Sweden and the Storkwitz project in Germany, which are all in a similar advanced stage of development. Furthermore, some projects, still at the early stage of exploration, exist. Two different exploration groups of the companies REE Minerals and Thor Resources drilled the Fen deposits in southern Norway in order to measure the inferred resource size. The Quantum Mineria Company has provided a first assessment of monazite sands deposit in the Matamulas in Spain. The firm Northland Resources, which holds the mine concession for the Hannukainen iron-copper-gold deposits in the region of western Lapland in Finland, has started to investigate the potential of the mine (ERECON, 2015, p. 36ff.).

All of these selected examples for the exploration and development of new mines illustrate the limited potential of primary mining to challenge China's virtual monopoly in the short term. The high prices of 2010 and 2011 induced some kind of "gold rush for Rare Earths" and to unrealistic projections of production starts that were based on wishful thinking. The required time to investigate the feasibility and environmental impact of a mine as well as the permitting systems in the deposits' countries have slowed down many mining projects. The decline of prices in 2012 led to reconsideration of the feasibility of some mines and made the access to financing more difficult (ERECON, 2015, p. 40). The requirement of high initial capital investments constitutes a market barrier for the entry of new mines while the estimates for their commercial exploitability are fluctuating with market prices. Therefore, most of the advanced projects have been postponed to a later starting date and it is doubtful whether projects in the early stage will be realized at all. Due to the delay of market entries of new mines, the ending of Chinese market power by 2019 as simulated by Pothen (2013b) might also be delayed. In a second simulation of Pothen (2013b), he models an entry delay of new mines of one and two years. The estimated result is an increase of total welfare losses up to -2.92 billion USD in the case of a delay of one year, and an increase up to -4.10 USD in the case of a delay of two years (Pothen, 2013b, p. 24).

Recycling, reuse and secondary sources

Research for recycling opportunities for REEs and the development of new recycling technologies is regarded as one of the most promising activity to counteract high prices on the global market and to secure the global supply. In another simulation of Pothen (2013b), it is shown that China's ability to exert market power declines as assumed recycling costs decline (Pothen, 2013b, p. 22). Furthermore, recycling was named a "low-hanging fruit" by the U.S. DoE because less than 1% of REEs embedded in downstream products are recycled, which leaves a large potential to ramp up efforts to increase recycling rates (U.S. Department of Energy, 2011, p. 128). However, there are different constraints and barriers for REEs recycling. First, recycling needs an efficient collection system due to their relatively short life duration, REEs-containing electronic devices for end consumers like mobile phones are promising end-of-life products for recycling. However, in many electronic devices and applications for end consumers, Rare Earths are contained in minor, dispersed quantities. Efficient recycling of these applications requires high collection rates, which could only be achieved by the cooperation of consumers and a supportive legal framework (ERECON, 2015, p. 48ff.; Golev et al., 2014, p. 55; Haque et al., 2014, p. 626f.; Schueler et al., 2011, p. 108ff.). For example, a law that bans the export of electronic scrap and discarded electronic devices would be required to safeguard high domestic collection and recycling rates (Schueler et al., 2011, p. 165). Another problem for the collection of recycling arises when REEs-containing products are exported to foreign countries in the first place. Seo and Morimoto (2014), who analyze the criticality of dysprosium for Japan, also assess the flow of end-consumer goods that contain dysprosium. Their results show that 30% of dysprosium embedded in automobiles, 6% of dysprosium embedded in home appliances, 61% of dysprosium embedded in devices of factory automation and 100% of dysprosium embedded in hard disk drives were exported to foreign consumer markets, especially to Southeast Asia, North America and the EU. Therefore, the collection system would also have to be installed in these regions. They conclude that domestic recycling is not sufficient to secure the domestic demand for dysprosium.

The second is the lack of information about the quantity of REEs available for recycling. In contrast to Japan, most countries have not surveyed the import and export quantities of REEs, their flow inside their economies and their resulting accumulated stock for some time. Therefore, it is unknown how large the recyclable base of Rare Earths is (ERECON, 2015, p. 60). Thus, the estimation of the recyclable stock is one of the main tasks before a recycling system can be established. Jung et al. (2011) estimate the potential of urban mining for Korea and Japan. Urban mining is defined as "the extraction of metals from discarded consumer electronics or automobiles for reuse after recycling" (Jung et al., 2011, p. 4). They report the potential value of rare metals, which include REMs, in Korean urban mines to be at least 85,800 tons with a value of 2.8 trillion Won at the time of publication. Especially the rare metals embedded in discarded automobiles are an enormous source for recycling. According to the authors, the total value could increase from 2.8 to 33 trillion Won by 2020 due to the increasing demand of rare metals. Japan's urban mining potential is estimated to be one of the highest in the world so that Japan could rely on its urban mine alone to satisfy its annual metal consumption for two to three years. If an efficient recycling system is established, urban mining can easily offset supply instabilities. Rademaker et al. (2013) analyze the recycling potential of especially NdFeB magnets for securing the demand for neodymium and dysprosium on the global and EU-27 levels. The authors focus on three waste flows of permanent magnets: from wind turbines to from hybrid and electric vehicles and hard disk drives. Due to their relative long lifetime, wind turbines, which contain the largest quantities of REEs of all applications, and hybrid and electric vehicles will not be a large source for recycled neodymium and dysprosium until the late 2020s. The recycling potential and the potential recycling supply ratio for both the world and the EU-27 will only increase after 2030, so Rademaker et al. (2013) consider recycling strategies to not be an adequate single solution to solve supply chain issues. Binnemans and Jones (2015) estimate the recycling potentials of all Rare Earths, which result in the more optimistic projection that the global recycling potential would be between 5,600 tons to about 10,700 tons of pure metals. While recycling cannot fully render primary mining redundant, it has the potential to complement it and offset a significant part of REEs mining.

The third barrier is the uncertainty about the profitability of recycling. The historical recycling rates of REEs were diminishingly low due to their low prices. The focus has moved to recycling since 2010 because of high prices that might render recycling profitable. Analogous to efforts to engage in primary mining, declining prices could made recycling unprofitable again. Jung et al. (2011); Schueler et al. (2011) and ERECON (2015) suggest that the collection and recycling system could be established as a network of public-private partnerships. In order to attract private companies, the long-term profitability of recycling would have to be certain. Due to the lack of fully developed commercial scale plants for REEs recycling, there is no information on yields and cost of recycling operations (Haque et al., 2014, p. 626). The risk that recycling might be proven not commercially viable even after prices increased is too high.

The last but not least constraint of recycling is the lack of knowledge in recycling techniques. Metals are normally recovered from electronic waste in pyro-metallurgical plants. Due to their high reactivity with oxygen, REMs easily oxidize in hydro-metallurgical techniques and become a part of the slag. Therefore, traditional techniques for electronic scrap recycling cannot be directly applied to Rare Earths. However, researchers from Germany developed a new process for the recovery from the slag of the pyro-metallurgical treatment of used NiMH batteries while Chinese researcher developed a recovery process based on leaching with sulfuric acid (Schueler et al., 2011, pp. 106–109). Another adequate technique could be the utilization of bacterial bio mining in bioreactors, in which the conditions that are favorable for the bacteria can be exactly controlled. Furthermore, genetically modified bacteria, which work more efficiently and faster, are currently being researched (Donner, 2011). In Japan, the Morishita Jintan Corporation and Osaka Prefecture University are jointly developing a microbe-filled capsule technology. The capsules are placed in a medium containing REMs or other metals, which are then absorbed by the microbes (U.S. Environmental Protection Agency, 2012, p. 5–7). The most economical way of recycling that generates no further waste and requires little input is the direct reuse of REEs materials in the current form and shape. This is especially possible for permanent magnets, for which recycling is technically complicated and very energy intensive (Binnemans & Jones, 2015, p. 7). As a disadvantage, the recovery for reuse requires intensive dismantling, which is predominantly based on the manual labor of workers. With regard to this disadvantage, there has been already been some research. Hitachi announced the development of a dismantling machine for recovering permanent magnets from hard disk drives and compressors that is eight times faster than human workers (Schueler et al., 2011, p. 106). In short, there are several projects that are researching adequate techniques for REEs recycling. Due to the broad diversification of REEs applications, specific recycling techniques might be required for each application. The USA, Japan and the EU are providing financial support for selected ongoing research projects. For example, the U.S. National Science Foundation and industry partners funded the Center for Resource Recovery and Recycling. At their locations at the Colorado School of Mines and Worchester Polytechnic Institute in the USA, and the Katholieke Universiteit Leuven in Belgium, the focus of research is on the developing of technologies to identify and separate electronic scrap, including Rare Earths, from waste streams. The U.S. EPA has provided 2.5 million USD for an UN project for tracking discarded mobile phones and other electronic wastes in order to recover REMs and other valuable materials. Japan formulated the goal of becoming the global hub of REEs recycling and made recycling of REEs mandatory. The METI has initially provided a third of a billion USD for 160 projects focused on ensuring a stable supply of REEs for Japan, which include recycling projects (U.S. Environmental Protection Agency, 2012, pp. 5–12). Nevertheless, despite of all research efforts and financial state support, most of the developed techniques and technologies for REEs recycling have been only demonstrated to be viable on the lab-scale. The 2015 final report of the European Rare Earths Competency Network stresses that “further research is required to take these processes to a commercial scale” (ERECON, 2015, p. 55). While recycling is theoretically the most adequate measure in order to reduce the dependency on Chinese REEs imports and to reduce the balancing problem, its realization is still in its infancy.

In addition to recycling, the recovery of REEs from secondary sources are also investigated. One of these secondary sources are the uranium-pregnant solutions and uranium extraction in Kazakhstan mentioned previously. Another secondary source is the recovery from existing REEs tailings itself. In Baotou, the recovery rate of primary mining was only 10% in the past (Information Office of the State Council, 2012, p. 10). Therefore, there are large quantities of REEs still located in tailings impoundments. As a consequence, Chinese researchers are investigating their recovery possibility. Researchers from the University of Leeds discovered a technique to recover REO as co-products from the processing of titanium dioxide mineral (U.S. Environmental Protection Agency, 2012, pp. 5–7ff.). Similar to the case of recycling, most of these activities are also still in the early stage and cannot secure short-term supply.

Reduction of Rare Earths use

In addition to recycling and recovery, the reduction of the total REEs use is also a viable solution to decrease the level of dependency on REEs imports and to minimize the impact of export restrictions. A reduction of REEs use is mainly achieved by the research and development of substitutes and/or resource-augmenting technologies that increase the use efficiency.

As already explained, there were almost no known and/or adequate substitutes for REEs in the year 2010, which is also incorporated in the different studies of critical assessment. However, there are some reported R&D activities that aim to develop alternative technologies that do not rely on REEs or materials, and which substitute REEs in existing technologies. For example, the U.S. company IBM was reported to have developed an alternative to indium-containing films for solar cells that are based on inexpensive materials like copper, zinc, tin and sulfur and is achieving a performance close to the level that is required for commercialization. Researchers from the University of California worked on a replacement for indium used on transparent conductors in electronic displays. In the field of magnets, the possibility to substitute REEs with iron nitride is researched in the Rare Metal Materials Development Project of the New Energy and Industrial Technology Development Organization of Japan. The Ames Laboratory is working on methods for making NdFeB magnets less expensive but also on magnets based on the Alnico[4] iron-alloy family or iron-boron-based alloys (U.S. Environmental Protection Agency, 2012, pp. 5–10f.). In the fields of batteries, lithium-ion batteries are seen to become the most used battery type in the near future. Consumers can choose to use either a NiMH or lithium-ion battery in Toyota's Prius models since 2010. In the application fields of mobile phones and notebooks, lithium-ion batteries have already superseded NiMH batteries (Schueler et al., 2011, p. 100f.). In the field of lighting, the transition from fluorescent light bulbs to LEDs, which contain less REEs, will reduce the total use of Rare Earths. When the use of organic LEDs and halogen incandescent, which both do not require any REEs, expands, the demand for terbium, europium and yttrium for lighting purposes will sharply decline. In the field of hybrid and electric mobility, the "Advanced Research

Projects Agency-Energy" awarded General Atomics and the University of Dallas with a 2.8 million USD for the development of a switched reluctance motor that incorporates the advances in electronic control and precision machining of motor parts in order to eliminate the noise problems of this motor type (U.S. Department of Energy, 2011, pp. 20–23). In Japan, both NEDO and Toyota are developing hybrid vehicles that solely relate on ferrite magnets (U.S. Environmental Protection Agency, 2012, p. 5–11). In the field of catalysts, producers are also working on next-generation catalysts with lower or near-zero REEs content. The U.S. firms Grace and Albemarle offer catalysts with a REEs content of 0.2 and 0.5 weight percent, respectively. The usual weight content of REEs-based catalysts is between 10 to 13% (U.S. Department of Energy, 2011, p. 17f.).

The dilemma of substitution is the time horizon. The commercialization of new materials usually requires between 12 to 15 years (National Academy of Sciences, 2000, p. 13) so that a materials-level substitution is a long-term solution. A systems-based substitution, which is based on the use of technologies and designs that do not require REEs, is not always a satisfactory solution. In many fields of application, especially in the field of permanent magnets, REEs-based systems are the most efficient, best performing option. Here, the substitution of REEs are resulting in cost reduction but also in losses in performance and efficiency. Thus, the R&D for resource-augmenting technologies might be the preferable solution for the reduction of total REEs demand. In the field of magnets, a project at the University of Delaware, which aims to develop high-strength magnetic material from neodymium, iron and boron nanoparticles, has received funding. The amount of required neodymium is thought to be smaller than in traditional NdFeB magnets while the magnetization should be on the same level. The Ames Laboratory is also researching a magnet based on nanostructured compounds made from combinations of REEs and transition metals. GE Global Research has received 2.25 million USD from the U.S. DoE for the project "Transformational Nanostructured Permanent Magnets", which should develop bulk nanostructured magnetic materials that include lower REEs contents (U.S. Environmental Protection Agency, 2012, p. 5–11). There is also some room for an international cooperation with China in order to increase the production efficiency of REEs utilization in the Chinese magnet production. Magnets are mainly produced in blocks and then cut to the desired shape. As consequence, between 20–30% of magnets are scrapped during the manufacturing stage and tons of neodymium and praseodymium are wasted due to problems in the direct recycling of magnetic materials. The patents for "press to shape" techniques are in the possession of Japanese and Western companies (Schueler et al., 2011, pp. 99, 106). A technological cooperation that exchanges magnet production techniques for Chinese produce magnets might reduce total global demand of REEs.

In summary, a systems-based substitution is possible in the short-term in order to reduce the total demand in Rare Earths but also implicates a step backward to last-generation technologies in many fields of application. Next-generation technologies that are on a comparable or even higher level of performance and efficiency than REEs-based technologies are currently being in the development or have been already developed but have not been yet adopted by producers and/or consumers of final products. Due to the long period required for the commercialization of new materials, materials-level substitution is not likely to be a solution until the late-2020s. As illustrated in a few selected projects, there are currently ongoing efforts in R&D of resource-augmenting technologies that reduce the required content of REEs in existing systems. It is unclear when and if these efforts will result in marketable goods or technologies. According to the Jevons paradox, these new goods and technologies might not reduce the total demand for REEs even when they require relatively lower amounts of them. The reduction of the neodymium content in NdFeB magnets might give the drive for building capacities of wind energy generation as part of global clean strategies a big push so that the relative decrease of REEs use per wind turbine is offset by the scale effect. Overall, the reduction of REEs use is rather achievable in the medium-to-long term instead of the short term.

Joint complaint before the World Trade Organization

On 13 March 2012, the EU, the USA and Japan announced that they "had asked the World Trade Organization to facilitate formal consultations with China over its limits on rare-earth exports" (Grasso, 2013, p. 7). While it was the first time that Japan filed a WTO complaint against China, the EU and the USA were confident that their complaint would be successful because, in 2011, the WTO decided in a similar complaint against Chinese export restrictions of raw materials including bauxite, fluorspar, manganese and coke in the favor of the complainants USA, EU and Mexico (Jebe et al., 2012, p. 581). The claims of the USA, the EU and Japan consequently followed the claims of the previous WTO dispute settlement process. The complainants argued that the export restrictions of REEs through imposing quotas, export duties, export licensing requirements and an implicit minimum export price system would violate China's obligations under the GATT 1994 and under its Accession Protocol. The three complainants stressed that this trade regime would especially violate WTO rules because it imposed prohibited quantitative restrictions on Rare Earths and is not administered in a uniform, impartial, reasonable or transparent manner. The violated, specific GATT 1994 articles are Article VII (Valuation for Customs Purposes), Article VIII (Fees and Formalities connected with Importation and Exportation), Article X (Publication and Administration of Trade Regulations) and Article XI (General Elimination of Quantitative Restrictions). The trade regime was also claimed to violate paragraphs 2(A) 2 and 2(C) 1 (Administration of the Trade Regime and Transparency), 5.1 and 5.2 (Right to Trade), 7.2 (Non-Tariff Measures), 82. (Import and Export Licensing) and 11.3 (Taxes and Charges Levied on Imports and Exports) of China's Accession Protocol (Jebe et al., 2012, p. 592ff.; Van Calster, 2013, p. 118). Here, especially paragraph 11.3 offers a huge possibility to challenge the Chinese REEs trade regime. This paragraph determines that "China shall eliminate all taxes and charges applied to exports unless specifically provided for in Annex 6 of this Protocol or applied in conformity with the provisions of Article VIII of the GATT 1994" (World Trade

Organization, 2001). Rare Earths are not included in Annex 6 so that the Accession Protocol cannot justify export duties imposed on them. Article VIII of the GATT 1994 allows fees and other charges on imports and exports when they are equal to the actual services rendered for them. These charges must not have the goal of protecting domestic industries or creating revenues (Matsushita, 2012, p. 411).

The Chinese defense before the Panel of the dispute settlement body[5] was also the same in both WTO trials. The imposing of export restrictions would be justified under Article XX (b) and (g) of GATT 1994, which allow exceptions for trade restriction as measures "necessary to protect human, animal or plant life or health" (Article XX (b)) or "relating to the conservation of exhaustible natural resources if such measures are made effective in conjunction with restrictions on domestic production or consumption" (Article XX (g)) (World Trade Organization, n.d. b). This argumentation emphasizes the narrative that China's primary goals of export restrictions of REEs are connected to environmental concerns and to promoting intergenerational equity through resource conservation. According to Charlier and Guillou (2014), who analyze the distortion effects of export quotas, quotas would only lead to a decreased total extraction quantity when the domestic demand elasticity is smaller than the foreign demand elasticity. Therefore, the imposing of quotas, and the subsequent increase of prices on the global market and the decrease of prices on the domestic prices lead to demand declines on the global market that are larger than the demand increases on the domestic market. As consequence, the total consumption would decrease (Charlier & Guillou, 2014, p. 327). Therefore, Article XX (g) formulates the requirement that also the domestic production and consumption have to be effectively restricted in order to reduce the total demand and production for exhaustible natural resources. An adequate measure would be the imposing of an additional consumption tax only for domestic consumer that brings domestic and global prices on the same level. Furthermore, export quotas are not generally regarded as an efficient measure for resource conservation. The best solution for resource conservation would be a direct tax on the extraction and production of natural resources instead of a combination of two measures. Consequently, the Panel assessed that China's reregulation measures, which even included measures for the domestic production sector in conjunction with export restrictions, were predominantly intended to establish a discriminating dual price system in order to secure the supply for domestic downstream industries. The Panel also judged that the Chinese restrictions on domestic production is not sufficient because they did not reduce the domestic demand and effectively promote the conservation of Rare Earths (Bond & Trachtman, 2015, pp. 8–16). The export restrictions are therefore not justified under Article XX (g). Furthermore, the Panel interpreted paragraph 11.3 of the Chinese Accession Protocol to generally outlaw the imposing of export duties so that China would not able to invoke Article XX (b) or other articles with general exceptions (Ribeiro, 2014, p. 86). This enforced the Chinese view that China would be a second-class member of the WTO that had to accept additional obligations on accession but received fewer rights (Hilpert, 2014, p. 12). Due to its strict Accession Protocol, China does not have the same rights as other WTO members do. Although the Panel judged that China could rely on Article XX (g) in order to impose export licenses, it also emphasized that China failed to explain why its system was justified under the provision. The Chinese system of export licenses would therefore be another violation of China's obligations. The Panel report of all findings was then issued to China, the USA, the EU and Japan as involved parties on 21 November 2013 and then circulated to all WTO members on 26 March 2014. On 25 April 2014, China appealed the Panel report so that the WTO Appellate Body, which reviews the Panel reports and has the power to uphold, modify or reverse their legal findings, initiated oral hearings (World Trade Organization, 2015). The result of the Appellation proceedings finally confirmed the findings of the Panel that China's system of export duties and quotas imposed on REEs is violating its WTO obligation and therefore has to be abolished on 7 August 2014 (European Commission, 2014).

As consequence of the WTO ruling, China abolished the system of export quotas on 1 January 2015, and finally terminated export duties on 1 May 2015 (METI, 2015). On the same day, the Chinese Ministry of Finance imposed an adjusted ad valorem resource tax system. The taxes are set at 11.5% for light REEs from Inner Mongolia, at 9.5% for light REEs from Sichuan, at 7.5% for light REEs from Shandong and at 27% for medium and heavy REEs ("China reforms resource tax", 2015). Thus, China switched to the first best solution of a direct tax, which lead to price increase of REMs. In the case of the highly demanded, critically heavy REEs, producers are likely to pass on a large share of the new tax to the consumers while a pass through is less likely in the case of excessively produced light REEs. As a consequence, especially heavy REEs prices would increase on the domestic and global market, which might lead to reduced demand and a delay of their exhaustion.

In summary, the joint complaint of the EU, the USA and Japan before the WTO has proven to be an effective short-term measure to decrease the urgency of fast developments in the fields of the 3Rs "recycling, reuse and reduce" and to ease the pressure of high REEs prices resulting from Chinese export restrictions. However, declining global prices have also induced a reconsideration especially of primary mining. The shares of Molycorp were initially sold in a July 2010 initial public offering at 14 USD per share. The share value increased due the China's imposing export restrictions and an investment boom in REEs-related securities, and finally climaxed at 79.26 USD per share in 2011. Due to declining price delays in the production start at Mountain Pass, Molycop reported annual losses for the years 2012 through 2014. Its share subsequently decreased to 0.36 USD in late June 2015, just before Molycorp filed for bankruptcy (McCarty & Casey, 2015). This illustrates the high risk of new REEs' primary mining projects that require high initial capital investment and a constant level of adequate high prices. Most countries and companies have a lack of experience due to the past abandonment of extraction of Rare Earths outside of China and might not be able to estimate effectively how high "adequate prices" are. Thus, primary mining cannot be regarded as a solution to reduce the import dependency of Chinese REEs especially after the abolishment of the dual pricing system as a consequence of the WTO ruling.

Implications for the future optimal extraction path

The measures of reregulation have several implications for the optimal future extraction path based on the Hotelling path. While the consolidation of the industry, which is supported by setting new high environmental standards, is expected to increase the Chinese market concentration in the field of REEs, this has no impact on the extraction rates based on a constant-elasticity demand curve. While production quotas were in effect before 2010, they were effectively non-binding due to a high level of uncontrolled extraction either in illegal mines or in mines that extracted REEs in excess of their quotas. Here, the consolidation should lead to the compliance of all legal REEs mines with allocated quotas, whereas inspection tours should curb illegal mining activities. The reduction of mining licenses should also eliminate the previously existing common-pool externalities and the resulting voracity effect. In addition, to be an auxiliary means to achieve consolidation, the environmental reregulation has also a theoretical impact on the optimal extraction path. The required investments in order to comply with the new and stricter regulations are fixed costs that are not directly included in Hotelling's original considerations. Siebert (1983) shows that an increase in fixed costs have an implicit impact on the extraction rates because they reduce the level of scarcity rents. As a consequence, the extraction rates in each period will rise and mines are exhausted earlier (Siebert, 1983, p. 267). At the same time, the raising of the volume-based resources taxes leads to an increase of the marginal costs of extraction. As discussed in Chapter 4, this will lead to initial lower extraction rates rather than in the original extraction path and a delay of exhaustion. The establishment of a dual pricing system through imposed export restrictions has two implications. First, REEs companies that are licensed to export will fully make use of their export quotas in order to benefit from higher global market prices. These high international prices are also an impetus for some economic agents to illegally mine and smuggle REEs out of China. The decline of prices on the domestic market have the same effect as increasing marginal costs. The initial extractions rates further decrease, and the date of exhaustion is further postponed.

It was discussed that the activities of exploration and development of new mines in the RoW were not very fruitful as most projects were delayed. Therefore, the impact on the optimal Chinese extraction path can be assumed to be infinitesimally small. The R&D of substitutes will only bring results in the long term. Due to the large variety of different REEs uses, it is more likely that substitutes for specific fields of end-use applications than one perfect substitute for all applications will be developed. Instead of a switch from a constant-elasticity demand curve to an inverse linear demand curve, as it is shown in Chapter 4, the elasticity of the demand curve will subsequently increase as the substitutability increases. This would lead to initially lower extraction rates that increase over time. When REEs prices are high enough to make recycling profitable and an adequate collection system is fully established, then recycling will have the same impact as the exploration and development of new deposits. The stock of resources available in urban mines is added to the stock of primary mines. The level of the price path sharply declines and extraction rates increase. Thus, the price level before the start of recycling has to be so high that recycling is still profitable after the price slump. The development of resource-augmenting technologies might have two diverging impacts. When they effectively decrease the total REEs demand, then the effect is that the demand curve shifts inwards. Net prices are required to decrease in order to increase the demand in every period. The time until exhaustion is lengthened. When resource-augmenting technologies lead to an increased total demand, then the net prices are required to increase in order to reduce the demand in every period. The date of exhaustion is also shortened. This would be an adverse effect neither desired by China nor especially the EU, whose most important strategy for securing resource supply is the promotion of efficient resource use.

The elimination of the trade restrictions as a consequence of the WTO trial would normally implicate a convergence of REEs markets and prices. When trade costs are neglected, Chinese REEs companies should be indifferent between the sale of REEs on domestic market or the global market. The adjustment of the tax system and the adoption of an ad valorem resource tax seems to be intended as a means to increase the REE prices on all markets and to lower extraction rates. This would delay the date of exhaustion. However, the largest impact on the Hotelling path has to be expected from a successful, full consolidation of the Chinese industry. When 80% of the production quotas is finally in the hand of six conglomerates under the control of the central government, discretionary power could be used in order to distribute Rare Earths rather to the domestic downstream industry than to foreign companies. The system of binding and enforced production quotas would transform the extraction path to be compatible with Rawls's criterion. This flat extraction path would be not optimal according to the Hotelling rule but might lead to a greater conservation and intergenerational equity. At the same time, it supports the goal of the Chinese government of retaining the lion's share of Chinese REEs in order to upgrade the domestic industrial structure. As a consequence, the physical unavailability of REEs outside China would again lead to increasing prices on the global market and to increasing efforts in the development of primary mining, and R&D in the fields of the 3Rs. According to the official stance of the State Council, it is the preferred long-term scenario that countries with REEs deposits would make active efforts in developing their own resources. This would help to diversify the supply and expand the international trade of Rare Earths (Information Office of the State Council, 2012, p. 31). Appropriately, Schlinkert and Van den Boogaart (2015) point out that the Chinese main interest is not the maintaining and protection of the virtual monopoly but the promotion of the transformation of the global REEs markets. The Chinese REEs consumption is still growing faster than the consumption of the RoW, and the country will become a net importer in the near future. Thus, the securing of resource supply in order to build up a leading position in high technology sectors is more important than any attempts to maintain market power (Schlinkert et al., 2015, p. 278).

Intermediate conclusion

As analyzed in this chapter, the impact of the Global Financial Crisis has given impetus for a new wave of reregulation and adjustments in the regulatory framework of the Chinese Rare Earths sector. While mild attempts of reregulation that aimed to eliminate basic underlying problems of REEs extraction in China – high environmental pollution, low market prices and fast depletion rates as consequences of excessive mining – were unsuccessfully conducted before the GFC, the GFC illustrated the urgency of an extensive and rapid reregulation due to the importance of REEs for rebalancing the Chinese economic growth path. The imposed measures of reregulation consisted of the reduction of domestic production quotas, production licenses, the promotion of M&As and the issuance of new industry standards in order to enforce a consolidation of the domestic industry towards the establishment of six State-controlled companies, the reduction of export quotas and export licenses as well as the increase of export duties in order to retain a larger share of the domestic production inside China, and the issuance of new and stricter environmental standards and laws as well as the raising of the resource tax in order to reduce the environmental impact of REEs mining and processing. These measures also changed the situation of the Chinese virtual monopoly that was in place since the later 1990s. Prior to 2010, Chinese REEs producers had a large accumulated market share but no monopolistic market power because they did not form a cartel in order to act as a unitary economic actor. Especially due to the export restrictions, China's market and price-setting power on foreign REEs markets increased, a dual price, which benefitted Chinese downstream industries and foreign mining companies and disadvantaged Chinese mining companies and foreign end-users, was established and global welfare was distributed in favor of China.

As countermeasures, the three main REEs consuming economies outside China, the EU, the USA and Japan, transformed their resource policy to embrace more R&D efforts in the 3Rs "recycling, reuse and reduction". In addition to State-funded projects, numerous research projects in the 3Rs emerged that aimed at the development of recycling techniques and processes, of material-based or systems-based substitution possibilities or of resource-augmenting technologies. Furthermore, high global REEs prices also fostered the exploration and development of new deposits and mines outside of China. However, the 3Rs were analyzed to be an adequate solution to reduce the import dependency of Chinese Rare Earths only in the medium-to-long term. Most projects in primary mining were delayed due to uncertainties about their economic feasibility and/or regulatory obstructions in the permitting process, whereas Molycorp, the firm that reopened its Mountain Pass mine, had to file for bankruptcy in June 2015. This led to reconsiderations of the adequacy of primary mining as adequate short-term means to secure the global REEs supply. The joint WTO complaint of the USA, Japan and the EU has proven to be a short-term solution as both the Panel and the Appellate Body decided that the Chinese system of export restrictions violated China's WTO obligation and had to be abolished. China failed to prove that its primary goal was the reduction of the environmental impact of REEs mining and production, and of extraction rates. As consequence, China eliminated export quotas and export duties in 2015 and readjusted the resource tax as a first best solution. While the WTO judgment reduced the urgency of the rest of the world of finding alternatives for Chinese REEs in the short term, it did not eliminate the necessity to develop mines outside of China and strategies of REEs recycling, reuse and reduction. When the full consolidation of the Chinese REEs industry is finally achieved, then the State's discretionary power instead of a discriminatory trade system could limit the physical availability of Rare Earths on the global market as a consequence of securing the supply on China's domestic market. This is reflected in the official position of the Chinese State Council that the rest of the world should make active efforts in developing their own resources. Furthermore, the extraction path after the full consolidation is expected to significantly diverge from the scenarios of the optimal futures extraction paths based on the Hotelling rule, which were modeled in Chapter 4. When production quotas become fully binding and enforceable, the extraction path will rather be based on the Rawl's criterion and adjusted to meet the demands of the domestic industry. As a side effect, this extraction path might lead to a delay of resource exhaustion and therefore to a greater intergenerational equity

Appendix

China's REEs export duty rates

Export duty rate (%)

Year / *Commodity*	*2007*	*2008*	*2009*	*2010*	*2011–2014*
Yttrium oxide	10	25	25	25	25
Lanthanum oxide	10	15	15	15	15
Cerium oxide, hydroxide, carbonate and others	10	15	15	15	15
Praseodymium	NA	NA	NA	NA	NA
Neodymium oxide	10	15	15	15	15
Europium and its oxide	10	25	25	25	25
Gadolinium	NA	NA	NA	NA	NA
Terbium and its oxide, chloride, and carbonate	10	25	25	25	25
Dysprosium oxide, chloride, and carbonate	10	25	25	25	25
Holmium	NA	NA	NA	NA	NA
Erbium	NA	NA	NA	NA	NA
Thulium	NA	NA	NA	NA	NA
Ytterbium	NA	NA	NA	NA	NA
Lutetium	NA	NA	NA	NA	NA
Other REO	10	15	15	15	15
Mixed Rare Earth chlorides and fluorides	10	15	15	15	15
Mixed Rare Earth carbonates	10	15	15	15	15
Mixed Rare Earth, yttrium, and scandium compounds and metals (including battery grade)	10	25	25	25	25
Non-mixed Rare Earth carbonates	10	15	15	15	15
Rare Earths Ore	10	10	15	15	15
Metals:					
Lanthanum	NA	NA	NA	NA	25
Cerium	NA	NA	NA	NA	25
Neodymium	10	15	15	15	15
Dysprosium	NA	NA	NA	25	25
Other mixed metals	NA	NA	NA	25	25

Source: Data retrieved from Tse, 2011, p. 8.

Notes

1 The State Planning Commission managed central economic planning and designed the Five-Year-Plans from 1952 to 1998, when it was renamed as the State Development Planning Commission. In 2003, it merged with other agencies in order to form the National Reform and Development Commission, which is currently the highest administrative body for economic, social and environmental regulation, controlling and monitoring.
2 The export rate is sometimes reported to be 17% in some articles, for example in Ting and Seaman (2013) and He (2014). It is not clear where this discrepancy stems from.
3 Although Greenland is geographically a part of North America, it is considered a part of Europe in most articles about global deposits due to its location within the Danish realm and its strong association with Europe even after Greenland's exit from the EU in 1984.
4 Alnico stands for aluminium-nickel-cobalt.
5 "Settling disputes is the responsibility of the Dispute Settlement Body (the General Council in another guise), which consists of all WTO members. The Dispute Settlement Body has the sole authority to establish 'panels' of experts to consider the case, and to accept or reject the panels' findings or the results of an appeal. It monitors the implementation of the rulings and recommendations, and has the power to authorize retaliation when a country does not comply with a ruling" (World Trade Organization, n.d. a).

Bibliography

Baotou Steel integrates 12 rare earth producers. (2012, December 28). *China Daily*. Retrieved from www.chinadaily.com.cn/china/2012-12/28/content_16066356.htm.

Batson, A. (2010, December 15). Not really 'Made in China'. *The Wall Street Journal*. Retrieved from www.wsj.com/articles/SB10001424052748704828104576021142902413796.

Baumol, W. J. (1972). On taxation and the control externalities. *The American Economic Review*, *62*(3), 307–322.

Biedermann, R. P. (2014). China's rare earth sector: Between domestic consolidation and global hegemony. *International Journal of Emerging Markets*, *9*(2), 276–293.

Binnemans, K., & Jones, P. T. (2015). Rare earths and the balance problem. *Journal of Sustainable Metallurgy*, *1*(1), 29–38.

Bond, E. W., & Trachtman, J. (2015). *China-rare earths: Export restrictions and the limits of textual interpretation* (EUI Working Paper RSCAS 2015/66). Retrieved from http://cadmus.eui.eu/bitstream/handle/1814/37056/RSCAS_2015_66.pdf.

Bradsher, K. (2010, December 29). In China, illegal rare earth mines face crackdown. *The New York Times*. Retrieved from www.nytimes.com/2010/12/30/business/global/30smuggle.html?pagewanted=pr&_r=0.

British Chamber of Commerce. (Trans.) (2011). *China's twelfth five plan (2011–2015): The full English version*. Retrieved from www.britishchamber.cn/content/chinas-twelfth-five-year-plan-2011-2015-full-english-version.

British Geological Survey. (2011). *Mineral profile: Rare Earth Elements*. Retrieved from www.bgs.ac.uk/downloads/start.cfm?id=1638.

Buetikofer, R. (2010, September 2). When rare earths get rarer. *The New York Times*. Retrieved from www.nytimes.com/2010/09/03/opinion/03iht-edbutikofer.html?_r=2&ref=global-home.

Buetikofer, R. (2014). *Seltene Erden und die Neuentdeckung der Rohstoffpolitik* [Rare earths and the rediscovery of resource policy]. Retrieved from http://reinhardbuetikofer.eu/publikationen/seltene-erden-und-die-neuentdeckung-der-rohstoffpolitik/.

Charlier, C., & Guillou, S. (2014). Distortion effects of export quota policy: An analysis of the China-Raw Materials dispute. *China Economic Review*, *31*, 320–338.

China reforms resource tax for rare earths. (2015, May 1). *China Daily Europe*. Retrieved from http://europe.chinadaily.com.cn/business/2015-05/01/content_20596832.htm.

De Beule, F., & Van den Bulcke, D. (2010). The global crisis, foreign direct investment and China. *BICCS Asia Paper*, *5*(6), 1–31.

Devarajan, S., Go, D., Schiff, M., & Suthiwart-Narueput, S. (1996). *The whys and why nots of export taxation* (The World Bank Policy Research Working Paper No. 1684). Retrieved from http://documents.worldbank.org/curated/en/895731468740209055/The-whys-and-why-nots-of-export-taxation.

Dong, B., & Torgler, B. (2010). *The causes of corruption: Evidence from China* (Fondazione Eni Enrico Mattei Working Paper No. 72.2010). Retrieved from https://papers.ssrn.com/sol3/papers.cfm?abstract_id=1628107.

Donner, S. (2011, February 10). *Biomining: Bakterien als Goldgräber* [Biomining: Bacteria as gold diggers]. *Wirtschaftswoche*. Retrieved from www.wiwo.de/technologie/biomining-bakterien-als-goldgraeber/5241056.html.

Economy, E. (2005). Environmental enforcement in China. In K. A. Day (Ed.), *China's environment and the challenge of sustainable development* (pp. 102–120). Armonk and London: M.E. Sharpe.

Elsner, H., Buchholz, P., Schmitz, M., & Altangerel, T. (2011). *Industrial minerals and selected rare metals in Mongolia: An investors' guide, prepared by the Government of Mongolia, funded by Federal Ministry of Economic Cooperation and Development of the Federal Republic of Germany through the Federal Institute for Geosciences and Natural Resources (BGR)*. Retrieved from www.deutsche-rohstoffagentur.de/DE/Themen/Min_rohstoffe/Downloads/investorenhandbuch_mongolei_endbericht.pdf?__blob=publicationFile&v=5.

ERECON. (2015). *Strengthening the European rare earths supply-chain: Challenges and policy options*. Brussels: European Commission.

European Commission. (2011a). *A resource-efficient Europe: Flagship initiative under the Europe 2020 strategy: Communication from the commission to the European parliament, the council, the European economic and social committee and the committee of the regions*. Brussels: European Commission.

European Commission. (2011b). *Tackling the challenges in commodity markets and on raw materials: Communication from the commission to the European parliament, the council, the European economic and social committee and the committee of the regions*. Brussels: European Commission.

European Commission. (2014). *WTO appellate body confirms: China's export restrictions on rare earths and other raw materials illegal*. Retrieved from http://europa.eu/rapid/press-release_MEMO-14-504_en.htm.

European Parliament. (2011). *Report on an effective raw materials strategy for Europe. Rapporteur: Reinhard Buetikofer*. Brussels: European Commission.

Fabre, G. (2013). *The lion's share: What's behind China's economic slowdown* (FMSH-WP-2013–53). Retrieved from https://hal.archives-ouvertes.fr/halshs-00874077/document.

Ferris, Jr., R. J., & Zhang, H. (2005). Environmental law in the People's Republic of China: An overview describing challenges and providing insights for good governance. In K. A. Day (Ed.), *China's environment and the challenge of sustainable development* (pp. 66–101). Armonk and London: M.E. Sharpe.

Fifarek, B. J., Veloso, F. M., & Davidson, C. I. (2008). Offshoring technology innovation: A cause study of rare-earth technology. *Journal of Operations Management*, *26*, 222–238.

Fliess, B., & Mard, T. (2012). *Taking stock of measures restricting the export of raw materials: Analysis of OECD inventory data* (OECD Trade Policy Papers No. 140). Retrieved from http://dx.doi.org/10.1787/5k91gdmdjbtc-en.

Frontier Rare Earths. (2012). *Frontier rare earths and Korea resources corporation significantly expand strategic partnership to develop the Zandkopsdrift rare earth project.* Retrieved from www.frontierrareearths.com/wp-content/uploads/2012/02/Frontier-Kores%20Update_23Oct2012.pdf.

Frontier Rare Earths. (2015). *Zandkopsdrift: The world's next major rare earth producer.* Retrieved from www.frontierrareearths.com/wp-content/uploads/2015/06/Frontier-Corporate-Presentation-June-2015.pdf.

Gang, C. (2009). *Politics of China's environmental protection: Problems and progress* (Series on Contemporary China Vol. 17). New Jersey et al.: World Scientific Publishing.

Goldman, J. A. (2014). The U.S. rare earth industry: Its growth and decline. *The Journal of Policy History*, *26*(2), 139–166.

Golev, A., Scott, M., Erskine, P. D., Ali, S. H., & Ballantyne, G. R. (2014). Rare earths supply chains: Current status, constraints and opportunities. *Resources Policy*, *41*, 52–59.

Grasso, V. B. (2013). *Rare Earth Elements in national defense: Background, oversight issues, and options for Congress* (CRS Report for Congress R41744). Retrieved from www.fas.org/sgp/crs/natsec/R41744.pdf.

Haque, N., Hughes, A., Lim, S., & Vernon, C. (2014). Rare Earth Elements: Overview of mining, mineralogy, uses, sustainability and environmental impact. *Resources*, *3*(4), 614–635.

Hayes-Labruto, L., Schillebeeckx, S. J. D., Workman, M., & Shah, N. (2013). Contrasting perspectives on China's rare earths policies: Reframing the debate through a stakeholder lens. *Energy Policy*, *63*, 55–68.

He, Y. (2014). Reregulation of China's rare earth production and export. *International Journal of Emerging Markets*, *9*(2), 236–256.

Hilpert, H. G. (2014). *China's trade policy: Dominance with the will to lead* (German Institute for International and Security Affairs Research Paper 1/ 2014). Berlin: German Institute for International and Security Affairs.

Holbig, H., & Gilley, B. (2010). Reclaiming legitimacy in China. *Politics & Policy*, *38*(3), 395–422.

Information Office of the State Council. (2012). *Situation and policies of China's rare earth industry*. Beijing: Foreign Languages Press.

Jacobsen, J. (2014, January 8). Analysts: Chinese consolidation of rare earths sector to have limited impact on global market. *SNL Metals & Mining*. Retrieved from https://www1.snl.com/InteractiveX/Article.aspx?cdid=A-26478811-12330.

Jebe, R., Mayer, D., & Lee, Y.-S. (2012). China's export restrictions of raw materials and rare earths: A new balance between free trade and environmental protection? *The George Washington International Law Review*, *44*(4), 579–642.

Jepson, N. (2012). *A 21st century scramble: South Africa, China and the rare earth metals industry* (South African Institute of International Affairs occasional paper No. 113). Retrieved from www.saiia.org.za/occasional-papers/a-21st-century-scramble-south-africa-china-and-the-rare-earth-metals-industry.html.

Jung, H.-S., Kim, H.-N., & Choi, M.-H. (2011). *Assessing the potential value of rare metals in urban mines: A comparative look at Korea and Japan* (Samsung Economic Research Institute Monthly Focus No. 8). Retrieved from www.seriworld.org/01/wldIssueV.html?mn=B&mncd=0203&p_page=5&key=20110920000001.

Kilby, C. (2014). China's rare earth trade: Health and the environment. *The China Quarterly, 218*, 540–550.

Kim, J. (2010). *Recent trends in export restrictions* (OECD Trade Policy Papers No. 101). Paris: OECD Publishing.

Korinek, J., & Kim, J. (2010). *Export restrictions on strategic raw materials and their impact on trade* (OECD Trade Policy Papers No. 95). OECD Publishing. Retrieved from http://dx.doi.org/10.1787/5kmh8pk441g8-en.

Lardy, N., & Borst, N. (2013). *A blueprint for rebalancing the Chinese economy* (Peterson Institute for International Economics Policy Brief No. PB13–02). Retrieved from https://piie.com/publications/policy-briefs/blueprint-rebalancing-chinese-economy.

Liu, H., Lei, L., & Ye, C. (2013). Study on rare earth management game between central and local governments in China. *Cross-Cultural Communication, 9*(1), 31–35.

Liu, L. (2009). Impact of the Global Financial Crisis on China: Empirical evidence and policy implications. *China & World Economy, 17*(6), 1–23.

Mancheri, N. A. (2015). World trade in rare earths, Chinese export restrictions, and implications. *Resources Policy, 46*(2), 262–271.

Market Wired. (2014). *Great Western Minerals reports feasibility study results for Steenkampskraal Rare Earth Element project*. Retrieved from www.marketwired.com/press-release/great-western-minerals-reports-feasibility-study-results-steenkampskraal-rare-earth-tsx-venture-gwg-1908184.htm.

Massari, S., & Ruberti, M. (2013). Rare earth elements as critical raw materials: Focus on international markets and future strategies. *Resources Policy, 38*(1), 36–43.

Matsushita, M. (2012). A note on the appellate body report in the Chinese minerals export restrictions case. *Trade, Law and Development, 4*(2), 400–420.

Mazza, M., Blumenthal, D., & Schmitt, G. J. (2013). *Ensuring Japan's critical resource security: Case studies in Rare Earth Element and natural gas supplies*. Washington, DC: American Enterprise Institute. Retrieved from www.aei.org/papers/foreign-and-defense-policy/regional/asia/ensuring-japans-critical-resource-security-case-studies-in-rare-earth-element-and-natural-gas-supplies/.

McCarty, D., & Casey, S. (2015, June 25). Molycorp files for bankruptcy as rare-earth prices drop. *Bloomberg*. Retrieved from www.bloomberg.com/news/articles/2015-06-25/molycorp-files-for-bankruptcy-proposes-debt-restructuring-plan.

METI. (2015). *Termination of China's export duties on three raw materials including rare earths*. Retrieved from www.meti.go.jp/english/press/2015/0501_01.html.

Morgenstern, R. D., Pizer, W. A., & Shih, J.-S. (2001). The cost of environmental protection. *The Review of Economics and Statistics, 83*(4), 732–738.

Morrison, W. M. (2009). *China and the Global Financial Crisis: Implications for the United States* (CRS Report for Congress 22984). Retrieved from www.fas.org/sgp/crs/row/RS22984.pdf.

Morrison, W. M., & Tang, R. (2012). *China's rare earth industry and export regime: Economic and trade implications for the United States* (CRS Report for Congress 42510). Retrieved from www.fas.org/sgp/crs/row/R42510.pdf.

Mueller, M., Schweizer, D., & Seiler, V. (2014). *Wealth effects of rare earth prices and China's Rare Earth Elements policy* (Center for International Economics Working Paper Series No. 2014–13). Retrieved from http://groups.uni-paderborn.de/wp-wiwi/RePEc/pdf/ciepap/WP88.pdf.

National Academy of Sciences. (2000). *Materials in the new millennium: Responding to Society's needs: Proceedings of the 2000 national materials advisory board forum*. Washington, DC: The National Academies Press.

National Research Council. (2008). *Minerals, critical minerals, and the U.S. economy*. Washington, DC: The National Academies Press.

OECD. (2013). *OECD economic survey: China 2013*. Paris: OECD Publishing.

Overholt, W. H. (2010). China in the Global Financial Crisis: Rising influence, rising challenges. *The Washington Quarterly*, *33*(1), 21–34.

Papp, J. F., Bray, E. L., Edelstein, D. L., Fenton, M. D., Guberman, D. E., Hedrick, J. B., . . . Tolcin, A. C. (2008). *Factors that influence the price of Al, Cd, Co, Cu, Fe, Ni, Pb, Rare Earth Elements, and Zn* (U.S. Geological Survey Open-File Report 2008–1356). Retrieved from https://pubs.er.usgs.gov/publication/ofr20081356.

Piermartini, R. (2004). *The role of export taxes in the field of primary commodities* (WTO Economic Research and Statistic Division Discussion Paper No. 4). Retrieved from www.wto.org/english/res_e/booksp_e/discussion_papers4_e.pdf.

Pigou, A. C. (1932). *The economics of welfare* (4th ed.). Retrieved from Library of Economics and Liberty, www.econlib.org/library/NPDBooks/Pigou/pgEW20.html.

Pothen, F. (2013a). *Dynamic market power in an exhaustible resource industry: The case of Rare Earth Elements* (ZEW Discussion Paper No. 14–005). Retrieved from http://ftp.zew.de/pub/zew-docs/dp/dp14005.pdf.

Pothen, F. (2013b). *The metal resources (METRO) model: A dynamic partial equilibrium model for metal markets applied to Rare Earth Elements* (ZEW Discussion Paper No. 13–112). Retrieved from http://ftp.zew.de/pub/zew-docs/dp/dp13112.pdf. 22.11.2014.

Pothen, F., & Fink, K. (2015). *A political economy of China's export restrictions on Rare Earth Elements* (ZEW Discussion Paper No. 15–025). Retrieved from http://ftp.zew.de/pub/zew-docs/dp/dp15025.pdf.

Prebisch, R. (1950). *The economic development of Latin America and its principal problems* (UN document no. E/CN.12/89/Rev.1). Retrieved from http://repositorio.cepal.org/handle/11362/29973.

Rademaker, J. H., Kleijn, R., & Yang, Y. (2013). Recycling as a strategy against Rare Earth Element criticality: A system evaluation of the potential yield of NdFeB magnet recycling. *Environmental Science & Technology*, *47*(18), 10129–10136.

Ribeiro, G. F. (2014). Export controls as industrial policy on natural resources regulatory limitations on China-raw materials and China-rare earths cases. *Brazilian Journal of International Law*, *12*(2), 78–92.

Ruettinger, L., & Feil, M. (2011). *Sustainable prevention of resource conflicts: New risks raw materials for the future? Case study and scenarios for China and rare earths* (Report 3.4). Berlin: Adelphi.

Ruettinger, L., Treimer, R., Tiess, G., Griestop, L., Schueler, F., & Wittrock, J. (2015). *Umwelt- und Sozialauswirkungen der Gewinnung Seltener Erden in Bayan Obo* [Environmental and social impacts of rare earths mining in Bayan Obo]. China and Berlin: Adelphi.

Sanyal, P., Brady, P. V., & Vugrin, E. D. (2013). *The impact of trade costs on rare earth exports: A stochastic frontier estimation approach* [Sandia report SAND2013–7751]. Retrieved from http://prod.sandia.gov/techlib/access-control.cgi/2013/137751.pdf.

Schlinkert, D., & Van den Boogaart, K. G. (2015). The development of the market for Rare Earth Elements: Insights from economic theory. *Resources Policy*, *46*(2), 272–280.

Schueler, D., Liu, R., Buchert, M., Dittrich, S., & Merz, C. (2011). *Study on rare earths and their recycling* (Oeko-Institute. V. final report for the Greens/EFA group in the European Parliament). Retrieved from www.oeko.de/oekodoc/1112/2011-003-en.pdf.

Schueller, M. (2006). Wirtschaftssystem und aktuelle Wirtschaftsentwicklung [Economic system and current economic development]. In German Institute of Global and Area

Studies (Ed.), *Die Volksrepublik China: Zur aktuellen politischen, wirtschaftlichen und gesellschaftlichen Situation* (pp. 25–36). Hamburg: GIGA.

Schueller, M. (2009). *China in der globalen Finanzmarktkrise: Wirtschaftspolitische Strategien und Strukturprobleme* [China in the time of the Global Financial Crisis: Economic policy strategies and structural problems] (GIGA Focus Asien 4/2009). Hamburg: German Institute of Global and Area Studies.

Seaman, J. (2010). *Rare earths and clean energy: Analyzing China's upper hand.* Paris: Institut français des relations internationales. Retrieved from www.ifri.org/downloads/noteenergieseaman.pdf.

Seaman, J. (2012). *Rare earths and the East China Sea: Why hasn't China embargoed shipments to Japan?* (Ifri-CIGS Op-Ed Series). Retrieved from www.ifri.org/downloads/ifricanonopedseamanecs.pdf.

Seo, Y., & Morimoto, S. (2014). Comparison of dysprosium security strategies in Japan for 2010–2030. *Resources Policy, 39*(1), 15–20.

Siebert, H. (1983). Extraction, fixed costs and the Hotelling rule. *Zeitschrift für die gesamte Staatswissenschaft, 139*(2), 259–268.

Siebert, H. (1990). Natuerliche Ressourcen und Weltwirtschaft [Natural resources and the gobal economy]. *Wissenschaftliches Archiv, 126*(1), 1–14.

Singer, H. W. (1950). The distribution of gains between investing and borrowing countries. *The American Economic Review, 40*(2), 473–485.

Statista. (2015). *China's Rare Earth Element export quotas from 2005 to 2014 (in metric tons REO)*, Retrieved from www.statista.com/statistics/215216/chinese-rare-earth-element-export-quotas/.

Steenkampskraal Thorium Limited. (2015, October 22). *The STL Group acquires the Steenkampskraal thorium and rare earth mine*. Retrieved from www.thorium100.com/blog/the-stl-group-acquires-the-steenkampskraal-thorium-and-rare-earth-mine/.

Terrascope project. (n.d.). *Mission 2016: The future of strategic natural resources Terrascope project of the Massachusetts Institute of Technology*. Retrieved from http://web.mit.edu/12.000/www/m2016/finalwebsite/solutions/newmines.html.

Ting, M. H., & Seaman, J. (2013). Rare earths: Future elements of conflict in Asia? *Asian Studies Review, 37*(2), 234–252.

Tse, P.-K. (2011). *China's rare-earth industry* (U.S. Geological Survey Open-File Report 2011–1042). Retrieved from https://pubs.usgs.gov/of/2011/1042/of2011-1042.pdf.

United Nations Conference on Trade and Development. (2014). *Commodities at a glance: Special issue on rare earths*. Geneva: UNCTAD.

U.S. Department of Energy. (2011). *Critical materials strategy*. Washington, DC: US DOE.

U.S. Environmental Protection Agency. (2012). *Rare Earth Elements: A review of production, processing, recycling, and associated environmental issues*. Washington, DC: Office of Research and Development.

U.S. Geological Survey. (2002). *Rare Earth Elements: Critical resources for high technology* (USGS fact sheet 087–02). Retrieved from https://pubs.er.usgs.gov/publication/fs08702.

Van Calster, G. (2013). China, minerals export, raw and rare earth materials: A perfect storm for world trade organization dispute settlement. *Review of European, Comparative & International Environmental Law, 22*(1), 117–122.

Van der Ploeg, F. (2008). *Voracious transformation of a common natural resource into productive capital* (Oxford Centre for the Analysis of Resource Rich Economies Research Paper No. 2008–02). Retrieved from www.oxcarre.ox.ac.uk/images/stories/papers/ResearchPapers/oxcarrerp200802.pdf.

Volling, T. (2016, May 2). Alice to serve as 'transport hub' for Nolans rare earth mining project, about 70% workforce will be FIFO. *NT News*. Retrieved from www.ntnews.com.au/news/centralian-advocate/alice-to-serve-as-transport-hub-for-nolans-rare-earth-mining-project-about-70-workforce-will-be-fifo/news-story/38a0b9f302286c1ca24b692f06a5a5c0.

Wen, D. (2006). *Wie China die Globalisierung bewältigt: Ein kritischer Blick auf die Reformpolitik seit 1978* [How China copes with globalization: A critical look at the reform policy since 1978] (Focus Asien No. 28). Essen: Asienhaus.

The World Bank. (2016). *World Bank data: Indicators*. Retrieved from http://data.worldbank.org/indicator.

World Trade Organization. (n.d. a). *Understanding the WTO: Settling disputes*. Retrieved from www.wto.org/english/thewto_e/whatis_e/tif_e/disp1_e.htm.

World Trade Organization. (n.d. b). *WTO analytical index: GATT 1994*. Retrieved from www.wto.org/english/res_e/booksp_e/analytic_index_e/gatt1994_07_e.htm#article20.

World Trade Organization. (2001). *Accession of the People's Republic of China*. Geneva: WTO.

World Trade Organization. (2010). *World trade report 2010: Trade in natural resources*. Geneva: WTO.

World Trade Organization. (2015). *China: Measures related to the exportation of rare earths, tungsten and molybdenum*. Retrieved from www.wto.org/english/tratop_e/dispu_e/cases_e/ds431_e.htm.

Wuebbeke, J. (2013). Rare Earth Elements in China: Policies and narratives of reinventing an industry. *Resources Policy*, *38*(3), 384–394.

Zhang, K., Wen, Z., & Peng, L. (2007). Environmental policies in China: Evolvement, features and evaluation. *China Population, Resources and Environment*, *17*(2), 1–7.

Zhang, L., Guo, Q., Zhang, J., Huang, Y., & Xiong, T. (2015). Did China's rare earth export policies work? Empirical evidence from USA and Japan. *Resources Policy*, *43*, 82–90.

Zhang, S. (2013). On problems in rare earth exports of China and countermeasures. *International Business and Management*, *6*(1), 21–25.

Zhao, S. X. B., & Zhang, L. (1999). Decentralization reforms and regionalism in China: A review. *International Science Review*, *22*(3), 251–281.

6 Conclusions

The main research goal of this study was to analyze the explicit impacts and implicit implications of the Chinese virtual monopoly in the Rare Earth Metals sector for China itself and the REEs consuming countries in the rest of the world. The rationale for focusing on this topic is based on their industrial importance as the "seeds of technology". Rare Earths are indispensable for many applications in the fields of high technologies, high technology consumer goods, industrial and medical appliances as well as modern weapons systems in national defense. Due to the emergence of new high-consumer goods and green technologies since 2002, their demand is increasing while their supply on the global market has been decreasing since 2010.

In order to reach the research goal, an introduction to the special characteristics of Rare Earths was given in Chapter 2. First, their special physical-chemical and geological properties were discussed because they directly affect the mining and processing routes and fields of application. Second, an overview of the global stocks of resources and reserves was given. Due to different geological definition and an unclear data situation, the exact sizes of the world's total stocks of resources and reserves as well as their global distribution are uncertain. However, it could be shown that the majority of explored and proven deposits and active mines are concentrated in China. Third, the mining and processing routes from extracted ores to individual refined and pure metals were reviewed especially in order to analyze the high impact of mining and processing activities on the environment and human health. Fourth, the historical development of the global Rare Earths production was discussed in order to illustrate the factors that helped China to supersede the USA as the dominant REEs producer and to establish its virtual monopoly. These factors include U.S. domestic factors such as the cancelation of public support for domestic mining and the creation of new obstacles through stricter environmental regulations, as well as Chinese favorable conditions such as the strong public promotion of the expansion of the domestic REEs industry, low wages, low environmental standards and increasing superiority in mining and processing technologies. Finally, the fields of application were shown in order to highlight the increasing economic importance of REEs especially for high technological consumer electronics and clean energy applications. As a consequence of their increasing economic importance, the expected demand for REEs is expected to significantly increase in the next two decades.

After the basic introduction, the scarcity of Rare Earths was assessed in Chapter 3. While Rare Earths are absolutely scarce according to the definition as exhaustible resource, several articles mention that Rare Earths would not be scarce or rare due to their relatively high geological abundance. In order to test the hypothesis that Rare Earths are not rare or scarce, eight different economic and non-economic indicators and their variations were theoretically discussed and then applied to REEs. Up to now, no other study has provided a similar full picture of REEs scarcity. While the indicators of geochemical scarcity and real market prices did not show a high scarcity level, all other indicators showed at least a medium to high level of scarcity. When the individual metals are analyzed, the heavy REMs, which are used in the emerging technologies of permanent magnets, emission control and electronics, are assessed to be scarce in the short-to-medium term. In the long term, their scarcity will even increase due to the expected exhaustion of the current active mines for heavy REEs. Consequently, Rare Earths were assessed to be scarce and of interest from the perspective of economics. The future increasing scarcity is also an integral part of the implications of the Chinese virtual monopoly.

Overall, the impacts and implications are different in three distinct periods: the first period from the late 1970s to 2009, the second period from 2010 to 2014 and the third and ongoing period since 2015. In the first period, the Chinese REEs industry expanded and gained its status of the virtual monopoly when the last mine outside of China was shut down. Towards the end of this period, the Chinese government realized the negative impacts and implications of its virtual monopoly. Due to the active promotion of the expansion of the domestic REEs, numerous mines and processing companies produced an excessive amount of Rare Earths, which were predominantly exported until 2004. Due to oversupply, global prices were decreasing in the 1990s and early 2000s. The Chinese producers, who had an accumulated global market share of over 90%, did not act as a unitary economic actor and therefore did not have the market power to set prices, which a pure monopoly would have. At the same time, unregulated mining and processing activities had a drastic impact on environmental and human health. Overall, the virtual monopoly of this period seemed to be not an advantage but a great burden for China. Consequently, the official Chinese view was that the Chinese REEs sector had to be adjusted. In light of excessive mining, high depletion rates of domestic deposits and high environmental impact, the government of the PRC claimed that Rare Earths were sold below their intrinsic prices on the global market while the country is threatened to run out of natural resources rapidly due to excessive extraction of REEs for exports.

In order to assess this Chinese claim, the Hotelling rule for the determination of optimal paths of extraction and price developments of a non-renewable resource was discussed in Chapter 4 as an adequate methodical approach. While the literature review on the empirical significance of the Hotelling rule showed that there is little empirical support for this approach, it is still regarded as a canonical model, whose empirical insignificance is mainly attributed to the strict assumptions of the approach that are seldom met in factual markets. Deviations from these assumptions lead to deviations of factual extraction rates from the optimal extraction path as predicted by Hotelling. Then, a relevant constant-elasticity demand curve and inverse linear demand curve were determined on the basis of historical data on Rare Earths production and real prices from the U.S. Geological Survey. The constant-elasticity demand curve, which reflects the discussed absence of perfect substitutes for REEs, was then used to model a historically optimal extraction path and its corresponding price path for the years 1965 to 2012. The comparison of the historical price path with the modeled historical price path showed that the hypothesis of an undervaluation of REEs on the global market cannot be confirmed because the historical prices were even higher than the modeled optimal prices in the 1990s in spite of the general trend of declining prices. This is an important result of this study because it disproves the Chinese narrative that REEs have been underpriced in the past. The prices of the 1990s and 2000s are rather the result of excessive supply instead of systematic undervaluation. Because the Chinese government is officially concerned about excessive depletion and the availability of Rare Earths for future generations, four scenarios of future optimal extraction paths were modeled. The changing parameter of these scenarios is the choice of the underlying social discount rate, which determines the level of extraction rates and the slope of the extraction path. The modeling of the four scenarios illustrated that the optimal extraction path is predominantly dependent on the interests of the Chinese economic actors. When the government is mainly concerned about the conservation of Rare Earths for future generations, then it should enforce the use of a low social discount rate through laws and regulations. When private resource owners are able to choose their relevant discount rate without state interference, then the extraction rates will be higher and the date of exhaustion will be earlier

Chapter 5 first discussed the implications of the Global Financial Crisis for the Chinese virtual monopoly and its reregulation. These implications were mainly the need to rebalance the economic growth path in order to sustain the Chinese long-term growth rates. In the strategies of rebalancing, Rare Earths play an important role because they are required for high value-added manufacturing sectors that were chosen as key strategic sectors for State promotion. In addition, the legitimacy of the Chinese Communist Party, which has been mainly based on high economic growth rates and economic development since 1978, was threatened to erode in the face of declining growth rates as a consequence of the GFC and emerging protests against the severe levels of environmental pollution and emissions. Thus, the necessity to reduce the environmental impact of REEs mining was enhanced by the GFC. The adjustments in the REEs export regime and in the regulatory frameworks of the domestic production sector and REEs-related emissions marked the beginning of the second period of industry reregulation. With regard to the domestic production sector, the main goal of reregulation was the consolidation of the industry towards the establishment of six conglomerates under the control of the central government that vertically integrate the completely mining and processing route and should amalgamate at least 80% of the total Chinese REEs production. The imposed measures of consolidation are the reallocation and reduction of production quotas and licenses based on the compliance of new industrial standards, and the promotion of M&As through state financial support. In the field of the export regime, the export quotas were significantly reduced, export duties were raised and the number of companies that are permitted to export was reduced. The main goal of these measures was mainly the reduction of REEs exports in order to retain a larger share of REEs for the domestic downstream industries. In the field of environmental regulation, the resource tax, which is based on the concept of the Pigouvian tax, was significantly raised in order to decelerate the rates of extraction and exhaustion. Furthermore, new and stricter laws and regulations for environmental standards and emissions were issued that force mining and processing companies to either invest in abatement technologies and facilities or exit the market. The impact especially of the restriction of REEs export was the strengthening of the market power of the virtual monopoly on the global market. The Chinese price-setting power and subsequently the international prices increased. In accordance to international trade theory, the domestic prices of REEs decreased as a consequence of export quotas. This led to the establishment of a dual price system that benefited Chinese end-users and foreign mining companies and disadvantaged Chinese mining companies and foreign end-users. Consequently, welfare was redistributed in favor of China.

However, there were also resistance against reregulation. In China, the resistance of some local government and the REEs companies in their administrative areas against the consolidation emerged. Local cadres are dependent on local tax revenues and economic indicators because these are the main determining factors in the Chinese cadre promotion system. When they would lose the control over the companies in their administrative areas through consolidation and the recentralization of regulatory power, then they would also lose the direct control over the parameters of their own promotion. Furthermore, some local cadres are personally benefitting from local mining and processing activities through corruptive networks. Their resistance against consolidation is also the protection of their personal additional income. Due to this resistance, it is not certain that the full consolidation will be achieved. In the rest of the world, especially the main REEs consuming economies, namely the EU, the USA and Japan, tried to challenge the strengthened position of the virtual monopoly on the global market. In particular, they changed their resource policy to promote all activities that would decrease the import dependency on Chinese REEs and would create additional international supply. These activities include the exploration and development of new deposits for primary mining as well as efforts in the 3Rs: recycling from urban mines, the reuse of reusable REEs materials and the reduction of the total REEs' demand through the development of resource-augmenting technologies and substitutes. However, it was shown that the lion's share of activities in primary mining were not fruitful because mining outside of China was proven to be financially risky and barely profitable. Furthermore, activities in the fields of the 3Rs can only be successful in the medium-to-long term because most developments and techniques in these fields are still being researched and have not reached marketability or commercial, large-scale applicability. The countermeasure that was successful in the short term was the joint WTO complaint of the USA, the EU and Japan in 2012. In 2014, the WTO Panel and Appellate Body finally decided that the Chinese export restrictions have violated China's obligations so that the export quotas and export duties had to be eliminated. The elimination of trade restrictions marked the beginning of the current ongoing period since 2015. The Chinese virtual monopoly lost their market power again. As a replacement for export duties, China adjusted its resource tax towards an ad valorem tax of up to 27%. In the view of economic regulation of negative technological externalities, this increased resource tax is the first-best solution because it directly reduces the total production and consumption. Nevertheless, the abolishment of the Chinese export restrictions does not eliminate the necessity to develop additional supply sources outside of China. When the full consolidation is achieved, China might be able to retain the lion's share of Chinese REEs for the domestic industries without reinstating measures that obviously violate international obligations. The creation of additional supply is even appreciated by China. Because the REEs consumption in China is still growing at faster rates than the consumption of the rest of the world, China will become a net importer of REEs in the near future while its virtual monopoly in upstream activities will subsequently erode. This would be no loss for China as long as high-valued downstream projects can be successfully established. Furthermore, international projects and collaboration would be required in order to prevent the increasing scarcity especially of heavy REEs, which will lead to increasing prices and might even create a major obstacle for the global drive for clean energy generation and green mobility. In the face of this long-term challenge, the Chinese export restrictions of 2010 might even be an event that turns out to be a wakeup call to pay more attention to Rare Earths and their important role for further economic development and sustainable development.

Especially the results of Chapter 5 have some important implications for policy makers. China will most likely harmonize REEs extraction rates only with domestic but not global demand in the mid-to-long term. Even after the elimination of export restrictions in line with the WTO ruling, it is not guaranteed that future Chinese exports will satisfy the future global demand. In order to reduce the import dependence on Chinese REEs and the indicated increasing scarcity especially of heavy REEs, it is therefore highly recommendable that the EU, the USA and Japan should adhere to the promotion of research for technologies and methods to recycle and reuse REEs and to reduce their total REEs demand by developing adequate material-based or systems-based substitutes. Thereby, secondary mining in the form of recycling is an even better solution than the promotion of primary mining because it can eliminate the balancing problem of REEs mining that more abundant REEs are extracted in excess of demand. Furthermore, a cooperation of these three economies with China is recommendable. As China will remain the main producing REEs country until the projects in the RoW provide significant quantities of REEs, it should be in the best interest of the EU, the USA and Japan to assist the Chinese efforts to upgrade the processing route at least to a certain level. The transfer of the "press to shape" technology for the permanent magnet production would reduce the amount of scrapped magnetic materials, would increase the relative resource stock of REEs and could increase the availability of permanent magnets on the global market.

As illustrated in this example, joint efforts for R&D related to resource efficiency might prove beneficial for both sides.

As the ongoing third period of reregulation of the Chinese REEs sector has just recently began, there are possibilities for further research. First, the effects of consolidation and environmental reregulation, which could not be quantified yet, could be measured. Especially the impact of these two fields on the domestic extraction rates is interesting to observe. When the production quotas can be enforced, the extraction path should be a flat line or a stepwise constant function in the case of quota adjustments. Second, the scarcity of Rare Earths, especially the indicator of critical assessment, should be reassessed regularly in order to recognize further upcoming needs of adjustments. Due to the development of new REEs-dependent applications, the total demand for REEs might increase and induce a higher level of scarcity on the one hand. On the other hand, successful activities in the 3Rs and primary mining might reduce the level of scarcity. This reassessment is important because the global market prices of REEs did not necessarily reflect their long-term scarcity as suggested by microeconomic price theory. Finally, the development of REEs-related downstream activities has some potential for further investigation, especially about specific supporting state policies and their efficacy.

Index

www.ingramcontent.com/pod-product-compliance
Ingram Content Group UK Ltd.
Pitfield, Milton Keynes, MK11 3LW, UK
UKHW011014180926
475701UK00004B/744
9780367590130